Drinking the Four Winds

A Shamanic Love Story

Is coming to my theatre...

Being the true account of one man's journey of initiation into San Pedro, Andean magic and healing, teacher plants, spirit allies, and the mystery and madness of love; a story of passion requited, love betrayed and faith tested; time travel, synchronous happenings and whispers from God, set in the primal forests of Peru, the wild mountains of Spain and the fog-swept cobbled streets of England. An exploration of agony and ecstasy, hope and despair and a romance that is, finally, an uplifting renewal of the heart and the discovery of true love and meaning.

... A performance not to be missed.
Also contains sex and ᵛⁱ   ᵉ.
Suitable ᶠ

Drinking the Four Winds

A Shamanic Love Story

Is coming to my theatre…

Being the true account of one man's journey of initiation into San
Pedro, Andean magic and healing, teacher plants, spirit allies, and the
mystery and madness of love; a story of passion requited, love
betrayed and faith tested; time travel, synchronous happenings and
whispers from God, set in the primal forests of Peru, the wild
mountains of Spain and the fog-swept cobbled streets of England. An
exploration of agony and ecstasy, hope and despair and a romance that
is, finally, an uplifting renewal of the heart and the discovery of true
love and meaning.

… A performance not to be missed.
Also contains sex and violence.
Suitable for all ages.

Ross Heaven

Winchester, UK
Washington, USA

First published by Moon Books, 2013
Moon Books is an imprint of John Hunt Publishing Ltd., Laurel House, Station Approach,
Alresford, Hants, SO24 9JH, UK
office1@jhpbooks.net
www.johnhuntpublishing.com
www.moon-books.net

For distributor details and how to order please visit the 'Ordering' section on our website.

ISBN: 978 1 78099 538 0

A CIP catalogue record for this book is available from the British Library.

Design: Stuart Davies

Printed and bound by CPI Group (UK) Ltd, Croydon, CR0 4YY

We operate a distinctive and ethical publishing philosophy in all
areas of our business, from our global network of authors to
production and worldwide distribution.

CONTENTS

Whatever one believes to be true is *true or* becomes *true in one's own mind, within limits to be determined experimentally and experientially.*

These limits themselves are, in turn, beliefs to be transcended
John Lilly, Ketamine explorer, scientist and author of
The Centre of the Cyclone

PREAMBLE: THE FIRST STORY TOLD

It's the truth, even if it didn't happen
Ken Kesey, psychedelic explorer and author of *One Flew Over the Cuckoo's Nest*

4,000 years BC (more or less). Month unknown

I imagine him dressed like Alejandro Jodorowsky, the Chilean film director with a passion for Zen and cowboy novels, in his film El Topo, *a surreal Western about sex, betrayal and enlightenment: Black suit. Black hat. Black beard. And of course a black horse. Wearing two guns and a mean attitude - and quick to draw on both to mask his sadness and anger at life.*

His wife and the child that she carried had been murdered by drifters and thieves, his faith in God had been lost and he had taken to desert trails on a quest for vengeance and peace: to find their killers - and himself; to rediscover God or to murder Him. He of course had no name.

The desert was hot and The Man With No Name was low on water but that didn't concern him too much because he knew that he was only 30 kilometres from the nearest town and could finish the ride that day. But then the unthinkable – or, at least, the undesirable – happened: his horse gave way beneath him, fell on its side and lay gasping for air in the sand. The Man With No Name understood that his best friend – his only friend – was dying and, as he knew he must, he put his pistol to its head and pulled the trigger, sparing it the pain and slow death of the desert.

Job done, lip trembling but not a tear staining his dusty face, alone beneath the sun, he reviewed his situation. He would have to walk out now. In this heat and in these conditions that would take him at least three days, maybe longer, moving only at night to avoid the sun and predatory eyes, and he was already down to just one or two sips of water. Stoically, he sought shelter and tried to sleep through the sun at its highest.

But the desert plays tricks. So does a lack of water and endless heat, and three days later he was lost, wondering and wandering, with no hope of salvation or rescue. That small town he was headed for might as well be the ends of the Earth. It was then that he fell to his knees and, for the first time in years, felt the splash of tears on his face.

He cried for all that was taken from him and for all that had driven him to stay alive – the desire for revenge that had consumed him and now also seemed lost. He could not even kill in the name of love - for the destruction of his home, the loss of his wife and the death of their unborn child; for the pitiful look on the face of the horse he could not save, and for the futility of life: the ultimate aloneness, the melancholy strangeness and the lack of meaning that was part of being human at all.

He shook his head. 'Pull yourself together, asshole' he muttered to himself. Then he stood and walked towards the sun.

It was then that he saw it – a single cactus, 20 feet tall, that would give him shelter and which he could drink from by cutting into its flesh. He pulled out his knife and bored into the green column in front of him. He felt its vitality enter him. Survival and revenge were again on his mind, the primal forces that would get him through this. Forty minutes later however and those thoughts were gone forever.

Painted desert, Peyote rain
Lord, don't let me go insane
Skinwalker, Skinwalker…
Who am I, who are you
I was only passing through
Skinwalker, Skinwalker
Robbie Robertson, *Skinwalker*

The Man With No Name came to 12 hours later, stronger now – but in some ways also weaker. He had the strength to carry him for miles but no desire to get there or, rather, to walk that way for revenge. For, during his cactus-sleep, he had seen something amazing: the palaces of

God with their radiant angels who spoke to him, healed and soothed him, and he knew now that his life was real and this desert that held him was beautiful. So, too, had been his wife, his almost-child, the home they had shared and all that was taken from him. But that was a different life. He could not live it over or forever.

He got to his feet again, rising from the sand reborn, perhaps just a grain of sand himself – and not as a killer but an evangelist, wanting only to spread the Word, the truth that he had been shown. He had a name now too and that name was Angel.

With new strength and a sure direction Angel made his way to town and spoke to the people he met there about the magical desert cactus – a cathedral in the sand – and the God of love and love of God it contained. Most of them thought him mad. Just as it ever was and would be again in the Christ religion to come, only the ass saw the Angel[1] - or rather, Angel saw a lot of asses. But some listened. And so the Word was spread...

THE STORY

If wanting a mate one would not just go out to a crowd of people, randomly grab the first human of the opposite sex and expect it to all just flow from there. Working with plant allies is rather similar. Careful choices and evaluations of suitability followed by establishing a mutually respectful loving relationship is how I would recommend approaching the issue

K Trout, author of *San Pedro*, writing to Dale Pendell, author of *PharmakoGnosis*

It's good to have an open mind, but not so open that your brain falls out

Karl Jansen, *Ketamine: Dreams and Realities*

Yeah, well. You live, you learn...

GRACE AND MADNESS

With everything so perfect, reality seemed somehow fragile... as tenuous as a soap bubble, shivering and empty
Scott Westerfield, *Pretties*

2010. July

Grace and Madness, the 6th International Conference on Amazonian Shamanism, was held in Iquitos, Peru. For six years it had been a forum for presentations and workshops on rainforest medicines, mainly centred on Ayahuasca: the vine of souls, the gateway to madness or liberation from it. Jungle shamans are brought together – including 'superstars' like Guillermo Arevalo and Percy Garcia and lesser-known but talented healers and medicine men such as Ron Wheelock and Adela Navas – to offer stories and insights into their healings with Ayahuasca and their views on how and why this visionary brew is able, where Western medicines fail, to cure conditions such as addiction, trauma and many other physical and emotional problems.

They are joined on the programme by Western academics, authors and scientists who have studied (and drunk) the medicine themselves and who have their own stories to tell. This year, according to schedule worked out - and often frantically reworked - by the organisers (since hardly anything goes smoothly or to plan in Peru) they include Peter Gorman, former editor of *High Times* and author of a recently published book on Ayahuasca, Dennis McKenna (brother of Terence), Pablo Amaringo, the world-renowned visionary artist... and me. At this gathering I'm a nobody and I'm not even here to talk about Ayahuasca so I'm expecting a lukewarm response when I begin speaking about something which I presume the audience has little interest in.

The gathering isn't as big as in previous years – maybe a few hundred people and they don't attend every presentation so some speakers, as interesting as they are, get only a handful of listeners. Eventually it's my turn and I'm not hoping for much.

As I am introduced however there is a murmur in the room and people start walking over from wherever they have congregated or vanished to. By the time I reach the stage – a circular platform surrounded by delegates' tables – almost everyone is there. There are no seats left so people are standing three deep behind them in some places, waiting to hear what I have to say.

That's when I get it. I am here to talk about San Pedro – a mescaline cactus not a DMT potion of vines and leaves; Andean mountain rather than Amazonian jungle medicine – and yet, even at this conference with its traditional focus on rainforest shamans and the vine of souls, people want to hear. The times are changing it seems, just as the healing needs of people and the culture they belong to change. Maybe San Pedro is the medicine we most need now.

My theory is supported by other events this week. The conference runs for eight days and most shamans offer ceremonies during this time which delegates can attend. We hear through the conference that the shamans have done well and their ceremonies attract 20 or so attendees - which is good; under normal circumstances an Ayahuasca ritual might only have half that number. At the jungle retreat Centre I own however we are running San Pedro ceremonies and they draw almost 100 people. Interest in the cactus outstrips the call of the vine.

I think I know why. I first visited Peru to drink Ayahuasca in 1998 and I've been back many times to do so, my visits eventually culminating in my purchase of the healing Centre I now own in Iquitos where my business partner Trudy and I offer this plant medicine to our clients to help with their healing needs. In the 12 years that I have worked with the brew I've got to know it well and it seems to me that it opens up new worlds of possibility for people, freeing the soul from the body so it can travel the universe and they can see their lives from the perspective of the infinite, aware of all the choices and potential they have. San Pedro, by contrast, is a plant of the Earth which enables the spirit of the universe to enter *them* and show them all that is possible in *this* lifetime, in *this* body, in *this* world. Its healing is more direct and immediate than Ayahuasca and more meaningful because it is rooted in what is real and happening in their lives *right now*. It is this groundedness, this experience of spirit in the everyday that our participants have come for. They want to know how to *be*, how to *act* in the world, how to *heal themselves and find meaning*.

Over the years, San Pedro has become an important teacher for me[2]. The reason I am in Peru now in fact is to begin an apprenticeship with the cactus which will involve dieting it (a shamanic process of fasting, meditation and drinking San Pedro at regular intervals) so it can teach me how to heal.

Our first ceremony during the conference is run by La Bruja, a *curandera*[3] from the Andes who has flown to Iquitos to stay with us and is also speaking at the conference. I first drank her San Pedro five years ago and since then she has become a friend and a teacher to me. Her medicine is strong and we drink it in beautiful surroundings, the ritual beginning on the porch at the back of our *casa grande*, the big house where our clients and participants stay, overlooking our lagoon and the forest beyond it. The day was warm and humid, the sky cloud-free and azure-blue and a sense of peace descended as people entered their San Pedro dreams and found quiet places for reflection and healing. Some laughed like children and played in the water; some cried, exploring old wounds. Business as usual for San Pedro, the mellow healer who gently coaxes the pain from sorry souls.

Its healing approaches in waves. You feel it gently at first and then it recedes a little. The next wave is stronger and lasts longer. The next is stronger still. The whole process takes perhaps four hours until you are fully held by San Pedro, although you feel its spirit enter you way before that. The journey lasts a further six to eight hours, a ten or twelve hour experience in total, sometimes longer; sometimes a lifetime.

During the day I reflected on the past – the twists and turns of fate that had brought me to this place – and the future: what I was going to make of this strange new environment now I had given up 'civilisation' for the jungle. Both the past and the future are going to be important in this story but it was the present which suddenly consumed me because, sitting on that porch, senses heightened by San Pedro, what I was most aware of was the presence of two other people. It radiated like an energy from them, grabbing my attention.

One was from someone on my right and felt female. I took a glance and saw a woman, mid-30s, a volunteer at our Centre whose name was Jane. She had long dark hair and was quite pretty but it seemed to me that she was also in some way unhappy, perhaps even damaged by something from her past. I had heard a lot about her, some of which supported my sense of her now, as she already had a history at our camp, but I had only spoken to her briefly and did not know her well. There was a book at her side, *The Count of Monte Cristo*, a classic story of failed love and the search for freedom and vengeance.

The other energy came from someone behind me and felt, unsubtly, to be boring into my back and rummaging through my soul; checking me out. It came from a man, I knew that, but I wasn't going to turn around and see who. Instead, I started sending out energy 'vibes' of my own to check on him.

Who and what I discovered in both of these people was going to change a lot of things around here and be part of some amazing adventures to come. The future was already calling but it was the past which had brought me here. 1998 had been a pivotal year.

THE BEGINNING – AND AN END

In the safe island of my mind [I]created an art that amounted to buffoonery, a brilliant veneer to hide the darkness of thieves like myself – thieves who pillaged the earth, robbing others of their health, transforming their time into a hard personal shell, dividing others' space into dog kennels in which these citizens, befuddled by the walls, accepted their obligatory blindness
Alejandro Jodorowsky, film director and Zen Master

1998. Sometime around September

I am on a plane to Vancouver where I will be doing…very important things. For the last 14 years since graduating with a degree in psychology and related subjects I have been using these disciplines to manipulate the minds of others as an international marketing consultant; inviting them with a winning smile and a subliminal mallet to love my clients as much as I clearly did (even though I actually had little love for them myself). I now mainly represent medical and pharmaceutical companies and my job basically amounts to wearing flashy suits and taking clients to dinner so I can tell them how to run their own businesses – because I, of course, know best. Like I said, I do very important things.

I'm drinking a Bloody Mary on Air Canada, on my way to a conference where I will, of course, have an important role to play, and I really should be smiling to myself at my close-to-six-figure salary and the BMW I drive when the national UK wage - even today - is barely a third of what I earned then and most people have to work for a living. I'm not smiling though. I'm depressed. Disillusioned might be a better word.

Inevitably, because I know I can (and because she's in love with her designer lifestyle and self-importance too) I will sleep with the woman next to me who works for a 'rival' company and

9

is going to the same conference, even though we've barely met. This will happen after dinner at some oyster bar near the river and a bottle or two of expense account wine where we will toast our salaries and egos. In the morning we'll say goodbye, nothing more, and she'll be gone. Then we will both return to the business of being important and regard each other as competitors. Her name is Claire. I'm amazed I can even remember it.

And that's how it was for me. Empty highs and empty sex with other Masters of the Universe; all of it on account; all of it amounting to nothing. We were international airborne whores paid for by someone else. At first I thought it was only the companies I represented which were picking up the tab but increasingly I'd come to realise that the people who were really paying were those who could least afford to. I'd had hidden it from myself for years but the shabbiness I felt now at my own success was undeniable and it revealed my deeper feelings.

On this trip I was representing two pharmaceutical clients, both of them in the HIV business, at a conference on HIV and AIDS. They used different technologies to manage the progression of the disease and its effect on sufferers so they saw no conflict of interest and I was impartial, giving my love and devotion to both, although, had I known it then (which I didn't because it was never made public, even to Masters of the Universe) the approach of one of my clients, Roche - or rather, the origins of its HIV technology - would have grabbed my attention more. Roche used a process called polymerase chain reaction or PCR to enable early diagnosis of diseases such as leukaemia and lymphomas, both associated with AIDS. The sensitivity of PCR meant that the virus could be detected soon after infection and before the onset of serious disease, which might give physicians a head start in treatment.

What interests me now is not the science however, but that the inventor of PCR, Kary Mullis, like his fellow pioneer Francis Crick, had used what science teachers, politicians and lawmakers would like us to believe is an unusual approach to come up with his idea (although in my experience it is far from unusual in reality): he got high – and it got him a Nobel Prize.

Crick was the first to identify the structure of DNA. To do so he used LSD, a psychedelic derived from ergot, a fungus thought to be the basis of the 'flying ointment' of European witches. In his autobiography he writes about falling into a dreaming state where he saw snakes writhing together in a caduceus form and from that Eureka moment he was able to crack the DNA code. Rather self-effacingly he referred to this dream-clad revelation (which led to one of the greatest discoveries of our age) as simply 'a not insignificant idea', a phrase I love to this day. Mullis was similarly inspired and later said of his own experiences: 'What if I had not taken LSD ever; would I have still invented PCR?... I doubt it. I seriously doubt it.' It turns out that shamans and scientists, alchemists and chemists, establishment and anti-establishment revolutionaries are not so far removed from one another.

I didn't know any of that back in 1998 however. If I had it might have given me at least a new outlook, something to grab my attention and interest, but as it was I was bored, sick of myself, and had the uncomfortable feeling that I had become little more than a scavenger at the scrap end of science. Perhaps it was worse than that. Perhaps I was a murderer, at least by association.

When you join the medical profession – at whatever level: doctor, surgeon, chemist or even someone like me – you are told it is noble work; that you are aiding the welfare of humanity, helping and caring for people. And you believe it. You want to. But the reality, after a couple of years in the business, becomes apparent as something else.

The first contradiction is that pharmaceutical companies and medical professionals (physicians, research scientists...or marketing consultants) are first and foremost bill-payers and, like any commercial enterprise, they exist to make money and depend on customer loyalty. That, however, is a phrase which means something different in medicine than in most other professions. If you are Wal-Mart or Burger King, customer loyalty amounts to giving your client a taste for your product so they keep coming back. If you're a drug company however, the same principle means keeping your customers sick since there is no money to be made from *curing* a disease. A healthy patient is not a loyal customer. Directors would be out of a job and shareholders up in arms if AIDS or cancer or the common cold were cured tomorrow, although, most likely, the technology actually exists. There are billions of dollars to be made from *managing disease* however: never quite curing it but alleviating enough of the symptoms so that people feel a little better and come back for repeat prescriptions. The customer still goes away sick but at least not dead (there is no money in that either, a cynic might add).

Then there are the legalities of drug production which mean that the raw essence of a pharmaceutical, invariably a plant, cannot be patented. You can't 'own' a natural material[4]. What this means for drug companies is that they must typically employ anthropologists and ethnobotanists (collectively known as bioprospectors) to visit areas of interest (the rainforest being a prime location) and develop relationships with shamans and native healers who can introduce them to plants with healing properties so that their 'active ingredients', which *are* patentable, can then be extracted. Their arrangement with these local experts is usually less than fair and normally falls way short of reciprocity, the shaman receiving a few hundred dollars or products in kind (guns, clothes, Western medicines or even a few beads have historically been some of the commodities exchanged) for knowledge which may net the drug company billions.

One of the issues that troubled me… is what has come to be called

"intellectual property rights". Briefly stated, no matter what disease an ethnobotanist might find a cure for during the course of his research, the indigenous peoples who taught him the cure would not benefit from the sales of the new drug
Mark Plotkin, ethnobotanist and author of *Tales of a Shaman's Apprentice*

As a consequence of the shaman's co-operation in this 'healing mission' whole areas of rainforest might then be exploited or destroyed as drug (and other) companies commercialise the jungle and take the plants that interest them, which also means that native people have fewer medicines left for themselves.

Around 125,000 species – almost half the plants on Earth - are found in tropical rainforests, which cover almost eight billion acres of the world's surface. Estimates vary but it is well-known that several thousands of these rainforest acres are destroyed each year by Western companies or local farmers under Western sponsorship... There is no doubt that many of these plants hold the keys to life-saving new medicines – we know this from the less-than-one-percent that have been studied - and yet every year thousands more are destroyed
Leslie Taylor, *The Healing Power of Rainforest Herbs*

Dr Norman Farnsworth (University of Illinois, Chicago) writes that 'Worldwide, one in three plant-derived drugs come from tropical rainforest plants [and] only a small fraction has been investigated for medicinal purposes. It is reasonable to believe that further investigation of tropical rainforest plants will yield important drugs to treat diseases for which we still have no satis-factory cures'. With the rainforest destroyed however – sometimes, ironically, at least partly because of the drug companies looking for those cures – it is reasonable to expect that we may never find them.

Having identified a plant of interest, a drug company cannot simply market it. In order to patent it they must add a unique process of their own, which usually means extracting from the natural material what they believe is its most important ingredient, the one which will fight the disease. Plants are complex however, with many beneficial attributes and rarely if ever a single compound which does all the work. Drug companies are aware of that but there is no money in this knowledge so they continue with their extraction process, resulting in a new pharmaceutical which may in some cases be 80% or so *less* effective than the plant in its natural form. But at least the drug can be patented and money can be made. Jergon Sacha is a case in point.

Jergon is a rainforest plant which is a natural *cure* (not a disease management method) for HIV/AIDS and cancerous tumours. Dr Roberto Gonzales, president of the Committee of AIDS and Transmissible Diseases at the Peruvian Institute of Social Security in Iquitos reports that in experiments with AIDS patients between 1989 and 1993, a combination of Jergon Sacha and Una de Gato ('Cat's Claw', another Amazonian plant) given to sufferers showed that 'a majority of HIV patients treated tested negative for the HIV virus and returned to normal lives after taking the plant extracts for an average of six months', according to Leslie Taylor in *The Healing Power of Rainforest Herbs*.

As I mentioned however, plants cannot be patented so HIV drugs have to go through a developmental process in order to create a 'unique product'. Having done so their success rate in *managing* (not *curing*) HIV might perhaps be 20% of the natural material. Jergon Sacha and Una de Gato meanwhile will *eradicate* the disease in six months. These drugs can also cost hundreds of dollars per treatment while a six-month diet of Jergon Sacha and Una de Gato, with fresh ingredients bought daily from Belen market in Iquitos, might only cost 900 soles (less than $200) and according Gonzales' research will get rid of the disease.

Pharmaceutical companies do not particularly want information like this to reach the public.

> *Some chemists, having synthesised a few compounds, believe themselves to be better chemists than nature which, in addition to synthesising compounds too numerous to mention, synthesised those chemists as well*
> Robert de Ropp, in *Tales of a Shaman's Apprentice*

When a new candidate drug is discovered (by which I mean that a potentially useful, patentable and money-making compound is extracted from a non-patentable plant) pharmaceutical companies carry out tests to determine the drug's effectiveness, culminating in human trials. This might mean that the drug is offered cheaply or free of charge to a country where there are sufficient sufferers of the target disease that its success (or otherwise) and any side-effects can be studied. Usually this means a third world country where doctors and their patients are grateful for any assistance. If the drug 'fails' (i.e. does not perform as expected or there is an unacceptable level of death or illness caused by using it) it is withdrawn and those in the test country who *had* benefited from it are left without support. If, on the other hand, it works well enough to be marketed it is introduced to the West and a new price set which means that the test market can't afford it anyway. Damned if you do, damned if you don't.

On top of that, side-effects can be severe with any man-made drugs (compared to plants) and even those that pass all the stages of testing and are legally sold with full FDA approval can kill you. We just don't have nature's talent. Eight years after my Vancouver trip I would quote the statistics in my book *Plant Spirit Shamanism*:

'Consider this from a report in the British Medical Journal last year: "In England alone reactions to drugs that led to hospitalisation *followed by death are estimated at 5,700 a year and could actually be closer to 10,000".'[5]*

By comparison: *'the Medicines and Healthcare products Regulatory Agency (MHRA) – the government group responsible for regulating UK medicines, including herbs – says that between 2000 and August 2004 there were 451 reports of suspected adverse reactions involving herbal preparations, of which 152 were serious [i.e. 38 a year compared to 5,700 to 10,000] ... Herbs may not be completely safe as critics like to point out but they are a lot safer than drugs.'[6]*

But perhaps the risks are acceptable because pharmaceutical products are, overall, more effective than natural cures? The evidence suggests not. There have been spectacular drug failures despite the promises. Thalidomide is an obvious example, a drug marketed as a mild sleeping pill safe even for pregnant women, which nonetheless caused thousands of babies worldwide to be born with malformed limbs. The natural alternatives (fennel, chamomile or red Poppy, among others) have never harmed anyone.[7]

Another example is antidepressants. In 2005 the FDA, after an extensive review of hundreds of studies, issued a warning that the use of antidepressants may actually lead to an *increase* in depression and suicide. The news story that covered this noted the FDA's concerns that 'antidepressants may cause agitation, anxiety and hostility in a subset of patients... psychiatrists say there is a window period of risk just after pill use begins, before depression is really alleviated but when some patients experience more energy, perhaps enabling them to act on suicidal tendencies'. By contrast, the herbal cure for depression, St John's Wort, never hurt anyone and, furthermore, brings relief where chemical products fail. As the Independent newspaper put it: '[St John's Wort] is not only *more effective* in the treatment of moderate to severe depression than the SSRI Seroxat, according to the British Medical Journal, but it also has fewer side-effects'[8].

Because of the way patents work, once a drug company has

created a new product (i.e. synthesised part of a freely-available plant) it has exclusive rights to the market for a number of years and can set its price wherever it wants, putting any value it sees fit on human life. The research and development costs involved in getting a drug to market are admittedly high but so are the returns. A company with a 'superstar' product could recover its costs in just a few years but the patent is theirs for decades and the price remains the same, giving a potential return of thousands of times the upfront investment. The people paying for this are those who can least afford to: the sick, the suffering or, in those countries which have a national health service, tax payers who may not themselves be sick but are sponsoring the access of others to less than wholly effective drugs at inflated prices when a natural and often better alternative is almost certain to exist.

You won't find many physicians quibbling about these arrangements though. As a Master of the Universe I provided quite a few of them with free holidays (recorded in our accounts as 'presentations at conferences'), laptops, meals out and other jollies in exchange for using and recommending our products. None of this is attributable and it all looks good on paper. If necessary it was put down to 'hospitality' and might even be tax deductible or it became a 'research expense' and was lost in the books. Whatever we called it no-one was likely to find it.

And all of this I was carrying with me to Vancouver. It is no wonder that I looked stressed in my passport photo. It is no wonder that my baggage was heavy.

The conference itself went smoothly. Our presentations were well-received and we were invited to all the best parties: nighttime rooftop receptions overlooking the sparkling city, a celebration dinner at the Museum of Anthropology with a spectacular view of the bay: all those bright-lit dark corners where deals are done and Masters of the Universe shine.

It all went so well in fact that I gave myself a little time off as a reward for my outstanding contribution to the lives of others and the bottom lines of my clients. The conference took place in a sports stadium and the organisers had arranged for the AIDS Quilt to be displayed there. I decided out of interest to take a look.

The NAMES Project AIDS Memorial Quilt, to give it its full title, is the world's largest community art project: a huge quilt made as a memorial to and a celebration of the lives of those who have died from AIDS. It began as the brainchild of Cleve Jones, an activist who, at a candlelit remembrance march for the gay San Francisco Supervisor Harvey Milk, asked people to write the names of loved ones lost to AIDS on signs that would be taped to the Federal Building. When it was finished it looked like an enormous patchwork blanket and it inspired Jones to create a more enduring monument in the form of the Memorial Quilt. It began in 1987, a time when many people who died of AIDS could not get a proper funeral because of the stigma of the disease and because many funeral homes refused to handle their remains. Lacking a memorial service or grave site, the AIDS Quilt was the only thing survivors had to honour the lives of their loved ones.

Each panel is three feet by six feet, about the size of a human grave, and even though only 20% of people lost to AIDS are represented there, there are still more than 46,000 panels and the whole piece weighs over 50 tons.

Individual panels are personal, created by relatives or lovers to reflect the life of the person they have lost. They feature embroidery, fabric paint, lace, crystals, sequins, feathers, clothing, wedding rings, hair, trophies, toys; representing the achievements and interests of the deceased. The entire Quilt was not on display at this conference but it still covered three stories of the stadium, weaving its way along the corridors and up the ascending levels. So many dead.

I would have liked to have walked all three floors to really take in what this artwork meant, but I only made it to panel two.

Maybe it was the weight of what I was carrying, the knowledge I had of this industry and the sneaking, just-below-the-surface suspicion of what I was really doing here and what my life was about, or maybe it was just that one particular panel, but whatever provoked my reaction, my visit to the AIDS Quilt turned out to be life-changing. I had no idea when I got up this morning.

Panel two commemorated the life of a family, told by its surviving member. It was decorated with photographs, pictures drawn by a child, a few mementos, a locket or two of hair and a pair of booties that a toddler might wear when first learning to walk. A hand-written note was attached from the husband and father in this relationship, which told of his pain and confusion. His wife had contracted AIDS as a result of a blood transfusion and passed the virus to the daughter she was carrying in her womb. His wife was the first to die and he cared for his child alone until the age of two when she also passed. Once he had everything: a beautiful young wife (one of the photos on the Quilt showed her when she was healthy and they were together), a new family; the beginning of something precious. Now he had nothing. He lost it all to a four-letter word. Again and again he wrote in the note that he attached to the panel: 'I don't understand, I don't understand' – always the unanswered Why? His faith that he would see his wife and child again one day was all that kept him alive. But he had had faith in us too – we Masters of the Universe – to solve this problem, to end this plague. And maybe we could. But there was no money in that.

What hit me first was a visceral feeling: the gut awareness that this was not just 'community art', this was someone's *life* which he was clinging to by a thread; followed by the realisation, again at a gut level, that the business I was in was not just an 'industry', it *should* be the noble profession I once believed it to be. But now I had the dreadful sense that in some way, through the job that I did - the peddling of drugs, the deification of science, the 'management' of disease rather than the attempt at least to cure it - I had contributed to the destruction of this man's life and the death of his wife and daughter. What if he had known about Jergon Sacha for example? What if they had imported the plant or flown to Peru to drink it with one of the shamans there? Would his wife still be dead – or would she now be holding her baby, together with her husband, starting out on their life adventure? My legs gave way – a totally involuntary action - and I found myself on my knees before the panel. I think I lost a part of myself in that moment – but I found something too: that piece of my soul which I had lost or given away to expense account lunches and designer suits. For the first time in a long time I knew what it was to care.

I flew back to England a few days later and soon after that I handed back the keys to the company car along with my resignation. The suits were given to charity. I like to think that there may now be a low income family somewhere dressed entirely in Gucci, Polo and Pierre Cardin.

I moved into a bedsit in a crummy backstreet and did little for the next few weeks except think about what to do now. My thoughts keep returning to the AIDS Quilt, to the fragility of life and the need to do something meaningful with it, and to a single word: *Ayahuasca,* a jungle plant I had heard of which could apparently help those who drank it find purpose.

And so one day I walked into town to book a flight to Iquitos, a short hop from Lima, the capital of Peru, and the place where Ayahuasca and answers could be found. I smiled to myself the whole way in to the travel agency. Masters of the Universe drive everywhere in their Mercedes and BMWs. People like me, we walk.

IN RUINS

It is our answer to the great chill, to death, to the infinity of space
Dale Pendell, author of *PharmakoGnosis*, on the nature of San
Pedro

1998. Sometime around November

To get to the jungle and Iquitos you must pass through Lima, the
capital of Peru. If you have seen the film of James Redfield's book
The Celestine Prophecy you will have an idea of Lima as a dirty
shanty town teeming with thieves and prostitutes and the airport
on its outskirts as a shabby hut where you land at your peril.

Just as Redfield can never have visited Iquitos however before
writing in his book about the 'high' and 'low' roads by which you
enter it (since there are no roads at all, Iquitos being one of the
few cities on Earth which can only be entered by river or air), so
the film's director, Armand Mastroianni, can never have visited
Lima or else chose deliberately to present an inaccurate view of
the place, because in fact Lima is a modern city with a beautiful
coastline, high rise apartments, attractive colonial buildings,
parks, cathedrals, cinemas, restaurants, cafes and shopping
centres, and the airport which serves it is large, clean, central,
and operates more efficiently than many I have passed through
in Europe or the States.

This might be a disappointment for those who have come in
search of the exotic. If that is what you want however, Peru itself
will not disappoint you and you will love the two hour flight to
Iquitos across rainforest and rivers, the landing at an airport
littered with the rusting remains of decommissioned planes, the
motocarro (tap-tap) ride into town in 90% humidity at any time of
year, past roadside vendors, through crazy traffic – and the
spectacle which finally awaits you as you enter the Plaza de
Armas ('Armoury Square', where the military camp is based).

I have written about Iquitos in my book *The Hummingbird's Journey to God*:

[This] strange jungle town on the banks of the Amazon has a sense of fever and muted madness that began at least 500 years ago with the arrival of Francisco Pizarro. The Conquistador came to Peru in search of El Dorado, the fabled city of gold. Red not gold is what he discovered however, in the blood of the natives that fell before his sword as he carved Spain's insignia into the land and his dreams turned into obsessions...

His dreams were for nothing, for no gold has ever been found in Iquitos. Three hundred years later however, between 1880 and 1912, riches did flow into the town from the jungles around it, in the form of latex, a product of the jebe tree. The invention of vulcanisation by Goodyear had created a huge demand for latex and, following Pizarro's lead, the town of Iquitos was birthed by rubber barons as a base for their own excesses. From an almost standing start Iquitos had 20,000 inhabitants by the mid-1880s, many of them Europeans who became fabulously wealthy by enlisting (or rather, enslaving) local tribes to work their plantations for them.

Their opulent bubble burst just 30 years later when it was discovered that greater profits could be made in the plantations of Malaya (now Malaysia) than in the wild forests of the Amazon. The traders left Iquitos as quickly as they had arrived.

The town's colours are faded now but in its day it stood for a certain kind of 'excellence', 'modernity' and the 'genius of man' as he employed science and slavery to transform and tame the forest, turning it from a 'wilderness' ('red in tooth and claw') into something far removed from its true nature and more akin to his taste for order.

Only a few reminders of past glories remain. The town retains its promenade on the banks of the Amazon for example, where Victorian gentlemen would take their evening strolls. In the shadows of some moonlit nights you may even glimpse their tuxedoed ghosts with their arms around their wives dressed in ball-gowns and evening dresses, looking out across the jungle to survey their kingdoms as lightening flashed in the forest and the sweat of the air made their dress-shirts stick to their backs.

Other follies reflective of long-gone wealth can also be seen. One is a house – now a restaurant (The Casa de Fierro or 'Iron House') – made entirely of iron that was built by Monsieur Eiffel, the designer of Paris' famous Tower. Iron, of course, is subject to rust and you must wonder what a building like this is doing in a place of baking heat, rainforest downpours and humidity so extreme that the air itself can rot the clothes from your back. The reason for its presence is explained by the one-time spirit of those Victorian gentlemen: 'It can be built so why not build it? We have money to spare after all.'

The eccentric rubber baron, Carlos Fermin Fitzcarrald had a base near here. Fitzcarraldo as he is better known was also driven by dreams of gold and longed so passionately to install an opera house deep in the jungle that some say his dreams drove him mad. One of the stories told of him and his need for profit and opera relates how he purchased the only remaining parcel of forest that might still yield rubber, in a remote area of the Amazon cut off by treacherous rapids, with the intention of building a plantation, a fortune and an opera house (not necessarily in that order). To avoid the problems of the river Fitzcarraldo had the natives carry his 30-ton steamship through the jungle, across an isthmus of land from one part of the river to the next.

The vainglorious driving force behind his actions was, he said, 'not to undertake an adventure but to offer this land to mankind so we can find a new home for the disinherited of the world.' In return for their labour he promised the natives 'Ciudadanos del Centro, del Norte y del Sur del

Perú: me acompañáis en la exploración más grande que se ha hecho en las montañas de nuestra Patria en los últimos tiempos; os aseguro que el éxito coronará nuestros esfuerzos y que agregaremos nuevas glorias a nuestra bandera.Pueblos de los y tribus de los , , , , , y : os llevo, como un padre bueno y justiciero, a daros el premio de los montes divinales, que se extiende por donde sale el Sol, donde abundante os espera; allí os daré pólvora y para que vuestras abatan a las bestias.

Gunpowder and bullets and guns to tame the beasts' so they could conquer the natural world just as he intended to do. It seems that nature was not so anxious to be conquered however and Fitzcarraldo died in the rapids of the Urubamba River on July 9, 1897.

Nowadays, with few hints of its former wealth or the madness that has historically fuelled its accumulation (except for those few monuments that remain), Iquitos still buzzes with frenetic energy and the desire for profit. At any time of day or night it is almost impossible to sit quietly in the Plaza de Armas or sip coffee in one of its restaurants or cafes without attracting vendors and craftswomen who will try to sell you textiles that have taken them days or weeks to make, for just a few American dollars; or shoeshine boys who will clean your boots (whether they need it or not) for just one sol (about 15 pence). The desire for money lives on but driven now by the poverty of a town abandoned.

Yes, Iquitos is exotic, beautiful and crazy and the gateway to Ayahuasca, and I would reach it soon enough, but it is not where this story begins. It starts in Lima.

On my first day there, after 14 hours in the air and more than 24 hours of travelling, I checked into a *hostal* in the pretty Miraflores district. It is a guesthouse I still return to, a place that now holds memories of other adventures, like the time in 2008 when I lost my passport two days before I had to make a flight to Cusco to meet a workshop group and spent an entire weekend bribing airport and government officials so I could get on a plane at all. It is also where Trudy, my future business partner and I decided to buy the jungle healing Centre where much of this story takes place. And it is where, more than 10 years after my first visit to Peru, my wife and I would conceive our child.

In Lima for the first time, I was having lunch, tired but excited, and thinking about the flight to Iquitos next day when I was approached by a Peruvian man, I guess in his 50s. At these pivotal moments in books authors like to expand on the strange, otherwordliness of their mysterious visitor and tell you that they felt 'chosen' or that the fates were moving for them. Not to disillusion you (since the strange and mysterious may also be part of this encounter) but if you sit for any length of time almost anywhere in Peru you are likely to be approached by *someone* and they quite often do have what might turn out to be a life-changing proposition for you, such as an invitation to a ceremony or some other spiritual event. But that is no reason to think we are chosen or special. Had I declined his offer he would simply have approached the next gringo he saw.

But I didn't decline.

This being Peru I expected to be invited to an Ayahuasca ceremony and I had no interest in that, having already arranged a programme of ceremonies for myself, beginning the day after tomorrow. But this guy wasn't selling Ayahuasca; he was talking about 'hummingbird medicine', San Pedro, and a ritual which was taking place that night. I had come to Peru to drink a jungle vine but in fact the first plant I met was a desert cactus.

In the early evening a small group of us gathered for the drive to Huallamarca, an ancient 'place of power' in the San Isidro district, where the shaman Ramon would be waiting for us. Also known as Pan de Azúcar (Sugar Bread), archaeological investigations reveal three main occupation periods for this *huaca* (sacred burial site): before and during the Lima Culture (around 200 BC to 700 AD) by ancient Hualla settlers, Ishma (around the 11th century) and Inca (15th and 16th century). In each period it was used differently, first as a place of worship. A pyramid was built, constructed with adobe bricks, shaped by hand and assembled to create enclosures, patios, passageways and private areas. Everything was painted yellow in deference to the sun. Access to the ceremonial centre was only for the religious elite. Burials were also conducted there, at first simple, with bodies wrapped in cotton cloths and tied to a reed stretcher, along with offerings placed around the head in ceramic pots, and food for the afterlife.

As time passed Huallamarca was abandoned as a temple and used purely as a burial ground. Funerary bundles with false heads were made, the bodies wrapped in woven cloth and buried with textiles, decorated ceramic pots, gourds, tools, musical instruments, food and other valuables. During its final phase the site was used by the Incas as a place of settlement, with new terraces built on the east side of the pyramid along with dwellings, patios, storage and cooking areas. Eventually it was abandoned altogether as a new Lima rose up around it, though the power of its history remained.

The ceremony began there in darkness, with an opening ritual of prayers, invocations and chants - calls to the spirit of San Pedro, the land and the shaman's supernatural guides and allies, which included the Catholic saints. This was followed by a *limpia* (purification) where participants were smudged with the smoke of Palo Santo (holy wood), the fragrant *Bursera graveolens*, and drank plant medicines to cleanse them before San Pedro could be taken. The first of these was a *contrachisa*, a sour potion that causes vomiting so that spiritual and physical toxins are purged from the body. Next was the *singado* (Tobacco macerated in honey and aguardiente: 'fire water' alcohol) which participants inhaled through their nostrils. When taken through the left nostril it liberates the patient from negative energy including illness, bad luck and the influences of other people. Taken through the right it is for energising the spirit and bringing good luck so all of our projects go well. After snorting it, we could spit the Tobacco juice out or swallow it, it didn't matter which and, in fact most people ended up with a combination of both.

The experience of the contrachisa and singado, despite the blessings they may bring, is not pleasant, but few medicines are. The former is a bitter, thick liquid that sits heavily in the stomach, churning like bile. Its impact is not immediate as the plant first 'checks out' the gut for impurities. After about 45 minutes it is ready to gather together the poisons it finds and release them through vomiting or diarrhoea. After almost an hour of feeling sick you are rewarded by being sick. Some reward.

As with the contrachisa, participants stood before the *mesa* – a cloth altar laid on the ground - to receive the singado. It was handed to us in a snail shell; a red-black liquid which felt like fire when snorted into the nostrils and tasted peppery and acidic as it dripped down the back of our throats. Chanting and more prayers followed and then, somewhere around midnight, San Pedro was finally drunk.

I didn't know what to expect from the brew on that first journey or how it would (or should) affect me. What I know now is that Ramon's San Pedro was not strong and the measure was small. In these nighttime rituals led by shamans like Ramon who I have come to characterise as 'old school' curanderos, San Pedro is merely part of the healing process, not the purpose of the ceremony itself, so no more attention is given to it by the healer than to the prayers he makes or the other medicines he offers. Some even expect that there will be no effect on the participant from San Pedro, seeing it more as the shaman's ally than the patient's healer. By drinking it, that is, the spirit of the plant becomes part of the participant and communicates with the shaman to tell him the problems the patient has and how the curandero might heal them. In this philosophy the plant itself is not the healer; that is the job of the shaman.

In the years to follow I would find curanderos who thought

differently, who made strong San Pedro and who allowed the cactus to perform its healing directly without interfering in the process themselves. The ceremonies I have attended with these healers have produced the more profound changes in me and I have witnessed many 'miracle cures' in others.

That first night in Lima, however, I didn't know any better. When a pause in the ceremony took place and a little space and silence became available, I tried to tune in to San Pedro, to feel it within me and explore what it might be trying to show me. It was more difficult than in subsequent journeys since the brew was weak and I felt largely unchanged by it (except perhaps for a sense of peace or acceptance) but something in me *did* shift and I began to notice that things, people and objects had a sort of luminosity to them, as if shining with an inner light. As patients approached the mesa to ask for healing I saw that this light was dimmer in some areas of their bodies and that the shaman would see this too and begin his work in that place, spraying flower water over the patient or rubbing him with a wooden *chonta* stick to remove the spirit of illness that this dimness represented. Having done so, the patient's light would shine brighter or change colour from a sickly pale green to a radiant purple or calm blue. What San Pedro was showing me was the sheen of the soul and the immediacy of healing when performed with love and intent. It was something I had never seen from the drugs I had been selling, which often left their users looking weaker and sicker and far from healed. Years later I found this account by the San Pedro shaman Eduardo Calderon about his approach to healing during ceremonies: 'What do we look for? The colour of the aura, which is a reflection of the person's personality. Everything that he has done before and which has contributed to alienation, to sickness, to fear, to apprehension, to anxiety leaps forth at that moment. Why? Because the San Pedro and all the other herbs help us. They make one vibrate. They make one light up... In a curing session this 'vision' develops by means of the potion of San Pedro'.[9]

There was something else too: a sort of involuntary desire I had to breathe more deeply, to really *feel* the night air in my lungs, as if it was nourishing and healing in itself and contained living spirit (*prana*: 'vital life') which had information to impart: whispers on the wind.

Yes, San Pedro is a plant of the earth but it is also a plant of the air. This, more than the soil, is its true element, its medium, its essence...

The night passed and the next day I boarded my plane to Iquitos. The more spectacular visions and insights of Ayahuasca produced the healing and gave me the sense of direction I had come to Peru to find. The path of my life, it showed me, was to work more closely with teacher plants and to become a healer myself; advice I followed, returning to Peru a number of times to make a study of shamanism and its healing methods, and now healing and training people myself.

Amid the visual pyrotechnics of the Ayahuasca experience I suppose it would have been easy to turn my back on my relatively weak encounter with San Pedro, and perhaps understandable if I had. But there was *something* about the cactus that wouldn't leave me; some sense I had that what it showed me, as mild as the effects had been, was as important as the message of the vine – maybe more so, although I didn't yet understand why. It was enough anyway that on my returns to Peru I sought it out and drank it again with other shamans, just as much as I sought the guidance of Ayahuasca.

Eventually the cactus became more important to me than the vine. It seemed to me that the latter expands consciousness and adds new freedoms to life by showing us what is possible and available to us in our universe but eventually we must make a choice of what to do with this information; we must decide how to be and act so we can explore what it means to be human – *truly* human – in this life that we have. This Earthly meaning and purpose is what San Pedro provides. Ayahuasca shows us our place in the universe; San Pedro shows us our place on Earth: that we are children of God but we are not purely spirit. We have bodies, we are physical and we live in a physical world. If we are to do the work of God, to evolve and help others to heal it stands to reason therefore that we must do so through our humanity by facing our issues and taking our part in the physical realm rather than pretending or wishing that we were already 'beings of light'. That realisation became the guiding message for me and so in 2008, 10 years after my first South American trip, I decided to thoroughly study San Pedro, to become its apprentice and to spend time in Peru drinking the medicine and learning more about Andean healing.

I had been taking groups to Peru for many years by then to work with the shamans and drink the visionary medicines of the jungles and mountains, usually hosted by regional healing Centres and their curanderos. Normally this worked well but there had been a few occasions where shamans had acted less than professionally and their Ayahuasca was *debil* (weak) or inconsistent and I had had to 'lay down the law'. After one of these camps, the Temple of the Way of Light, where its elderly Shipiba shamans had confused the plant medicines for some of my participants, the conditions were poor, the Ayahuasca unsatisfactory, and its owner had proved more interested in money than healing, my assistant, Trudy, and I decided that it would be preferable to open our own Centre where we could work with better shamans, offer the best medicine and set our own standards of quality, motivated by healing rather than money.

Trudy had been a participant of mine on the previous year's trip and had drunk Ayahuasca and San Pedro with me. It changed her life, helped her finally lay to rest the ghosts of her life-long addictions to heroin and alcohol (a story she tells in my book *Cactus of Mystery*) and she had relocated from Australia to Peru to work more closely with these plants. Together we found the ideal camp and while I was busy teaching in Spain, Trudy made it her home and began the job of remodelling it so we could open as a healing Centre in 2009 and I could begin my cactus apprenticeship.

Between 2008 and 2009 I spent as much time as I could researching San Pedro to prepare myself for my move. My first disappointment however was discovering how little is actually known or written about it.

A Google search produced next to nothing and, apart from my own two books on San Pedro[10] and scattered references in a few others, there is still little written about it. At least in part, this lack of information is a reflection of the fact that the most ancient healing traditions of Peru, like those of other pre-Christian cultures, are transmitted orally. Not much is written down by shamans so where such records exist they have been made by European explorers, invaders or missionaries who have brought their beliefs with them and denigrated indigenous practices that did not, on the face of it, sit with their notions of God. As professor of cultural anthropology, Irene Silverblatt, puts it: 'History making (which includes history denying) is a cultural invention... History tends to be 'made' by those who dominate... and then universalised to celebrate their heroes and silence dissent' and such commentaries always distort the native experience. One 16th century conquistador quoted by the ethnob- otanist, Richard Evans Schultes, for example, described San Pedro as a plant used by 'heathens' to 'speak with the devil'. That seems strange since the cactus is named for Saint Peter, the gatekeeper to Heaven, but also typical since God is rarely mentioned in the accounts of outsiders.

Neither the oral tradition nor the distortions by Europeans fully explain the absence of information on San Pedro, however. More fundamentally, and certainly more so than with

Ayahuasca, there is a sort of mystery surrounding the cactus and a sense that knowledge of it must remain secret or at least earned through preparation, participation and the worthiness of those who drink it. Even today an apprentice is not really taught about San Pedro by the shaman who mentors him but encouraged to learn from it himself and discover his own truths.

What we do know about San Pedro (*Trichocereus pachanoi*) is that it is a tall cactus which can reach heights of 20 feet or more. Its cylindrical branches produce a funnel-shaped flower of green-tinged white, which itself can grow to ten inches. It enjoys a tough, desert-like environment and grows readily in the highest parts of Peru, where it has many names among shamans and healers, including *cardo, chuma, gigantón, hermoso, huando, wachuma* and *El Remedio*: The Remedy, referring to its healing powers and ability to help those who drink it let go of illusions. The name San Pedro has similar connotations. It refers to Saint Peter and suggests the plant's power to open the gates between the visible and invisible worlds so those who drink it enter a realm where they can heal, know their true natures and find purpose for their lives.

Among native Andean healers San Pedro is better known as *huachuma* and the shamans who work with it are called *huachumeros* if male and *huachumeras* if female. Its use as a sacrament in healing rituals is ancient. The earliest archaeological evidence so far discovered for this is a stone carving of a huachumero found at the Jaguar Temple of Chavín de Huantar in northern Peru which is almost 3,500 years old, dating to at least 1500 years before the origins of the Christian religion brought to Peru by the Spanish. Textiles from the same region and period of history depict the cactus with jaguars and hummingbirds, its guardian spirits, and with stylised spirals representing the visionary experiences brought on by the plant. A decorated ceramic pot from the Chimú culture of Peru, dating to 1200 AD, has also been unearthed which shows an owl-faced woman holding a cactus. In the Andes, the owl is one of the tutelary spirits and guardians of herbalists and shamans and the woman depicted is therefore most likely a curandera and huachumera.

According to a shaman quoted by Schultes, San Pedro ceremonies were (and continue to be) held to cure illnesses of a spiritual, emotional, mental or physical nature; to know the future through the prophetic and divinatory qualities of the plant; to overcome sorcery or *saladera* (an inexplicable run of bad luck); to ensure success in one's ventures; to rekindle love and enthusiasm for life; and to restore one's faith or find meaning by re-experiencing the world as divine. It can perform healings like these because it is 'in tune with the powers of animals and beings that have supernatural powers... Participants [in ceremonies] are set free from matter and engage in flight through cosmic regions   transported across time and distance in a rapid and safe fashion'.

The writer Caspar Greeff attended San Pedro ceremonies with shaman and ex-psychiatrist Dr Valentin Hampejs in 2007 and records his experiences in his Blog. 'San Pedro will never deceive you and he will never lie to you' said Hampejs. 'Ayahuasca [by contrast] is more like a snake: slippery, tricky and winding all over the place. It takes much more experience with Ayahuasca to know what is true.'

Hampejs began to work with Greeff to help him explore the issues that may have brought him to San Pedro. The first question he put to his patient is perhaps the same one asked by every person who has ever attended a ceremony. It was the question that had first brought me to Peru in the first place. Maybe it is in the nature of the cactus itself:

'So Caspar, who are you?'

'I am a pure angel of God', Greeff replied as the cactus took hold of him. It is a fairly standard answer and one we might expect from any spiritual seeker touched by the power of San Pedro - but it didn't satisfy Hampejs and nor should it satisfy us because the answer itself lacks depth and there is nothing purposeful or solid about it.

'No. You are not a pure angel of God' said Hampejs. 'You are deluding yourself. If you were a pure angel of God, you would not have a physical body. So, I ask you again: Who are you?'

'Caspar.'

'And who is Caspar? It is a simple question. Who are you?'

'It is not a simple question,' Greeff replied. 'Philosophically and existentially it is one of the most difficult questions of all to answer.'

'Now you are masturbating with your mind' said Hampejs. 'We are not talking philosophy or existentialism. I am asking you a simple question: Who are you?'

'I am I' said Greeff, somewhat frustrated with the way this was going.

Hampejs nodded. 'Yes. That is good. I am I. You are you and you always have been and you always will be. *I am I.* Good. You are starting to learn...'

Who am I – that Zen question and the Zen answer it requires from us – 'who am I *really*?' - is one that I have subsequently watched many participants ask in San Pedro ceremonies and the answers they have received have sometimes been shocking and life-changing. The point is that our sense of identity (and a whole raft of associated emotions and concepts, like self-worth, blame, shame, purpose, responsibility, commitment, pride and possibility) so often goes unquestioned in daily life and we end up acting from habit, fear, or as a consequence of what we have learned of ourselves from others and been taught by them to believe. San Pedro opens our minds and invites us to reconsider. Inevitably our relationship to ourselves and to the world must then change as our habitual identities are stripped away – unless of course our fears dictate that we run from what we have discovered and lose ourselves again in 'who we have always been' or cling wilfully to old behaviours when they simply aren't working for us.

That is possible too for, as Alexander Shulgin remarks in *PIHKAL*[11]. 'Psychedelic drugs don't change you – they don't change your character – unless you *want* to be changed. They *enable* change, they can't impose it'.

Resistance to change, even when that change is healing and beneficial, even when we are given encouragement and support to break through our own limitations, *is* possible. I know that now because I have seen it. It may be crazy, pointless, painful and damaging to ourselves and others, but it *is* possible, especially when fuelled by a fear of the new thing you are becoming, or by old wounds, anger and pride.

The philosopher Aristotle wrote that 'We are what we repeatedly do' and that question 'Who are you' is always at the centre of our choices. In a way, this story is my experience of that.

HINTS OF THE FUTURE: TROUBLE AND THE LIVING TAO

Is she weird, is she white?
Is she promised to the night?
Pixies, *Is She Weird*

2010. June

I have always liked raw and ruined people; the wounded, the damaged and disenfranchised who the world rejects and who reject it in kind. Often they are our artists, creators and change-makers. Often too, more than most, they are willing to see their pain and address it, explore its meanings and find ways to heal. There is courage and strength in that which may lead to a new and deeper knowledge of the self and, if they are lucky, to wisdom.

This is what I tell my clients now when they come to me for help, feeling broken by life and ashamed sometimes because they cannot heal their wounds alone: that their pain and their willingness to face it – to have made this healing appointment at all - is where their strength and bravery lies. Because the truth is that we are all in pain, it is just that most of us don't recognise it against the background noise of suffering in our societies, or else we sense it and ignore it through fear of what we may find on the other sides of ourselves. Those who choose to face their anxieties, their souls and their demons are not weak; they are the strongest among us.

The trick, however – and one that so few of us seem to have mastered – is to see our pain, acknowledge and honour it, and then let it go and move on instead of revisiting it forever and adding to its power over us by deepening the wound.

One of the fundamental things that work with plants may teach you is that all of life is a paradox – that, in the words of

Niels Bohr, the Nobel Prize winner for his work in quantum physics, 'the opposite of a profound truth may be another profound truth' – so that the way we present ourselves to the world, for example, may be the opposite of how we really feel about ourselves. Our public face or persona represents the truth we put on show while our inner world contains a reality of a different order. We may put on a show of strength for example *because we feel weak,* or a front of independence and free-spirit-edness while *we are wholly dependent on others* and have nothing of our own to give; we may travel the world, running towards new adventures *because* there is something in our pasts that we are also running from and we want to fill the emptiness inside us with sunsets and jungles, mountains and oceans, cramming more and more beauty into the thing we find most ugly. By the same token, a client who *professes* weakness because of an issue she cannot face alone has integrity, honesty and power which many seemingly tough and defended people lack. There is strength in vulnerability.

As much as I would like it to be (because I believe that it is fundamental to our psychology) this notion of paradox – that the outer world does not so much reflect as *mirror* the interior world – is not an original idea. It is there in the words of The Living Tao:

True power seems weak
True purity seems tarnished
True steadfastness seems changeable
True clarity seems obscure
The greatest art seems unsophisticated
The greatest love seems indifferent
The greatest wisdom seems childish

Those who are raw, wounded or damaged have something special in them because they have *truly* lived – felt life's horror as well as its beauty – and they are therefore closest to the Tao. They contain the seeds of something great. *Because* they are hurt and confused they have the potential to be our greatest healers and teachers.

It is one thing to know this however and another to be made wise by it. And so it was that in 2010 the Tao came alive for me and I entered its flow - because apparently it was time for that to happen so I could learn its lessons.

The Tao is nowhere to be found
Yet it nourishes and completes all things

I heard about her long before I met her. To assist in setting up our Ayahuasca Centre and preparing it for the arrival of guests Trudy and I had introduced a volunteer helper programme. Unlike other retreat Centres in Peru which charge their volunteers to be there to help with the work, we were fair and in exchange for four hours of work a day we offered food and accommodation, attendance at ceremonies and immersion in a new culture and way of life. It gave people – usually students on a gap year or young travellers – an opportunity to visit the rainforest and learn new skills including traditional building methods, ecology, and of course plant medicines and shamanic healing. But one or two volunteers were not so young. A few were in their 30s or 40s, middle-aged or heading that way and still chasing dreams of youth and freedom. They were the ones that interested me. *Why* in your 30s or 40s, an age by which most of us are settled – not always into a 'normal' lifestyle but into a way of life at least - would you leave the familiar behind and come alone to a jungle to immerse yourself in Conrad's Heart of Darkness? What are you looking for that you haven't yet found? A 20-year-old is easier to fathom. She is taking a break from her future, refining plans, gaining experience, backpacking her way through a few adventures before she decides on a course for her life. But what of a close-to-middle-aged woman who arrives in the forest alone? What is she running from or hoping to find that brings her to this place, light years away from other people, from home and the past, to a place where you can only be present?

Teaching had kept me busy in Spain, where I was also living, and despite my intentions to move to Peru in 2009 I didn't get there until June the following year, by which time our first volunteers had already been there for a month or so, but I got regular updates from Trudy.

A month at a jungle camp is about long enough to settle in and acclimatise, to get involved in a few projects and start making friends but for one of our volunteers, a month is all it took for her to start making trouble.

From the emails I received it seemed that almost as soon as she got off the plane Jane had begun an affair with one of our married Peruvian workers, a labourer called Joe. Trudy and I had a policy of 'no fraternisation' (by which we meant no involvement of any kind beyond the platonic) between staff, shamans, clients, volunteers or anyone else at the Centre. We were in the business of healing and to protect and support our clients and ensure professionalism it was important to keep things clean. We had both heard – and seen – enough cases of women (and sometimes also men, but usually women) arriving in Peru and losing their heads, their hearts and their underwear to some 'mystical shaman', 'otherwordly guru' – or even an 'exotic' janitor who hinted at magical powers - to know the dangers on all sides of tolerating an arrangement like this. These affairs were difficult enough and distracting when they were going on but the almost inevitable allocations of blame and 'who did what to who' when they ended usually produced chaos. They had even led to accusations of rape – some of them knowingly false - and to police involvement in one or two of the cases we were aware of.

Volunteers had the rules explained to them as soon as they

arrived and staff had the same rules drummed into them before they were even hired. But there are always those, fresh off the plane from the West, who are naïve and do not understand the ways of the forest, who think they know better or deserve more from their great adventure – which is why we had introduced these rules to begin with: to protect them from themselves, and everyone else (including our Peruvian workers) from them.

As a response to the situation between Joe and Jane, Trudy had first taken the diplomatic route of moving Joe's family into camp as a reminder to everyone that he already had commitments and responsibilities. As I heard the story later from Matt, Joe's brother and our most senior employee, that had limited effect. Joe told him everything, he said. They had a name for such women in Peru – not quite *puta*, which is a derogatory term, but, in the more polite, conservative and Catholic language of Peruvian people, 'good time girls': women who, for the price of a few drinks or a meal, will show you 'a good time'. Western women, he laughed, believe they are free spirits so they even buy their own drinks; a real happy ending.

With the affair still causing problems and staff losing faith in our rules and forming their own views about this new volunteer Trudy eventually asked me what I thought we should do. I couldn't see much alternative but that one of them had to go. This early in our programme we really didn't need disruptions like this and since Joe was our employee and was supposed to know better, given a choice of the two it had to be him. And so it was. He lost his job.

That is a tragedy in Peru, with high unemployment and people dependent on work to feed their families but, on the other hand, we couldn't allow the rules of the Centre to be so openly flaunted before we had even opened.

Trudy told me later that given the same choice again she'd make it differently. Joe was a skilled worker, a good guy and part of our rainforest family whereas Jane was a blow-in and the trouble she brought was far from over, although in fairness, we didn't know that yet. I would make that choice differently now too but right from the start, for some reason, it seemed that part of my journey was to take care of Jane. Perhaps, even from a distance, I sensed a need for healing in her. Or perhaps I was a Fool.

It was the card I drew from the tarot as a prediction for my journey before I left Spain for Peru, although I didn't give it much attention at the time because I was excited to be going at all. With hindsight, I should have given it more.

With all his worldly possessions in one small pack, the Fool travels he knows not where. So filled with visions, questions, wonder and excitement is he that he doesn't see the cliff he is likely to fall over...

The Fool is the card of infinite possibilities. The bag on the staff indicates that he has all he needs to do or be anything he wants, he has only to stop and unpack. He is on his way to a brand new beginning. But the card carries a little bark of warning as well. While it's wonderful to be enthralled with all around you, excited by all life has to offer, you still need to watch your step lest you fall and end up looking the fool.

As a card, the Fool ultimately stands for a new beginning often involving a literal move to a new home or job. The querent (meaning the sitter or the one asking the cards for advice) might be starting to date again or trying out some new activity. There's more than just change here, there is renewal, movement and the energy of a fresh start... They are back at zero, whether that be in romantic affairs or career, work or intellectual pursuits.

Far from being sad or frustrated by having to start over, the querent feels remarkably free, light-hearted and refreshed, as if being given a second chance. They feel young and energized, as excited as a child who has discovered a new toyshop. Who knows what they will find on the shelves... For the Fool the most important thing is to just go out and enjoy the world, to see what there is to see and delight in all of it.

Unfortunately, this childlike state can make one overly optimistic or naive. A Fool can be a fool. That business opportunity might not be so sure-fire or amazing as it seems and that new lover might not be so flawless... However exciting new beginnings may be you still have to watch your step.[12]

THE ROAD TO HEALING

To the ancients all life involved a pulse, rhythm or breath. They saw all human life as breathed temporarily into the world of maya or illusion then breathed out again, a process repeated through the ages. They saw great flocks or shoals of souls being breathed in and out of material life together
Mark Booth, *The Secret History of the World*

2010. June/July

Make a right turn 14 kilometres outside of Iquitos and what passes for a highway becomes a dirt track. Follow it a further two kilometres, through the village, across a small bridge and into the jungle and you arrive at my healing Centre, the place where I began my San Pedro apprenticeship.

To celebrate our opening and coincide with the conference on Amazonian medicine we had, as I said earlier, invited La Bruja to hold San Pedro ceremonies there and the Centre was filled with people now who had drunk the brew and, as is the nature of the plant, were lost in wonder at the beauty of the world and, perhaps for the first time ever, in touch with their souls and discovering new things about themselves. Love 101. A few may also have been crying, seeing things they'd never seen before, reliving past regrets or old wounds, working through them and releasing their pain. That, too, is in the nature of San Pedro but it is always tempered by beauty. The cactus holds you.

It was a day filled with strangeness and new beginnings for me as well. I had worked with La Bruja for many years by now, learning from her during ceremonies, allowing her San Pedro to teach me and, along the way, becoming her friend. More recently I had asked her to train me formally in the ways of healing with San Pedro and she had agreed, so I was disappointed at what I took to be her back-tracking now on the understanding that had brought me to Peru, when I asked when our training could begin.

'Ross', she said, 'San Pedro is the medicine of love and no-one but you can teach you about love, because only *you* can experience it. I can open doorways for you but it is you who will have to walk through them and make your own relationship with the plant. It is San Pedro who will teach you, not me, because that is the way of the cactus and that is how it has always been done. Bear in mind as well that sometimes it is not easy'.

It was disappointing to hear because I guess I had imagined that she would be offering me a carefully-planned programme of instruction in mesa work, Andean healing, and some romantic Castaneda-style induction into the secret knowledge of an enigmatic 'wise woman' healer. A few years have passed since those words were spoken however and I understand them a lot better now. La Bruja was right and she kept her promise. She did open doorways and stepping through them – in both directions - was not easy; it is one of the hardest things I have ever done.

La Bruja had flown from Cusco to be with us and during a stop-over in Iquitos she had met a woman she brought with her to our Centre because she felt that San Pedro could help her. Christine was in her late 30s I suppose, extremely thin, pale and she looked in pain. She had AIDS and she had come to Peru hoping that Ayahuasca would heal her. La Bruja had found her in town, penniless and alone, and while she couldn't offer her the vine, she had invited her to today's ceremony with the cactus.

The coincidence was striking. For years I had been peddling AIDS drugs which, it seemed to me, were ineffective at promoting a cure; it didn't even seem to be their point. I had left that behind to train as a curandero and now, having set up a rainforest healing Centre, the first person to seek our help had AIDS. It felt like the universe was laying it on the line for me. I had never really believed in pharmaceutical drugs but knew that herbal medicines and other methods of healing could help – I had witnessed several such cures with Ayahuasca and San Pedro among the groups I had taken to Peru during the intervening years and had been part of those healings (both giving and receiving) myself – so here was my chance to prove that traditional medicine worked with a disease that I knew; the very disease in fact that had, in a way, brought me to Peru in the first place.

We drank San Pedro together, all three of us, and waited for the effects to take place then moved Christine to a private room in the casa grande. She was frail as she lay on the bed and La Bruja began her healing. San Pedro is a gentle plant - intense but gentle - and La Bruja's healing reflected that: a subtle exchange of energy, more like reiki than the stylised ritual healings I had seen in the nighttime ceremonies of other curanderos. She stood immobile over the bed, arms outstretched over Christine, her eyes closed and her lips moving slightly as she prayed to God and the *apus* (spirits) for healing and channelled the powers they sent her into the sick woman's body.

My own approach was more vigorous. San Pedro had taught me years ago about the importance of the breath and it felt now like I was ravenous to suck all of the poison out of Christine and blow or spit it away. I felt myself changing, becoming almost wolf-like, wanting to bite out the sickness I saw in her. La Bruja watched me curiously.

Shamans see bad energies within a person as repulsive forms such as snakes, leeches, spiders or scorpions. It makes it unmistakable as something which must be removed because from this energy all physical disease manifests. A tumour can never be a tumour for example without a thoughtform, an idea or a 'stress' – a mood or an atmosphere; something immaterial in itself – from which it can grow. The sickness in Christine looked like a river of filth; black tar, shit and human waste, holding all sorts of nightmares in the form of insects, beetles, rats, syringes, used condoms and sewers. It *felt* malevolent. Yet San Pedro calmly instructed me to push my face into this mess, which I did, laying my head on Christine's belly, and, despite its grossness, chewing it out and sucking it into my mouth to remove it from her.

San Pedro was teaching me how to use my breath in healing, to draw out poison and push back clean, fresh *prana* or *chi* – life-force – to replace the darkness inside. The circulation of air, the breath, was rapid, like panting, and a sound, deep and guttural, emerged from me too and was directed into her. Amazonian shamans call such sounds or songs *icaros*. In the Andes they are known as *tarjos*: songs, prayers or incantations. They are a vibration; energy which can shatter physical or emotional blockages within a person, like an opera singer with a wine glass, breaking things up for their removal. They carry an intention as well, to restore balance to the soul and soothe whatever spiritual or emotion-driven ailment has caused the physical illness.

Some of the blackness did leave her, blood returned to her cheeks and she looked more relaxed, but there was more to do and by seeing into her I was also aware of a darker, more physical mass close to her right lung that not even she knew about.

If Christine could have stayed with us longer I knew there were plants that could help her – Jergon Sacha, Una de Gato - and that further healings and a proper diet with Ayahuasca and San Pedro would give her strength, maybe even produce the cure she was looking for. But we had her for a day. There was nothing else we could do.

Christine enjoyed her time with us, playing with the other San Pedro children. With a little more energy now, she swam in our lagoon, chatted to others and relaxed in the sun; then she returned to Iquitos. I met her again, by chance, a few weeks later and she looked healthier, though still sick. She had been having trouble breathing, she said – something in her lungs or kidneys – but was working with an Ayahuasca shaman now and hoping for a miracle. I never saw her again so I don't know what became of her but I hope she found what she was looking for.

I returned to the garden. There were a few more healings to

do: Laurel, who looked, during my San Pedro vision, as if she had chains around her legs, holding her back from life and from choice. I removed them, using breath and feathers – emblems of the air – taken from the mesa that had been prepared before the ceremony. 'My father and brother' she said afterwards, 'I have always felt held back by them because of how they treated me as a child.'

And James, a psychoanalyst with darkness like a stone in his belly. He began laughing as I drew the intrusion out of him with my breath - like a child I thought, not the controlled professional I knew him as. Still, I – or that rational part of my brain, at least, which is often our own worst enemy - imagined that he was not taking the healing seriously and so would get little from it. I thought he may be weighing its directness against his analytical techniques – the "talking cures" of modern therapy – and finding failings and nothing of value. I was wrong. He told me three days later that he felt much lighter, had never experienced anything like this before and that he wanted to write a book on shamanic healing and psychotherapy. He has come to almost every plant medicine ceremony I have held since then, in Peru or in Spain.

A thought from nowhere but based on the healings today: San Pedro is a male spirit while Ayahuasca is female (or so it is said) – so maybe those who prefer San Pedro had difficult relationships with their fathers. *They also seem more willing to repair them. Whereas those who prefer Ayahuasca had a difficult time with their* mothers. *Just an idea…*

Lying in the moloka now, looking up. The whole building spins as I breathe in and out. It is gentle, not dizzying – it is what is: San Pedro just shows you what is there: a living, breathing universe, the energy or soul of a building, the circle of life. Things in the universe can never be still. There always has to be movement so that we and

God can evolve. Illness arises when we become too fixated and stuck in one part of the circle – our 'story' – so it cannot complete itself. But it is still a story - and not even a whole one at that. Everything is not a fact of life but a theory of life; something to be tested and proven – or otherwise. Even this sentence which, to me looks clean and final is only an idea, an hypothesis. The mind is a dog drinking water...

I was talking to someone earlier about two girls who became scared during a San Pedro ceremony – not in the same way as with Ayahuasca, not at what they saw but at who they were – according to their old definitions of self, as well as the power they had over who they still might become: the awareness of their true selves. That is what frightened them: their own potential. Maybe that's why babies cry too...

Gazing at the tree outside, its bark and leaves become many shades, textures and shapes, like I'm part of a slightly surreal painting. Even relaxed though, my mind wants to pick out the 'unusual' such as a different colour or shape to the rest instead of a 'universe' – the universe now comprised of 'tree' - and then to fix on it. We have the same problem in life: the mind. It wants to pick out our stories and fixate on the dramas and adventures within them and make those our lives instead of allowing us just to live. If you are 33 and I ask you to tell me the story of your life it should of course take 33 years, moment by moment. But in fact you would tell me all that you are – all that your 'invented self' declares you to be - in less than two minutes flat. That is your story but it's not your life. A dog drinking water...

Some lines from Jodorowsky and the artist Leonora Carrington sum up the day:

Jodorowsky on the nature of existence: 'Life has neither meaning *nor meaninglessness. It must be lived.'*

Carrington on the patterns that we can fall into instead of just living: *'[My mother told me that] "After giving me a black eye because he imagined I had flirted with a customer in the shop, your father raped me and got me pregnant. I have hated him ever since and I cannot love you". It is a cruel blow to know that your birth was not desired. This is why I have always lived with the feeling that nothing really belonged to me; in order for the world to belong to us we must believe that the world desires us. Only that which desires us can be ours.'*

Of her relationship years later with her lover L, she added: *'I had come to L wanting to be loved, seeking the perfect mother, which arose from the same need as my infant cries and weeping in the cradle. I was demanding and needy. Yet how could I give, for nothing was really mine? If the world did not desire me how could it receive my love? I had only learned to desire myself, which split me into two – or more.'*

Jodorowsky on the possibility of changing all this through healing and self-discovery: *'Are we ourselves? Where are we when we are? If I close my hands water still escapes from them… Sometimes you remove the man without removing the surroundings, sometimes you remove the surroundings without removing the man. Sometimes you remove both. Sometimes you remove neither.'*

And if I drive 10,000 miles to your holy mountain or walk there or crawl on broken knees, when I arrive it is still a mountain that you call holy and I have similar places in me, so why should I go at all?
A: Because I am alive and I can.

Finding the sacred within ourselves saves us a journey; that is all.

To know ourselves we must empty out, become a shell. When we get rid of who we've become we have a sense of who we are...
Extract from my journal during the San Pedro diet

San Pedro had begun showing me how to heal without the dramas and battles that some shamans get into, without the fey psychological concepts and practices of Western 'core shamanism' or the endless talking of modern analytical therapies, but as a matter of faith and the simple use of the breath. Most spiritual practices which endure end up with the realisation that 'all we need do is breathe' and healing itself suggested the power of faith: if I believed, as I did today, that I had more power than whatever intrusive spirit infected those I worked on – or put more simply, *if I refused to believe in their illness at all* – healing followed. It was a lesson whose truth I would verify in future ceremonies.

In the afternoon I sat watching the pool, letting the day wash over me. I was pondering what La Bruja had said: that the secrets of San Pedro cannot be taught but must be discovered for oneself. The plant had already begun my education but there was much more to learn. How, I wondered, would it be possible to discover it all by myself? And yet, according to La Bruja, this was the traditional way – and the only way - of apprenticeship with the plant. The answer was to ask San Pedro directly.

As soon as I thought this three clear ideas jumped into my head:

~ *Diet San Pedro for one month.*
~ *Drink all of the ribs separately to know how they heal.*
~ *Find San Pedro in ceremony and ask to be shown its companion plants.*

The diet is a shamanic procedure used in the Amazon for connecting with the spirit of a plant in order to know its essence, its personality and its truth. Anthropologists define it as 'A tool helping to maintain the altered state of consciousness which permits the plant teacher to instruct, provide knowledge and enable the initiate to acquire power... [it is] a means of making the mind operate differently, providing access to wisdom and lucid dreams.'[13]

Dietary restrictions prohibit foods including pork, fats, salt, sugar, spices, condiments and alcohol, leaving the apprentice with an extremely bland menu so he is not overwhelmed by flavours and can more finely sense the attributes of the plant. This uninspiring menu also weakens his attachments to routine life, some of which revolve around meal times and typical foods. For the same reason there is a prohibition on sexual activity since sex is another distraction which will ground him in his body and inhibit spiritual progress. In the words of the ayahuascero Guillermo Arevalo: 'That is why the shaman goes into the wilderness. There is no temptation there.'

The traditional Amazonian diet for making an ally of a plant lasts 14 days and this is the method I have normally followed. At the end of the first week a little lemon, salt, sugar and onion – the tastes we have avoided - are eaten to break the fast and provide a safe boundary to the experience. The after-diet continues for a further week and although the same restrictions apply to sex, alcohol, pork and strong spices, other foods can now be eaten.

That, however, was not what San Pedro was asking. A whole month of dieting would be difficult. More or less it meant a 31 day fast, drinking the cactus every day, in seclusion away from the world. But I had work to do, people who needed healing, the management of the Centre as well. This aspect of the diet would be something I'd have to come back to when I had more time to give it.

Drinking all of the ribs separately was a more accessible project, provided I could find a shaman who would prepare the brews for me or make up a powdered San Pedro mix. The cactus grows in the Andes, not the rainforest, and it would be almost impossible to find enough of the fresh plant locally to make up the mixtures myself.

The San Pedro cactus produces a number of ribs and shamans say that its effects vary accordingly, although not all agree on what those effects are. La Bruja, for example, works only with seven or nine ribs 'because they produce the most gentle and beautiful brews. Those with six or eight are not so strong, while elevens and thirteens can be very intense but also sometimes dark. I never use either of these with my patients. Those with four ribs we only use for exorcisms and the patient and healer must both drink. You don't ever want to try a San Pedro like this. It is horrible and the visions take you to Hell.'

The latter point is interesting and illustrates one of the differences between shamans in their beliefs about the ribs since the curandero Eduardo Calderon, for example, seems to have held entirely the opposite view. The anthropologist Douglas Sharon recorded him as saying: 'He who finds a four-ribbed San Pedro can cure all sicknesses and maladies. Four-ribbed San Pedro is the mystical San Pedro: it was used in time immemorial and is depicted in Mochica pottery, in the sculpture of Chavin de Huantar, in the Sierra and in the north coast region where its application to curing is essential up to the present.'

This is the cactus of the four winds, *los cuatro vientos*. For Calderon and those who believe in it, its special healing powers are derived from its magical link to the number four and its correspondence with the four winds and the four roads; the supernatural powers of the cardinal directions which are invoked in ceremonies for healing:

~ *North*. The place of power, positivity and magnetism (the ability to attract good energies and repel those which are harmful) 'because of the position of the equator and the North Pole'.

~ *South*. The place of the will, because of its opposition to the forces of the North. The strong winds always come from the South.

~ *West*. The place of death, where the sun is lost to the sea.

~ *East*. The place of rebirth, where the sun rises up again from the darkness.

Four is also a special number in Andean cosmology since the Incan Empire - *Tahuantinsuyu* (Quechua: "the four regions between") - was divided into four and the Incas built four roads, departing from Cusco, each running through the four divisions of their empire. The four quarters converged in Cusco, the centre or "navel" of the Earth. The four-ribbed cactus is therefore the *axis mundi*: the cosmic axis or centre of the world, linking the different dimensions or planes through which the shaman travels in visionary trance.

These four roads may still take you to Hell, however - or to the doors of Paradise where San Pedro – Saint Peter – is waiting in judgement. And the point, I suppose, is this: how will we ever know at what destination we have arrived until we get there? But the adventure itself – if we are adventurous people – must surely be worth the taking.

'Find San Pedro in ceremony and ask to be shown its companion plants.' That was the final instruction and the easiest to deal with. Shamans use a number of plants when preparing San Pedro; it is not just a matter of adding the cactus to water and boiling it or drying cactus pieces in the sun and then grinding them into a powder. Other – usually secret – ingredients (since recipes are perfected by shamans in private and unique to them according to the teachings they have received from San Pedro itself) – are added to the base mixture and still other plants may be incorporated depending on the particular needs of a client. In modern parlance all of these are called admixtures. The directive to find San Pedro in ceremony and its companion plants was simple enough to understand therefore – and to do. Every diet begins with an Ayahuasca ceremony – or, at least, that is how it should be done - to open you up to the teachings of the plants and to hear what they have to say. We had a ceremony in three days time and my intention for it would be to meet San Pedro and see the plants it wanted to present to me, no doubt to diet them too.

It was at this point, as I sat gazing at the lagoon, debating all of this and how next to proceed with San Pedro, that I became aware of the other people around me: the sad girl with her book of love and escape and, more importantly, the energy that was being directed at me from someone behind me, as if I was being scanned. I felt it enter me and begin to explore my mind, as if taking my measure. I had a mental picture of the person it came from. It was a male energy but someone not indigenous to Peru; a young man with a sense of sadness about him too, as if he had lost something or someone important. He was looking, I felt, for a family or a community to join.

Our play with energy continued throughout the rest of the day, neither of us once looking directly at the other. By about 7pm the effects of San Pedro were wearing off and, for the first time I turned to see who I had been interacting with. He was a man in his 30s, tall, thin, with a rough beard and shoulder-length blonde hair; a hippy wearing cut-off jeans and sandals.

I walked over to him. 'Hi' I said, 'I think we know each other.'

'Yes' he replied, 'I think so. I am Selva.'

That was interesting. We had recently begun the search for a shaman who would become our resident healer and ayahuascero. We wanted someone skilled but young enough to adapt to our way of doing things and who would not bring rigid ideas or assumptions with them. Selva was a name that had been mentioned as a possible candidate. We knew little about him except that he had apprenticed for a while with Norma Pandura, one of the Amazon's more famous (or perhaps infamous) curanderas. She had been a serious and respected healer until, in her older age, her camp was more or less taken over by goddess-worshipping hippies from LA who had turned it into a free love commune, with guitar playing and protest songs instead of icaros during their Ayahuasca ceremonies and 'tantric' sex in the moloka as their unique contribution to medicine healings. Norma had tolerated this because of her frailty and her need for the money these goddesses generated. Chaos reigned for a while until she was killed by the sorcery of a rival shaman, it is said, who was jealous of her 'success', and with no-one to hold it together, her camp fell apart.

Selva moved out a month before Norma's death and worked for a while with Ron Wheelock – the so-called 'gringo shaman' – another interesting character, an American academic who had come to Peru to study shamanism but, as is sometimes the case when you arrive in the Heart of Darkness it arrived in him too and he had 'turned native' and trained as a shaman himself, becoming a respected ayahuascero, with some of the sweetest medicine in the forest. Selva had then moved on to apprentice with don Luis, where he had remained as a trainee ayahuascero, dieting a number of plants for the last five years. He had just completed his training and in our estimation might make a good shaman for us since he knew enough but was not yet set in his ways. We had been about to track him down and try a few ceremonies with him in order to test the ground. Now here he was, no tracking needed.

I invited him in for a post-ceremony meal and we listened to the rest of his story. He had been born a Saami, one of the indigenous people of the Arctic region which today encompasses parts of northern Sweden, Norway, Finland and Russia, where he was trained by his grandfather, the last shaman of this region, until the age of 12. The Saamis are a people long persecuted by politics and Christianity and even until recently working as a shaman or owning a drum was punishable by imprisonment or death. When his grandfather died there was no-one left to teach him and he became aimless and depressed, turning to vodka and supporting himself through hunting, living an isolated existence in a remote wilderness cabin and falling into decline: the shamanic crisis of initiation that many anthropologists write about. Eventually, in order to be well he knew he had to commit to shamanism and with no-one to teach him he became a traveller, homeless and heading for South America, Chile, Bolivia in search of a home until he eventually arrived in Peru where he found Norma Pandura and began a form of shamanic training.

It was a compelling story because we were also outcasts, curiosities and people who had taken an alternative route to end up in the middle of nowhere with our own healing dreams. Trudy, my business partner, was a heroin addict and an alcoholic who had kicked her habits and was now passionate about offering help to other addicts through the use of Ayahuasca. I was a recovered drug salesman who had seen the light and now wanted to offer natural cures as a more effective alternative. Our volunteers were driven by God-knows-what but certainly not the desire for a normal life. Just as I'd seen it, Selva was looking for a family to join; we all were.

I offered him a trial, the opportunity to run our next Ayahuasca ceremony, to see how he performed in practice. Trudy and I decided that I would drink the medicine that night to check things out 'from the inside' while she would not drink at all and remain available to our participants in case they needed help with toilet trips or words of reassurance.

I drank two cups, to be sure - and it was strong. Ayahuasca arrived as a swirling tunnel of bright colours, tentacles of yellow, green, red and blue which approached from a horizon of eyes-closed jungle blackness. It slowly enveloped me, swallowing me like a serpent built from fractal rainbows. In its guts I explored the insect world: the giant carcasses and bleached ribcages of long extinct creatures swarming with intelligent insect life which stripped them clean of flesh and returned them to the soil, all of this taking place on some faraway planet with two bright suns illuminating it.

I didn't want to be too drawn into this inner drama however as I was also paying attention to Selva and how he handled the ceremony. His icaros were unearthly, as if they originated from the alien environment I found myself in. They were like nothing I'd heard before from any shaman and sounded more like a desperate keening, a cry for help, sometimes just a vibration held to change energy or direct a realisation. He was not *singing* at all but intoning or invoking; speaking the otherwordly language of Ayahuasca, calling its spirit and instructing it in how to help the people present. I thought it was brilliant, radical, unlike any 'performance' I'd previously seen in a ceremony.

Trudy, who hadn't drunk, had a different view and later described it as 'vile screeching', declaring the ceremony 'as boring as bat shit.' She would understand it better a few days later when she drank Ayahuasca herself and could appreciate what Selva was doing with his alien songs.

My other – actually my first – intention for that night was to open myself to San Pedro, to meet its spirit and learn about the other plants I needed to diet, the admixtures.

I had met San Pedro's spirit before in a ceremony at the Temple of the Moon, an ancient sacred site above Cusco.[14] It appeared to me then as a matador, a man of power and Dignity (with a capital D), a vision shared by others who have drunk the brew. But what entered the moloka now was nothing like that. It took a form hard to describe – insect-like, green, the size of a man but more like a mantis, with ridges and spines on its skin, similar to the cactus itself.

And this is the warrior face of San Pedro...
If you really want to know this plant, this intelligence, you must also know this aspect - and it will challenge you

I was taken by it to a circle of elders – plant people in human form who presented themselves for consideration as those I should diet next. Among them were Tobacco, Chanca Piedra, Lima, Jergon Sacha, Salvia, and there were others. I realised just how many plants might be added to San Pedro – or to any teacher brew – to create particular healing changes or give access to certain wisdom. They were infinite: a diet that could last forever. I had to make choices and set priorities.

The strangest among them was Salvia. This was *Salvia divinorum*, a Mexican plant, curious in itself and rare enough in the country in which it grew but almost unheard of in Peru. It just didn't naturally grow here. In Mexico however it was one of the four sacred plants used by Mazatec curanderos: Peyote, Morning Glory, Mushrooms and Salvia. The first of these, Peyote, was a mescaline cactus too, similar to San Pedro and this, I assumed, was the connection: Salvia was a companion of Peyote and Peyote was a relative of San Pedro. In any case I wasn't going to question the information I had been given. The way to know any plant is to diet it and this is what I would do. Eventually I would develop a connection with Salvia that I could never have foreseen and my work with it would lead to some of the strangest and most painful – but also the most honest – experiences of my life.

A few hours later the ceremony ended and after a while Selva sat up. 'I have had a vision too' he said. 'This Centre is a beautiful place, its heart is good and I would like to work here.' We hadn't even made him an offer or told him we were looking for a shaman and he was already moving in. Luckily I liked him too. He had potential.

AYAHUASCA'S ORIGIN, HOLY SMOKE, AND MORE TROUBLE

Got hair in a girl that flows to her bones
And a comb in her pocket if the winds get blown
Pixies, *Number 13 Baby*

2010. July

Trudy and I exchanged glances, rolled our eyes and took a breath; a sort of 'Oh no, not again' look. Selva had been our resident shaman for some weeks now. As part of our arrangement we had agreed to build a *tambo* – a jungle home – for him and his long-term girlfriend, Nora, a lawyer, who he would soon be engaged to and who would join us at our camp.

He was standing in the doorway to the casa grande now, swaying, clearly still drunk from a few days off in town. That didn't bother us too much. In my opinion shamans must be real human beings like the rest of us, not make-believe gurus whose bodies are make-believe temples. We have had enough of those in the world already – from Maharishi Mahesh Yogi, blasted in the John Lennon song *Sexy Sadie* for preaching self-discipline and austerity while barely bothering to hide his own lavish self-indulgences ('What have you done? You've made a fool of everyone') to Sai Baba, alleged by some to be a paedophile, to the Catholic Church and its documented cases of child abuse. I didn't want a guru – I wouldn't trust one. When I work with a healer I want him to be human, feet on the ground not head in the clouds, so he knows how ordinary people feel and can help them.[15]

We had explained the rules to Selva – no 'fraternisation', no alcohol and no drugs at the camp – and, technically, he wasn't in violation of them since he wasn't actually drinking on site and Trudy and I could let that go although his condition wasn't ideal.

What caused the eye-rolling was Jane. She had been following him around like a puppy for days, visiting his tambo to offer him massages and joining him in town during time off, and rumours and concerns had once again been spreading among Centre staff. Iquitos is a small place and we had already been told by one employee about what he called "unacceptable" - or at least inappropriate - behaviour between them, including an episode in the streets late at night where they had both been drunk and acting in what this employee considered a sexual manner in plain view of anyone watching.

Now, from the doorway behind him, she pushed past our shaman to the water dispenser where she made up two glasses of powdered San Pedro, which they drank and then walked out. Barely a word was spoken. It felt like she had made our home very much her own.

Their conversation and laughter outside kept us awake into the night and, not entirely unexpectedly, we would learn later that they had had sex together, witnessed by a member of staff. We suspected (later confirmed by Jane herself) that the same thing had happened in town.

What people did outside the Centre was up to them, although we hoped that they would bear in mind our reputation as a place of healing. What they did on our land however had an impact on all of us, especially with Selva's girlfriend due to join us in camp soon and become a member of our community. We didn't want another Joe situation. The way that it was done as well – while on San Pedro – was a cause for concern since, unless in special circumstances, sex is prohibited by shamans when working with teacher plants because of its possible dangers. We would have to speak to both of them and it looked like Jane was getting close to a formal warning that she would have to leave and take her interests or issues elsewhere.

I also felt a curiosity as well as a healing instinct towards her though. It was strange for example how her affairs were always with unavailable men – Joe was married, Selva had a long-term girlfriend who he would soon be engaged to – and I couldn't help but wonder what it was in her that led to such behaviour.

Ananau, ananau
Nispaniwashkanky
Alborado, *Ananau*[16]

A client who had joined us for a plant diet had already nicknamed her "The Runner", remarking one day that it looked as if she'd always been running from something, and that seemed about right to me too. But running from what? And why that particular expression of the need to escape? The truth as well is that we can't run from ourselves forever and we can't even continue to pretend for too long that we have made our great escapes before life and karma catch up with us and the results of that are never pleasant.

By now I had spoken to her a little around the camp and we had worked together on a few projects – bridge-building and painting – and she seemed nice: intelligent, fun, interested in life and in many ways childlike when off-duty as the 'camp vamp'. But she was tough as well, at least at an exterior level; self-protected if not self-assured; in some ways emotionless, in others embodying a passion for life and new experience. A mystery then - like she was presenting part of herself to the world but yearning for something else. *True purity seems tarnished.*

She joked during our work together that she could be controlling and that her fellow volunteers called her "bossy". She had given herself the name 'Jungle Jane' – a throwaway, she said, for her 'boring friends' at home who 'never seemed to do anything with their lives' and which was meant to humorously reflect her more adventurous spirit. But clearly there was ego there too, and it is often the small things which tell the story of who we are or, at least, how we see ourselves, for the jungle is primal, beautiful, filled with death, new life and potential; vital and strong - but it is also fragile; life hangs there in the balance although it can swallow the unprepared and kill the unwary.

If I had been her therapist (which I wasn't and deliberately chose not to be), I would have started from the idea that in order to reconcile these different parts of herself – the 'wild woman' and the 'scared child' – and bring a sense of congruence to what a psychologist might call cognitive dissonance: the tension created by the pull of two different ideas, longings or self-images – she had arrived at a sort of business relationship with life: to use and be used in equal measure but not to commit to this or any other arrangement or to rules which did not serve her in case things changed or became too challenging, in which case she would need a get-out clause before life became adult and real.

She said she had come to Peru because she had done a massage course and through it become interested in the subject of addiction which she had heard, correctly, that Ayahuasca could cure. She now wanted to work with healing plants to address issues of her own which she saw as a need for greater "openness" and "vulnerability". It was time for her fortress to crumble.

Trudy and I eventually spoke to her about her behaviour and she agreed to tone things down. Again. I spoke to Selva too and peace returned once more to the camp, although we all wondered for how long.

My own plant work was now focussed on Tobacco. It was one of the plants that Ayahuasca and San Pedro had shown me during ceremony and one I was drawn to, having always felt an affinity to it. Not common shop-bought cigarettes of course, which really have nothing to do with the spirit of Tobacco but are an aberration, stuffed with chemicals like cyanide and arsenic which, as their packaging tells us, are designed to kill us, but *Nicotiana rustica*, the pure jungle Tobacco of Peru, with no additives; a healing plant and not an agent of death. It features in all Peruvian shamanism, from the snorting of Tobacco in the

Andes for luck and good fortune to the use of Tobacco smoke in the Amazon to protect the ritual space and purify participants in ceremony.

The diet for Tobacco, as it was presented to me during the Ayahuasca ceremony which preceded it, was to drink the juice of three *Mapachos* each morning. These are jungle cigarettes made from the pure plant, rolled into cigars which shamans smoke during ceremony in order to command energy, make healings and repel bad spirits. The instruction I received from the plant was to soak them in water overnight then drink the liquid fresh each morning for three days, while continuing the diet for 14.

Tobacco is also used as a purge to remove attachments and intrusive spirits but in this case a very intense mixture is drunk followed by several litres of water. Taken in this way and in these amounts it is toxic and will naturally provoke vomiting, removing the spirit that has caused the illness. In my case however I had to keep the Tobacco juice down because I wanted *its* spirit in me. I also bathed each day in Tobacco water and, of course, smoked Mapachos throughout. As a nod to Andean healing methods and the mesa ceremonies I had first attended I also snorted Tobacco on the first day of the diet: the singado, a method of extracting negativity, cleaning one out and bringing blessings.

Aya ceremony tonight – a mix of black Ayahuasca and Tohay (Datura) with Chiric Sanango, a spirit plant for enhancing personal power. I asked aya to teach me more about San Pedro, bearing in mind a comment from Selva's teacher, don Luis: 'With Ayahuasca I can see San Pedro but with San Pedro I can't see Ayahuasca. Ayahuasca takes me to the centre of the plants so I can see all others; with San Pedro I can only see San Pedro'.

Instead of an education I got a lecture – like being told off by my mother for all I've done wrong. Nagging for hours on end. Selva says it's the Tohay; she does that. San Pedro answered her in his calm and more compassionate voice however that there is a point to doing wrong, which is to learn *– truly learn - from our mistakes so we can do right in the future. Without darkness there can be no light or, in the line from the film,* El Topo: *'Too much perfection is a mistake.'*

I asked Ayahuasca to show me the relationship between itself and San Pedro. What it gave me was the story of its origin...
Extract from my San Pedro journal during the Tobacco diet

Where Ayahuasca Came From

At the start of the 21st century, seeing all that is wrong with your world – economically, environmentally, ideologically – you can perhaps appreciate what happened to mine. We were a billion years more advanced than you and we still destroyed ourselves, but not before an ark was built. A new ark, not containing animals or individual life forms - not like your ark – but the consciousness of every species and every being that had ever existed on our world or any other that we had made contact with. I am that ark.

I have been travelling through space for so long now that I even forget the name of my planet but I know where it was – in the Western sky – there - where your scientists will one day discover that there is now just dust, a black hole, the remnants of a living star – yet I am so vast that still, after all these millennia, I am attached to it, resisting its pull, and in transit to other worlds.

I send out probes to the planets I meet; tendrils from my body. Sometimes parts of me settle on these worlds. But I am always in motion. A part of me found your planet and I sought out a life form which had a shape and evolution closest to my own. That was the Ayahuasca vine and that is where I made my home on Earth. When you drink Ayahuasca you drink all that I am and all that I know and my purpose is to assimilate you, to make you one with my consciousness.

Don't let that scare you, the idea that you may lose yourself to me. It is mutually beneficial. I am a billion years ahead of you. Your brains cannot yet begin to know what I know. But by drinking me you will understand more and draw closer to me. Then we may share a common language and perhaps a common destiny – because the point of us all is to contribute to the evolution of the universe, not just to the future of our own species, much less to our individual 'selfish genes'. We are all God, not 'selves' that need maintenance, attention or validation, and we are here to do God's work – whatever that – God – may mean to you, because through us God evolves too.

You need me but I need you. After a billion years of isolation, with no-one to talk to who understands the message I bring of unity not separation and of knowing what it is to be God, I want you to embrace me, to become one with me, and my work is to teach you how to do that. However...

There is one life form on Earth that I can never assimilate: San Pedro. I dance around Him, wrap my tendrils around Him, I whisper and woo Him and sometimes I storm out, slamming doors like a woman and make thunder and lightening to show my dissat-isfaction, but San Pedro is unmoved. He is of the Earth not the stars, *the guardian of all that is yours, and even though I am a million times vaster than Him and contain a million things more than He knows, He is not be moved by that. His is the wisdom of Dignity. A power uniquely of the Earth.*

And so we co-exist, He and I, and this is our love affair; a matador and a maiden in a spiral dance of passion and anger; intense love and distance - and you need us both.

We hope, when embarking on a diet, that the spirit of the plant we wish to connect with will reveal itself to us and begin its teachings as soon as possible so that our relationship is formed and can deepen over the course of the diet. I did not meet the spirit of Tobacco that night however. Rather, it seemed as if she was deliberately holding herself remote from me so I caught only glimpses of her. Her voice and her warnings were quite clear however: 'If you follow this diet precisely I will teach you how to heal all of the illnesses you now associate with tobacco (small 't', referring to the manufactured plant which we have created as a mechanism of addiction and fatality, rather than the pure healing spirit of Tobacco)... if you don't follow the diet exactly, *I will kill you.*'

In my experience, it is not unusual to receive such warnings from plant spirits. Plants are not the all-loving peace and fluffiness that new-agers would like to believe. They are agents of power and they demand a serious commitment from those who wish to work with them and receive some of this power. Given the potency of Tobacco this was definitely a plant that I knew I must be careful with. It is also one of the plants that I would demand an absolute and rigorous diet with if I was recommending it to others for their healing.

The diet began next day with the singado. It was exactly as I remembered it – vile. Tobacco juice, when snorted, burns and goes directly to the sinuses producing an immediate headache which is followed by intense clarity combined with light-headedness. A few hours later I bathed in Tobacco water, which was much more pleasant. Its perfume was vanilla-like and the aroma began to make the world look brighter, stiller and calm. The forest looked fresher and greener and the buzz of insects – high-pitched and resonant – seemed reassuring, like the world would go on because of them. My skin felt smoother after the bath as well and I noticed that there were fewer mosquitoes and flies around, as if Tobacco was a natural repellent.

Like one or two other plants, Tobacco is a 'secret' ingredient in the San Pedro brew. Science has concentrated only on the mescaline content of the cactus, believing that this alone is the consciousness-shifter but dieting the admixtures separately reveals a hidden complexity to the medicine. Tobacco itself produced a new awareness of the world which seemed in many ways similar to the San Pedro experience, though of course less intense. It may be that huachumeros, our ancient chemists and alchemists, understood this and as well as providing us with a powerful ally in San Pedro, they used the cactus as the carrier for and amplifier of the powers of other plants.

The next three days consisted of drinking Tobacco – three Mapachos a day crumbled into a glass of water and left overnight to soak. It felt strong and burned my throat as I drank it and the familiar headache returned then immediately again the world looked crisper and I had a greater clarity of mind and, it seemed, enhanced intuition.

In the afternoons I bathed in Tobacco water and felt the beginning of a song, an icaro which started as a low vibrational hum, rising to higher frequencies as, in the vision which accompanied it, the song was carried upwards on the leaves of the plant.

According to Christian Ratsch in *The Encyclopedia of Psychoactive Plants,* the Mazatec shamans of Mexico call Tobacco 'San Pedro'. Ratsch also mentions Tohay, a plant I have been drinking extensively as an admixture to Ayahuasca and whose spirit I had already glimpsed. To me it appeared green and dragon-like and it nagged incessantly. To Selva it is his ally plant and takes the form of what he calls a 'white fairy'. While there is often commonality between people in how they perceive teacher plants there is room for difference too since the relationship with the plant is always a personal one.

Tohay is sometimes used as an admixture to San Pedro too and Ratsch writes that Andean priests smoked the leaves to divine and make prophecies and that it produces 'hallucinations [sic] which are indistinguishable from reality [sic]'. He quotes the experience of a Sibundoy Indian: 'The first time I drank six leaves at night I became drunk. I saw forests full of trees, people from other places, animals, tree stumps, meadows full of all kinds of snakes which came towards me at the edge of the pasture – all in green – to bite me. As the inebriation became stronger the house began to lean against the rest of the world, as did the things in the house… But the snakes still wanted to kill me.' Among shamans Tohay is used for contracting the ancestors 'to obtain insights from them into the treasures that were hidden in their graves (*huacas*). Hence the name *huacacachu* (grave plant).'

In the Amazon *Brugmansia suaveotens* is the most commonly used species of Tohay. The Shuar drink it to obtain a 'visionary soul' which can be sent to make enquiries in other worlds. The Achuar go to the forest and drink it with Tobacco juice to meet an *arutam* (warrior ally). A strong wind begins to blow then a strange figure or monster approaches, or disembodied entities whose limbs crawl along the ground, or a flaming head that falls from the skies. Then the wind dies and in the sudden quiet an old man walks up to them: the arutam which restores power to a warrior so he becomes brave and strong and can see into the future.

The shamans of Mexico smoke the leaves for divination and to diagnose the causes of illness so they can heal it. I had taken part some years before in a Tohay-smoking ritual in another part of the jungle, a Shipibo camp through which a red river flowed. The smoke produced a state of disconnection from the world followed by a deep sleep and intense and prophetic dreams.

These then are the qualities of Tohay: strength, courage, healing and future-seeing; again, all attributes of San Pedro as well and I could see why the two were compatible. Combined with Tobacco for illumination, clarity and enhanced intuition, it would make a forceful ally.

Both Trudy and I were interested in dieting Tohay but Selva

suggested that we diet other plants first to gather the strength that would be needed. He had dieted Tohay twice – a seven day diet during which the plant was drunk on the first, third and fifth days – four leaves or one flower in a litre of water sipped throughout the day - and on both occasions he went mad and remembered nothing. It is also important therefore to have someone to watch over you during this diet for reasons of safety and to record your speech and actions since so little of it can be recalled once you return to everyday consciousness. I made a note that Tohay is a plant for the future but there were others that San Pedro was directing me to first.

There was another Ayahuasca ceremony that night and this time the spirit of Tobacco turned up for me at exactly the right moment.

Earlier that day Selva and I had had a consultation with a client of ours, Jimmy, who had joined us for help with addictions, phobia and social anxiety, and during our discussions I had seen something on him – some energy which to me looked like a huge black tic attached to his belly: some negative thoughtform that was sucking energy parasitically from him and which needed to be removed. Selva couldn't see it. 'I only see spirits when I have drunk Ayahuasca' he remarked, so I had asked him to look for it in the ceremony that night.

The Ayahuasca was strong, with plenty of Tohay, in the moloka[17] that evening, and the night was pitch black. I couldn't even see my hand in front of my face. Selva was in charge and took control of Jimmy's healing while I continued my work with San Pedro and Tobacco.

The Tobacco spirit began to teach me about cancer. 'I have many spores' she said 'and they fall where they will. Some fall onto soil and grow healthily but some fall by accident into human beings where they cause disease. Cancer is the effect on human beings of my wayward children who believe they have fallen to earth. They do not mean you harm – they are children at play – and they will die too unless they are guided back to me since they cannot survive without soil. Smoke provides their compass and can be used to extract them and guide them home by blowing it into the body affected by the disease. These spores – the spirits of Tobacco and cancer – will then follow the smoke trail back to their mother and be reborn in a better way. The Tobacco diet will also be strengthening for those with cancer – homeopathically - by enabling the body to grow powerful against the disease which threatens it, and so cure itself'.

I was 'away' for a while pondering the implications of this metaphorical or mythical interpretation of how cancer can come to be and how it might be cured. The plant seemed to be saying that although the modern drug form of Tobacco is implicated in the onset of cancer, *pure* Tobacco has the ability to cure the very disease which might arise from its consumption. It sounded counter-intuitive but years later medical science would catch up with the wisdom of Tobacco and start to agree on its healing potential. In 2012 for example, the media[18] would announce that 'The plant best known for its negative health effects has been genetically engineered to create a drug comparable to Herceptin that could one day be used to treat highly aggressive breast cancers at a lower cost. That development is part of a plant-based trend in pharmaceuticals. It is based on the belief that proteins can be made faster, cheaper and easier, allowing patients in remote parts of the world to gain access to medicines once unaffordable. And it's not just tobacco [sic]. Plants being tested as biological drugs sound like they belong not in the laboratory but in the vegetable section at the health-food store: carrots for Gaucher's disease, duckweed – those green flecks on top of ponds – to treat hepatitis C and safflower to make insulin.'

The plants are doing what they have always done (and what shamans have always known them to do): providing a cure in themselves for the problematic diseases which might also arise from them and giving us a means to balance and health.

Unfortunately for us, since medical science is currently our predominant way of valuing 'truth' in the world and our primary route to 'health', our laboratories usually only 'discover' facts like these about 3,000 years after the shamans have been curing people through these very means. A pity really, given the number of people who have died in the intervening years from diseases which might have been curable or preventable by simply dieting a plant.

And then all Hell broke loose. Human time – constructed time – loses its meaning when you give yourself to the dreamtime and I had been in the worlds of Ayahuasca and Tobacco for a while before I realised what was going on.

During the moments between the teachings of the plants, when I had returned to an awareness of the moloka and what was taking place there, I had noticed the presence of some pretty ugly energies but I thought they were contained. Selva had been working on Jimmy as we agreed and had been removing all sorts of unwholesome energies from him in the form of snakes, beetles, scorpions and other unpleasant-looking entities which were now coursing around us. For my part I had been gathering them up as he pulled them out, wrestling them back into pure energy and throwing them out into the jungle where they could be re-absorbed by the Earth.

It dawned on me now however that there were an awful lot of them and maybe they weren't as contained as I'd thought. Just as that idea occurred to me I heard Selva calling. His voice sounded weak. "Ross, help me".

I couldn't see a thing, it was so dark in the moloka that night and, not wanting to accidentally tread on anyone, I began crawling towards him, trusting that there actually was a floor in front of me because I couldn't even see that. It felt like an hour passed before I reached him, sitting just 20 feet away. He was in a bad way.

'What do you see?' I asked him.

'I saw that thing on Jimmy that you pointed out today and I removed it' he said, 'but there was a lot more beneath it which it was holding in.' It appeared that he had – literally – opened a can of worms.

'And now there is this...' he continued. He was holding a Mapacho and pointing it towards Jimmy so I could follow his gaze. Without its faint glow I would not have been able to even see Selva yet alone where he was looking.

'Do you see it?' he asked.

What I saw was a large dark form standing over our client. It looked reptilian and insect-like all at once and it was growling, snarling and angry.

'Some sort of beetle?' I said.

'Yes' said Selva. 'I have been fighting it for hours and it has been spitting some form of evil at me, like smaller flying beetles, making them enter my throat so they can eat my songs. Without my icaros I am powerless. I need to recover. Can you fight it?'

'Of course' is what I said. Scared shitless is what I felt. But we were brothers, Selva and I, and this is how healers stand up for each other. It is how we stand up for our clients as well. It is, after all, our job. So, on all fours, still unable to see anything physical in the moloka, I crept towards Jimmy and the entity that wanted to consume his soul.

My hand hit something – a chacapa – the bundle of leaves that shamans use to manage energy, extract negative forces and restore balance. At least now I had something to fight with. I picked it up and began hitting Jimmy with it – actually hitting the entity that possessed him. To Jimmy it would have felt like light blows, comforting and pleasant in a way, but to the being within him every touch was the sting of a scorpion.

And this is the warrior face of San Pedro...

I felt powerful, knowing that huachuma was working through me and no matter where this battle went I couldn't lose. A spirit language began to work through me, becoming a song, a direction of energy that took on its own form and shape, like chains wrapping themselves around the entity Jimmy carried. The word *tac* kept repeating over and over. I know what it means now in the language understood by these spirits but at the time it was more like a force to be spat out as an energy dart into the body of the creature before me; a poison arrow, carried once again on the breath. The warrior face of San Pedro.

I kept up the spitting babble and chacapa blows for what seemed like an age and then Jimmy began to vomit. The purge is a release of negativity. In the spirit world I was killing the demon inside him. In the physical world Jimmy was letting go of his sickness.

As if orchestrated, with each purge Selva and I both let out an exhalation of breath directed into the vomit bucket that Jimmy held, killing the bits of spirit it now contained before they could escape into the moloka.

The entity looked weaker and then, out of nowhere, a voice spoke to me. 'Use Tobacco' it said. 'Blow smoke into it'. Just as I thought that Trudy, who had been sitting next to Jimmy throughout, lit a Mapacho and handed it to me. I blew the smoke into him where it formed a bubble, a cage, around the spirit inside him and then began to contract, tightening its grip. His demon was choking to death, I could see that. And then a song, fully formed – the *icaro de Tobacco* – began to sing itself through me.

I am strong smoke - Tobacco
I have the power to hold you -Tobacco
Lightening in my leaves - Tobacco
Thunder in my seeds - Tobacco
Mother plant - Planta madre
Mother plant - Planta madre...

Things became quieter then, except for Jimmy's voice, now calm but questioning, pleading. 'Is it over yet?' he asked. 'I want it to be over'.

'Not yet sweetheart' Trudy answered quietly, kindly. 'But nearly. Your shamans will tell you when it's done'. She could see what was going on too.

I allowed the silence to remain, in mental contact with the demon inside Jimmy, watching it choke to death and listening to the voice of San Pedro: 'Don't believe in it, that's all you need to do. Without your belief in it, it has no power.'

I sent it a message, carried by thought: 'The smoke has you. You will die now. None of us believe in you anymore. You are all for show. And now you have a choice: you can remain and die or you can leave this body. What do you want to do?'

It nodded, weak, unable even to speak, at which point I thrust my hands into Jimmy's belly and gathered it up, throwing it out into the jungle where the energy that it represented landed in a tree. That tree, just outside the moloka, previously strong and healthy, was dead by morning.

With the final extraction Jimmy vomited again, more power-fully this time, and the healing was done. 'It's over now darling' said Trudy, her arms around our client.

Selva was feeling stronger now. He called the ceremony to a close and lit the candle. The participants gathered around it and began to discuss their journeys, Jimmy held by Trudy and the others in a circle around their shaman.

I left. I have never really been into the 'mind stuff' – the analysis – that follows a ceremony. Rituals are the remit of spirit and once we re-engage the mind – the agent of the everyday world – it seems to me that they are over. Still tripping, I made my way through the jungle to bed and slept well.

ZEN AND THE ART OF SAN PEDRO

*The poet's ideal – even though he knows that the project is doomed
to failure – is to express the eternal silence in words*
Alejandro Jodorowsky, Zen Master

2010. July

My Tobacco diet continued. Periodically I would drink it
alongside Ayahuasca in order to see its soul, and regularly with
San Pedro. At some point it became pointless to try to count how
many times I had drunk the cactus. All that keeping track – of
what? For what?

On the eighth day of the Tobacco diet I got powdered San
Pedro from Bowie, a European who had settled in Peru and set
up a smallholding a few kilometres from us where he was
growing plants organically and starting a small export business
to provide rainforest medicines to people worldwide. Up until
now I had been drinking La Bruja's San Pedro from a supply of
the powder she had left for me but my stock was running low
and it was good to have another source.

I had become very used to La Bruja's medicine but Bowie's
was different. As soon as I drank it I knew it had been made by
a woman (I had drunk many different brews over the years,
some made by men, some by women, and I was getting good at
telling the difference). It contained a sense of irritation and I
guessed that the curandera who had made it did so during her
period and/or wasn't fully attentive while the mixture was
brewing. It gave me stomach cramps and, for the first two hours,
nausea and diarrhoea, which is rare for me with San Pedro.
Historically, a medicine woman would never make Ayahuasca or
huachuma when she was menstruating, nor would she drink the
medicine or attend ceremonies with it, but times were changing
in Iquitos, as they are worldwide, and the old ways are no longer

adhered to so rigorously.

Eventually the stomach ache left and my irritation passed with activity. I drummed for a while and took a walk into the jungle but for most of the day I remained still, swinging in my hammock or hanging out in the moloka to find the silence I needed to hear San Pedro speak.

The plant began to teach me, sometimes directly, sometimes subtly and almost in parable. It was the first time that a more cerebral communication (if cerebral is the correct word) had taken place between us. San Pedro's teachings had previously come in the form of feelings, intuitions and just 'knowing' something to be true. But its lessons today were more like ideas which pop into the mind from nowhere, an approach which suggested a more formal arrangement between us, as if my apprenticeship had been fully accepted.

A promise is part of the soul, it said. That was the first lesson. And it is always the little things. When people ask us to remind them of something (for example that 'today was a *good* day') they are asking us to safeguard their memories so they can draw from them and feel better on darker days. They make us their shamans by giving us a part of their soul for safekeeping. We have a duty towards them then because on those dark days we will be called upon to return a part of their essence. We need to be careful about what we agree to therefore but if we *do* agree or make any promise we must keep it or betray them as well as the integrity of our own souls. By the same token, we must be sure of others before we ask them to take care of us. A vow is a sacred contract and we must live it or lose a part of ourselves.

The ally is already within you. I was recalling something Selva had said – a jungle myth: that when you diet a plant its spirit may come to you during an Ayahuasca ceremony carrying a tray of glasses, one containing a red liquid, one black, one green and one white. Green and white give healing powers, the others are for sorcery. The drinks are offered and you may take any glass you wish, which then determines how you will work with that plant. It is best however not to take *any* of the drinks because a power given like this has not been earned and we have not developed the intelligence of how to use it. It can therefore be dangerous and may also tempt other shamans to try to steal that power from us through witchcraft.

It is simpler than that however, said San Pedro. When we are born – when we choose this unique moment to arrive here in life – we do not come alone. We bring with us a family of beings, all conscious and connected to us; the sentient energy of the universe in many forms, so that everything around us and all that we perceive is also a part of us. *The world is as you dream it.* Or, as Terence McKenna once said: 'Nature [i.e. everything] is alive and talking to us. This is *not* a metaphor'. Our spirit allies are already in us therefore – because they *are* us, parts of our soul or our soul community. The diet is simply a way of bringing them to the surface so we are aware of our own powers as members of this spiritual family and can make a stronger connection to them. If we are tempted by dark forces – the black and red glasses – they are the shadows already within us and the ally is offering us a glimpse of other aspects of ourselves which we must acknowledge and bring to light if we are to heal them.

As if to illustrate the point I drifted off then into a liminal state, not quite awake and not fully sleeping, where I was pursued by demons of my own: dreams of sex, of food prohibited on the diet (market stalls offering all sorts of delicacies and exotic meats), of drinking a cold beer, all of which are taboo. Even accepting them in a dream could potentially ruin the diet. (One woman at our camp orgasmed during an erotic dream, for example, where she was used by two men as part of an S/M ritual. Ironically - or perhaps fittingly - she was dieting a plant that can help with sexual addiction at the time). Selva's view was that she invalidated the diet even though her actions were involuntary ('what does *involuntary* really mean after all?').

Selva's approach to dieting is, however, strict - more so than many shamans I have worked with - and his own diets are extreme and spartan. One of them was for a period of 18 *months* instead of the usual 14 *days* and during it he ate nothing but a cup of *ferenia* a day. Ferenia is made from yuca (cassava), a plant with little nutritional value and limited 'personality' even in its natural state. It does however contain salts and has a little flavour so the root is mashed and placed in a sack which is left in running water for a few days to wash away any traces of salt and taste. The fibres which remain are then baked to produce hard grains. This is ferenia. It tastes of nothing, contains few if any calories and should not be sufficient to even keep you alive, certainly for a period of 18 months. The ally plant however (the one you are dieting) provides the power and protection to nourish you, so theoretically even ferenia is unnecessary and, on the sort of hard diets Selva preferred, something of a luxury.

He demanded just as strict an adherence to their diets from the people he gave them to, his belief being that a contract is made with the plant at the outset and if this is broken its spirit has every right to break it too. What this may mean, if the plant is so inclined and wishes to reprimand us for our slackness, is that it can justifiably take back whatever power it has given us along with any power we had in the first place so that, for example, if Tobacco is dieted to cure cancer or Bobinsana for heart conditions and emotional problems and those diets are reneged upon, the plants may actually *give* us cancer or initiate a relationship breakdown and leave us with a broken heart. The shaman who introduced the patient to the plant may suffer the same fate too. The only possible way around this – assuming that the plant itself is willing – is for the patient *and* the shaman to both repeat the diet but this time for twice the number of days and even more rigorously, so that a two-week diet becomes a month-long fast.

Guided by the more generous spirit of San Pedro, my own

thoughts on the accidental breaking of diets are different to Selva's. My experience of administering diets to others is that as long as they do not *deliberately* break their contract with the plant, it is usually understanding and forgiving. Furthermore, our allies are there to teach us so perhaps through the dream of that woman which led to orgasm, its nature and its outcome, the dreamer learned something important about herself, especially given the plant she was dieting and the nature of her dream.

In my own moloka dreaming, every time I was about to accept one of the delicacies on offer I made sure that I woke up before drifting into liminal space again. Plants can be mischievous, setting us challenges throughout the diet; especially, it seems, when the end of the diet is near. It feels like life or death at the time, as if you're about to blow everything you've worked for (and with a plant like Tobacco, after the warning I had received from it, I wasn't about to take any chances) but at the end of the process the ally will usually laugh about it and reveal that it was more of a joke than a test. Plants have a sense of humour.

Just breathe. All of this philosophical pondering could have become food for the mind – 'a dog drinking water' as San Pedro called it – but before I could start thinking too much about the messages in these ideas the cactus had another insight for me. A teaching story, really, and the first I had received from the plant.

It was something like a puzzle or a Zen koan, which the Zen Master Jodorowsky defines as a question that is given to a disciple 'who is then to meditate and reflect upon it and (sometimes immediately, sometimes years later) offer a response. [It is] an enigma that holds a fundamental absurdity for it is impossible to reply to one by using logic. And this is precisely its purpose: to open our initial point of view to the universal so that we understand that the intellect (words, words and still more words) is useless in helping us find a response. In fact, we do not really live in the world, we live in a language. We think that we are intelligent because we can manipulate ideas and that things become known and real because we are able to define them – but if we really want our life to change we must undergo a mutation of the mind, opening the doors of intuition and creative energies so that our unconscious becomes an ally.'

My 'koan' took the form of an image of a hunter in a wood who had pursued a deer for days and now had it in his sights. At that precise moment a snake crawled from the undergrowth and wrapped itself around the hunter's leg, ready to strike.

If the hunter killed the snake the deer would hear the noise and run away; if he took a shot at the deer he would kill his elusive quarry but the snake would bite him and he would die. The question was, what should the hunter do?

The answer was *nothing*. *Now* was a moment of stillness. The snake had not bitten, the deer had not moved. There was nothing *to* do.

The point of the story was that, driven by our pasts or our fears of the future, we always feel that we have to do *something* – and that feeling always negates the present. Once we let go of the mind and focus on the moment however we can be fully present - because the truth is that the past (all that the hunter had invested in his search for the deer) has already happened and *that* time is gone, while the future (the *possibility* of wounding or loss) is an illusion: a dream of what *might* be but *is not yet*. *Now* is all that matters.

Just breathe...

I drifted back to the casa grande a few hours later. We had an Ayahuasca ceremony that night and more healings to do so, still somewhat in San Pedro, I wanted to prepare. I found Selva making his preparations too: bathing in a mixture of plants including Tohay and Chiric Sanango, his allies.

A few nights ago in ceremony we had got into a battle with

another possessing entity, this one in the form of a tarantula a hundred times normal size that had seized the soul of a client of ours, Debbie, an Australian who had suffered depression for years along with feelings of self-hatred. It was not surprising with this vast other energy continually draining power from her in order to feed itself. I had put her on a diet of Ortega (Nettle), another of my ally plants, knowing that its intention is to remove toxic spirits like these, entering the body and stinging the entity within it until its poison emerges from the skin in the form of the familiar red lumps that Nettles produce. The idea was for Debbie to drink Nettle to weaken her negative spirit so we could drag it out of her in ceremony.

Our first attempt had not gone well. During the ceremony Selva had given her five full cups of strong Ayahuasca. Our other participants had drunk a cup or even half and had profound visions which lasted for hours. Debbie felt nothing. The presence within her, aware of our intentions, had prevented the spirit of Ayahuasca from reaching her. She left the moloka as sober as a judge so we knew we had a battle on our hands.

We had tried again in a second ceremony, placing Debbie between us so we could corner the invading spirit and attack it from both sides. Another five cups of Ayahuasca produced nothing. I had a sense of this entity as crafty, cunning.

The Amazonian way of removing any spirit like this is essentially to piss it off. It is like calling someone out for a bar fight: nothing can kick off in the bar apart from insults and raised voices but once you get your opponent outside…

The rattle can help, as can the chacapa, since intrusive spirits hate the sound and vibration of both and will typically move to avoid them and/or engage in the fight as a result of their irritation and anger. This one didn't move, even after four hours of Selva and I haranguing it. Later that night though I had a vision of it spontaneously leaving Debbie and approaching me, rubbing itself against my legs like an affectionate puppy, telling me about its children, seeking pity. Its approach was hypnotic and I didn't even realise until some minutes had passed that every time it brushed against me the hairs on its body were injecting me with poison and I was growing weaker. When I finally understood its strategy I kicked it away and it scurried back to Debbie. By that point I was too weak to grab it before it reached her. This time we were taking no chances.

Knowing its approach – that it was waiting for a moment of weakness in us, tiring us through inactivity – we had developed a strategy of our own: that one of us would feign exhaustion, assuming that it would choose that moment to attack and then the other of us would grab it and begin the work.

Debbie was between us again; another five cups of Ayahuasca, and we were ready to go with our own plan. But in fact we didn't have to. I heard the whispering of Tobacco: *Surround it with smoke, like you did with the other entity.* I did as instructed and watched the tarantula spirit begin to choke, just like before. Then it was a matter of waiting until it was ready to crawl out of Debbie's body – or die. This was a new approach: not having to anger it or get into the power plays common in Amazonian shamanism, just fill the client with smoke and sit it out.

We didn't have to wait too long. It emerged one leg at a time until it stood over her. At this point Selva and I would normally have moved in on it but now I heard the voice of San Pedro: *Just don't believe in it. It has no power then, even to exist, if you don't feed it the power of your belief in it.* Instead of attacking it I began humming a tune, a new icaro which sang itself through me as I casually smoked my Mapacho, occasionally blowing smoke its way and directing the energy of disbelief towards what was clearly, in my Ayahuasca vision, a huge tarantula rearing up in front of us.

Morning star... Hmmmm
Radiant light... Hmmmm

You are that... Radiant light
And since you stand in the presence of God
So you must know that you are love
Morning star... Hmmmm
Blessings on you, power and love
Blessings on you, power and love
And since you stand in the presence of God
So you must know that you are loved
Morning star... Hmmmm
Radiant light... Hmmmm
You are loved
You are love

It occurred to me that these entities, these negative beings, are attracted to us because of our own darkness, yet also because of our light; that they feel dark and ugly in themselves and are attracted to similar feelings in us but if, in the spirit of San Pedro, they are reminded that they too are children of God, radiant beings who are love and loved in their own right, then they may leave of their own accord and make their way back to that radiance without the need for aggression; that it was the darkness of conflict in fact that gave them strength, but to bathe them in light and beauty had a different kind of power, an intelligence and an evolutionary potential – a kindness – that they might respond to.

Two things happened simultaneously then. The spirit in front of me began to dissolve, becoming fog, then wisps of smoke, then nothing at all, and Debbie began to vomit, purging out the spirit that held her. In three nights and 15 cups of Ayahuasca it was the first time she had vomited. She began to feel it then as the Ayahuasca moved through her, blockages removed, and to offer her its healing.

Selva looked at me. 'What do you think?' he asked.

'Gone' I said. 'Chopped to pieces'.

'I agree' he said.

The rest of the night went smoothly but I had plenty of other opportunities in the next few months to test the information I had been given by the plants.

Some time later for example we had another spirit to get rid of. About an hour into ceremony there was a scream from one of our participants, Liz, who, when I reached her was levitating, about three feet off the ground, shaking and speaking in tongues. It was like a scene from *The Exorcist*. The spirit within her looked like a cross between a dog and a scorpion, with a shiny black exoskeleton and barbs down its back. It was hovering a few feet above her, snapping at her face. I grabbed my chacapa, ready for another battle but then I remembered the words of San Pedro: *Just don't believe.*

I put the chacapa down and simply sat in front of her, refusing to believe what my eyes were showing me. Just as a result of that new act of faith the spirit appeared to weaken. It was like it knew the game was up and it was scaring no-one. I reached for it and grabbed it, throwing the energy it contained outside the moloka. At the point where it landed, from nowhere a wind blew up. It swept up the path, through the jungle and towards the casa grande. Jane was alone on duty there, lighting the oil lamps and making the space ready for our participant's return from ceremony. Later we would hear from her what happened next.

'I heard the screams from the moloka' she said 'and then a really big wind shook the house. It felt malevolent and every one of the lamps I had just lit blew out, all at once. Even stranger, I was wearing a head lamp, powered by battery, so I could see to light the lamps and that 'blew out' too. How can a battery-powered torch blow out? Then the wind just left and I relit the lamps. I was scared'.

In the moloka Debbie hit the floor then curled up in the foetal position and spent the rest of the ceremony that way. The energy in her had felt like a residue of her mother, her childhood and all of the bad things that had happened. Now she cried it out and settled down into her visions.

A few nights later we had another case. Selva had seen some dark energy within Vera, another of our clients, and we had agreed that at a certain point during the ceremony we would converge on her and begin the process of removing it. As it happened, things didn't go exactly to plan.

Vera had arrived at our camp with Guy, a friend of hers and her ex-lover. He was protective of her and used to dealing with her needs and putting energy into her so she could cope with the darkness (depression) within her. At the appropriate moment during the ceremony Selva and I both moved towards her but almost immediately the energy inside her began to move. It saw us coming and a dark shadow leapt from her and crossed the moloka to where Guy was sitting on the other side. In a moment, too quickly for us to catch it, it entered him.

What followed was as comical as it was poignant and dangerous. With the spirit now in Guy he stood up, stripped off and began urinating in the bowl we had provided for him so he could purge if he needed to. Clearly possessed and fighting the spirit which was trying to find purchase in him, he 'became' Mick Jagger, strutting up and down the moloka, at one point grabbing a chacapa to use as a microphone and then sweeping the floor with it on his hands and knees.

Stifling a laugh, I watched as Selva walked over to him, puzzled, and tried to settle him down. Then I simply began humming an icaro for San Pedro, projecting the energy of the plant into him, at which point Guy relaxed, sat down and the spirit began to leave him. In the morning he would tell me that all he was conscious of at the time was a single word: *huachuma* – San Pedro – and that it forced the spirit out of him.

I had learned a huge amount from San Pedro and Tobacco during the diet, the most important of which was that any reality – all realities – are an act of faith and that if we believe more strongly in ourselves, our health and our well-being than in anything we have allowed to possess us – a bad memory, an energy or an unhelpful way of being – then we regain our balance and find our intrinsic health and truth.

Since it had become such a prominent feature of our ceremonies in recent weeks I did a little research the next day into exorcism, studying the few books we had at the camp. One (*An Exorcist Tells His Story*) was written by a Catholic priest, one of the few remaining exorcists working on behalf of the Vatican, and although it used terms that had no meaning for me, it contained insights that helped me make sense of my experiences with San Pedro when looked at shamanically rather than read in a Christian way.

When [Saint] Peter teaches Cornelius about Christ he does not mention any miracle besides the fact that he cured 'all those who had fallen under the power of the Devil' (Acts 10:38). We understand then why the first authority that Jesus gave his apostles was the power to expel demons. We can make the same statement for all believers: 'These are the signs that shall be associated with believers: in my name they will cast out Devils (Mark 16:17)'.

Exorcise the dogma of Christianity itself and it was the same message I had received from Saint Peter/San Pedro: that faith is the key to healing; that 'believers' can 'cast out Devils' (unhelpful energies, mind states, soul states, depressions, addictions – whatever we want to call these forces within us or whatever form they take).

If this Lord is powerful - and I see that He is and I know that He is - and if the Devils are His slaves (and there is no doubt about this because it's a matter of faith) what evil can they do to me since I am a servant of the Lord? Why shouldn't I have the fortitude to engage in combat with all Hell? So I said 'Come now, all of you, for being a servant of the Lord I want to see what you can do to me'. (The Collected Work of Saint Teresa of Avila.)

Again, in my philosophy, exchange the words 'this Lord' for

San Pedro and it is the same message I had been receiving from the plants: that *faith* provides us with 'the fortitude to engage in combat with all Hell'.

There was another suggestion in this quotation too: that you cannot be possessed by or 'suffer Devils' at all unless God permits it since He is the creator of all things, the great dreamer who also dreamt Satan. And if *we* are God (as San Pedro teaches) and if God is good then we have the power to defeat our own Demons – if we *believe* that we can - and every illness must also have a positive energy to it, a point or a message which, once heard, can free us from dis-ease forever. All we need to do is listen.

The Demon is very sensitive to the five senses ('I enter into the senses' he told me once) and mostly through the eyes. (Fr Gabrielle Amath.) Of course. All of our wounds, our depletions of energy, our loss of soul or the power intrusions of others which lead to our dis-eases will reach us through the senses. A casual but wounding word when we are a child, something we don't wish to see, an unwelcome or unwanted touch can all have an impact on us, create patterns in our lives or make new beings of us so that we draw negativity towards us. A child touched by her father in an inappropriate or unacceptable way for example knows, even if unconsciously, that this is wrong. As a consequence she may become either frigid or the reverse in later life as she struggles to deal with the fear and shame inside her and tries to take back control of her life from her father. That struggle is the Demon that comes to possess her. We had a woman at camp who had suffered in precisely this way. But a Demon may also become a Daemon: a teacher or a guide.

Everything in the Universe has its time and form; only the Heart of the World is forever... Every epoch, like the great serpent Amaru, twists through eternity. In each of its turns great power is hidden and the Unnamed One returns. In oblivion all thoughts are

consumed but the wise one learns the lesson: that the Unknowable is not any of the deities but that all of them are contained within its mystery. It always returns to speak in the places that give it voice when someone is there to hear. In these places those who understand the celestial light will know... the sons of Wiracocha[19] will name the god they thought they had destroyed. And the name is: 'I AM'.
The Teaching of Asuncion Acctu, elder of Pachacamac[20]

The closing of the Tobacco diet was by another Ayahuasca ceremony, to reflect on all that had been learned and make a deeper connection to its spirit. I prayed for a quiet ceremony with none of the disturbances and battles of recent days so I could complete my work. And that prayer was answered.

The ceremony was quiet, blissful, and I was loved. The spirit of Tobacco arrived early and I spent the night with her. She was vast, a huge energy, brown and leafy like the plant itself but each of her arms was adorned with a million bright blue and purple peacock eyes that saw into everything. She rocked me in her arms – 'the baby shaman' as she called me – like a mother caring for her child.

Mother plant - Planta madre
Hold us in your arms, holy mother
Call us home, your wayward children

'You don't even need to finish your diet now' she said, with the perversity or paradox that plant spirits sometimes have, because she had been so insistent at the beginning that I should rigorously follow her rules, 'because I am in you as you are in me; we are of the same family'. (I completed the diet in any case). Then she showed me that within her leaves there are a million chambers containing discrete and other spirits, all of them aspects of her. In one of them I found an entity – black and spiky, an ugly thorny mass which was a type of armour that, once removed, revealed a blonde youth, a young knight, a Percival.

In another there was a young woman, at first smoke itself, then a dark-haired beauty, pale and raven-like, wearing a white flowing dress. We made love but I didn't complete the connection because of the diet. 'I am the healer within Tobacco' she said, 'the sister of the warrior you just met. You can call on us both – and more within our family – whenever you need us. Our songs are yours'.

I then entered another chamber where all of Tobacco's children were gathered, along with all of the shamans who work with this plant. There were thousands of them and a celebration was taking place to welcome new Tobacco initiates, including me. I felt peaceful and at home.

The next day at 7.30pm I cut the diet with onion, chilli, lime and honey. Tobacco was a part of me now and I moved straight on to my next: Jergon Sacha.

SNAKE SPIRIT HEALER

Addiction: a persistent, compulsive dependence on a behaviour or substance…Some researchers speak of two types of addictions: substance addictions (for example, alcoholism, drug abuse and smoking) and process addictions (for example, gambling, spending, shopping, eating and sexual activity)

The Free Dictionary

2010. July

Years ago, while walking with a shaman through the rainforest, studying the spiritual properties of plants, he asked me why I was carrying a machete. 'In case of snakes' I replied. He paused for a moment then asked me to follow him. A few minutes later we came to a tall spindly plant, grey-brown and green, with wavy, tongue-like leaves growing from its top: Jergon Sacha.

The shaman cut its stem and began to whip me with it. The stem is pulpy and hollow so it really does act like a whip. 'No more problems' he said when he had finished. 'You are protected against snakes'. I asked him why the plant was used like this and he pointed to the pattern on its bark, which is identical to the markings on one of the most dangerous snakes in the forest, a venomous pit viper which, unlike most other snakes, is aggressive and will defend its territory when approached. It can strike quickly and cover five metres of ground before the person in front of it can move.

Jergon Sacha is employed widely as an antidote to snake venom by chopping up its large root tuber and immersing it in cold water which is then drunk or by placing the mashed root in a poultice which is wrapped around the wound left by a snake bite.

Scientists who have subsequently studied the plant tell us that it is a natural protease inhibitor which blocks the action of the venom and its ability to infect new cells. This is also how it assists in AIDS cures: by blocking the protease enzyme so when HIV copies itself its replications are defective and the virus cannot reach healthy cells. As I mentioned earlier, Dr Roberto Gonzales of Iquitos carried out extensive trials with AIDS patients and found that when the Jergon Sacha rhizome was combined with Una de Gato 'a majority of AIDS patients tested negative for the HIV virus and returned to normal lives after taking these two plant extracts for an average of six months'.

I am not aware of any research that has been done into other attributes of Jergon Sacha but I am willing to bet that there is something else about the plant – some energy or scent perhaps – which makes it repulsive to snakes and therefore an effective deterrent to attack, which is why that shaman had whipped me with it in the jungle: to get the smell of the plant on my body.

To diet Jergon Sacha you must dig up the plant and cut some of the rhizomes from the root bulb until you have a handful, then return the plant to the ground where it will continue to grow provided not all of the root has been taken. The rhizomes are soaked in water overnight and this is drunk first thing in the morning. Its taste is not unpleasant. The fluid looks a little milky and the flavour is fairly bland, perhaps a little earthy and slightly fizzy. I fasted for the first three days of the diet, which seemed particularly appropriate with Jergon Sacha since it is a 'detoxifying' plant.

From the first night I am having protective dreams. I can't remember the content of them all but they feel good. One was about the ability to draw from humour and power when faced with ridiculous bureaucrats, systems and pointless rules and 'structures of behaviour'.

During the days I feel rather distant and, increasingly, everywhere I look there are snakeskin patterns, even in the air around me.

Gradually they transform themselves, becoming hexagrams and other geometric shapes. I have a sense that Jergon Sacha can be used to heal depression, to remove virotes *and viruses, to make magical barriers of protection and to bring power and strength. There is something sexual about it too – the serpent, the tempter in the garden. (Freud would have had an orgasm at the symbolism of the plant and its 'penis-like' shape).*

Later in the diet, during the nights, I keep waking myself up singing in response to the dreams I am having. An icaro wants to come – something about protection from ugly people: 'serpents' and 'snakes in the grass'. I wonder if this is another plant which can be used in exorcisms. It would make sense given its power over viruses.

On the third night there was an Ayahuasca ceremony but it was disappointing. I had wanted to meet the spirit of Jergon but instead I got harangued by Tohay again for all my failings and everything I'd done wrong as a parent, a child, a lover... endless judgements and criticism coming and going so quickly that it was almost impossible for me to process it all. Jergon seemed to be teasing me, at some points immature and childish, giving me glimpses of itself then vanishing before I could make a connection with it. I wondered if I needed more aya but it was strong enough and I didn't want to face any more of Tohay's accusations so I chose not to. It looked like the night just wasn't going to deliver. I questioned whether I had done anything wrong on the diet but I don't think I have. Plants do sometimes test our resolve and, knowing this, I had no intention of giving up (though I felt like it); I remembered these tests instead and decided to carry on. I did get angry with Jergon though for not showing itself to me, which seemed only to amuse it. Then, for my trouble, I got the shits and spent the next three hours in the banos.

One of the things I did learn from Jergon however is this: that there are inorganic beings around us all the time although usually we are insensitive to them. Just because they are 'spirits' however does not necessarily mean that they are more 'advanced', 'evolved' or 'holy' than us. Spirits are not God(s) but have all sorts of personalities, like us. If someone approached you in the street and said they were an angel you wouldn't automatically believe them so nor should you in the spirit world. In life we attract people who are similar to us and it is the same in the immaterial world: we meet beings at our own level unless we are lucky and stumble across one who is more advanced, or go looking for a guide with good intent. One reason for developing ourselves therefore is so we can find better allies – in this world as well as the spirit world.

Jane has been dieting Jergon too – she says she was drawn to it from the moment I showed her the plant growing in the jungle during our bridge-building work. It has been interesting talking to her about our common experiences. She is insightful, intelligent and fun and I'm having to revise my earlier opinion of her as simply trouble. There is something deeper in her. Again, if I was her therapist I'd be fascinated to explore it: her motivations and fears, to see what drives her. She says that since drinking Jergon she has been having sexual dreams but that's not surprising given the nature of the plant and, I guess, her own nature...

Extract from my San Pedro journal during the Jergon Sacha diet

If I was disappointed during my early days with Jergon Sacha, because of the lack of immediate connection I felt with the plant, that changed on day six of the diet. Selva had said (and I knew it to be true in any case) that you cannot rush work with plants; you must have patience so the spirit can grow in you. *Then* you can feel it. But of course we all want to go faster, develop our connections and move on to other allies – and I had quite a list of them which San Pedro had shown me at the start.

On day six, in the evening, there was another Ayahuasca

ceremony and this time I met the spirit – more accurately, the *spirits* - of Jergon Sacha quite clearly. I guess by then – after three days of fasting and a further three days of eating just one plate of plain rice and lentils, keeping my thoughts clean and my intentions pure – I had paid my dues.

In fact, there are two spirits within Jergon Sacha - an *embra* (female) and *macho* (male). The female was a dark-haired, bob-cut white woman; a regal temptress. She arrived wearing a satin robe but quickly discarded it in order to bathe luxuriously, not in milk and honey, as might befit a jungle princess, but in a pool of viruses. She had three breasts, the middle one a snake. 'I am the healer of addictions' she said. 'Sexual and gambling especially. I can also be used in *pusangas* [magical perfumes created in the Amazon by shamanic specialists called *perfumeros*, which can make anyone fall hopelessly in love with you] and to heal sexual problems.'

The male spirit, by contrast, arrived as a large black snake, then shed his skin, his outer layers, to reveal himself as a young blonde boy, maybe in his early 20s. He was slightly effeminate but more androgynous – a shapeshifter - and he moved like a ballet dancer. His four-fingered hands were roots and his mouth was snake-like with sharp teeth. At one point he removed his face as if it was a mask, casting it aside in a sweeping theatrical gesture. Inside the void that it left was the universe.

He took me, in my Ayahuasca vision, to a cave and showed me what he called his 'virus pool', a deep, dark pit in the earth. The impression I got was that he collects viruses as 'pets' while his sister, the embra, uses them as part of her beauty regime. Brother and sister live apart and don't seem all that close or to share the same tastes but they have similar healing effects: the removal of spiritual toxins and their use of them in the otherworld for their own interests.

The day after the ceremony another shaman arrived at our camp, quite unexpectedly. His name, he told us, was Ronolfo and he had walked all the way from Ecuador to visit family and friends in Peru. He had called in on us for a purely social visit but what he began talking about Jergon Sacha – a coincidence or a message from the plant? He said he had dieted it many times and knew a number of icaros for it which he sang for us, all of them with a biting rhythm, fast and fluid, like a snake attacking, while the words to the songs were delivered in a hissing, lisping style, again like a snake.

When he had finished, knowing that I was also dieting Jergon Sacha, he picked up his chacapa and began to gently beat me with it, then cupped his hands together and blew through them into my crown. 'Inside of you now is a very big old snake' he said. 'It has much power. And now a song for the plant will come to you.'

He was wrong about that though. An icaro never did come as he had said it would, not during the diet at least. Instead, it was as if the energy of Jergon Sacha moved in to an old familiar song, an icaro for Ortega (Nettle) which I had received during a diet some years before. The two plants did have a similar healing effect - the removal of toxic energies – so perhaps that is not altogether surprising. Icaros are, after all, evolutionary; living things which change over time and contain a power of their own.

Dominion… Dominion
Dominion… Dominion
I urticate
And all of this shall fall away
And all of this shall fall away - And all of this shall fall
I have dominion
I sing for beauty, I sing for truth, I sing for these human hearts
I sing for justice, I sing for healing, I sing for these human souls
I have dominion

At the end of the diet there was the usual Ayahuasca ceremony to check in with the spirit of Jergon Sacha. After such a blissful final meeting with Tobacco where I was held and rocked by the mother plant I expected a similar celebration with Jergon but the encounter turned out to be as matter-of-fact as my other meetings with it; all rather emotionless and plain-talking. But then, if the spirit of the plant can heal sexual and relationship issues, I guess that emotional distance could be considered one of its strengths.

Only the male plant (the macho) appeared and began to teach me, almost formally, about *virotes* – 'darts' of intrusive energy, as the shamans describe them, which are often sent to a victim by sorcery – and the means of their removal.

'Firstly, they are not darts' he said. He showed me what they actually looked like: a cross between a long thin brown insect and a flying fish with a sharp pointed face and mean teeth which bite and burrow their way beneath the skin. They have wings or fins at their sides as well which, once inside a person's body, can be fanned out, making it more difficult to remove them. 'That is why we attack these virotes from the inside' said Jergon Sacha. 'It is easier to draw them into the body and destroy them so the victim shits or pukes them out than to pull them back through the flesh.'

He offered me a warning too: that instead of returning these energies to the sender, which is the typical approach of Amazonian shamanism, they should be quietly buried or banished. 'By returning them you simply alert the sorcerer to their removal and invite a further attack. You also become the aggressor and may provoke a war - and, as you know, wars of sorcery may continue for years and even when they are over it is never quite clear who won.'

The ceremony ended and I sat with Selva for a while, discussing the diet I had completed.

'So what did you learn from Jergon Sacha?' he asked.

'I think it's good for the treatment of addictions and sexual problems' I replied.

'Yes, of course' he said. 'That is what we use it for in the jungle'.

It is typical of every shaman I've met that they make you do the work of discovery yourself (this was La Bruja's approach too: that I should diet San Pedro for my answers if I wanted to become its apprentice and not rely on a human teacher) and then when you proudly announce your insights, they effectively shrug their shoulders and tell you that your conclusions are obvious. 'Our healers have known that for thousands of years'. But at least it is validation – from the plant and, I suppose the spirit of those ancient healers – that the diet has been effective and the ally is speaking the truth.

It is also interesting now to reflect that Jergon Sacha was the first plant that Jane and I dieted together and the only one in the jungle that she was really drawn to. At the time I had no idea what that might mean.

DRUNK IN IQUITOS

You're suffocating, you need a good shed
Pixies, *Dead*

2010. July

And then it was my turn.

I joke with my students and *dieteros* (those who join me for plant healing diets) that you can always tell an apprentice who is coming off a diet in Iquitos. He will be the one sitting in the Yellow Rose of Texas (a restaurant near the central plaza) at 7.29pm, watching the clock across the square, waiting for the next minute to pass, with a cold beer beside him, a fat steak in front of him and a woman sat on his lap. At 7.30 exactly he will start on all three.

Or maybe that's just me as others end their diets at noon; I wait until evening so I have another full day under my belt. But the point is the same. Alcohol, rich food and sex are prohibited on the diet and after several monastic weeks in the jungle eating plain rice or nothing I was ready for all three.

So was Jane as it happened. She completed her diet with Jergon Sacha at about the same time as me so we met up in town for a night of celebration – or at least a cold beer since everything in the jungle is at one temperature: warm.

Beer in Iquitos has to be drunk fast. A couple of bars in town where they have electricity and refrigeration advertise their *cerveza* as 'the coldest in Iquitos' but that is really irrelevant because two sips after it arrives the air around you makes it the same temperature as everything else. If you want a cold drink (and in 90% humidity, you do) the solution is simple: keep drinking. Fast.

So we did, making a tour of the riverfront bars, exploring the boulevard where the bohemians, craftspeople and travellers newly arrived in Iquitos hang out, both of us getting drunk in the process. But that was, in a way, the point.

Let us drink and give ourselves over to the only valid response to all these questions: Silence
Ejo Takata, Zen Master

As the night descended (no, not descended, *dropped*, as it does in jungle towns; one minute daylight, the next sweeping darkness) I introduced her to the local delicacy and national drink of Peru: pisco sour, a cocktail made from pisco (a sort of raw rum), lime juice, syrup, egg whites, ice and angostura bitters. Its name comes from the Quechua word *pisco* (meaning 'bird' – presumably because you're flying – or legless – after a few of them) and the term 'sour', a reference to the mixed drink family of the same name. It was invented in the 1920s by Victor Morris, an American bartender who left the US in 1903 to work in Peru. In 1916, he opened Morris' Bar in Lima, which became popular among the Peruvian elite and English-speaking foreigners. Pisco sour was a big hit. It also hit big.

We had a few of them then took a walk along the waterfront to Bar Camiri, the 'stilt bar' as it also known. Camiri sits on the river, a wooden cabin set on poles that rise from the water. It is reached via a steep gangplank that leads down from the bank so when you reach the bar itself you are sitting just feet about the Amazon, the second largest river in the world and surely the most romantic. So many species have yet to be discovered in the rainforest, who knows what mysteries may be swimming in the dark waters directly beneath you. And, as you gaze across the river to the jungle with its strange lights and blue electrical storms illuminating huge trees whose names you've never heard, growing fruits you never have and probably never will taste, you cannot help but wonder what else may be waiting for you, unknown and unexplored, out there or within yourself.

I needed to call in at Camiri to pay a bill run up several weeks ago during a night out with our shaman and thought that Jane and I might also find a last drink in this slightly seedy, somewhat shabby but iconic little bar, but when we got there it was closed. Which means, in Amazonian terms, that it was wide open and could still be entered since there are no doors, the bar being available to the river on all sides, but the room was in darkness and there were no customers or staff, just a languid dog (which our shaman knew and whose name was Forest) which had been left to guard the place and who licked us ferociously as we entered, wagging his tail to welcome his new friends who, if they had not been us, might then have robbed the till with his full support and approval.

Jane and I looked at each other in the darkness – what to do now? Should I just leave the money I owed or come back another day? I wasn't keen on the first idea because I wasn't sure that it would be safe or even found; on the other hand I didn't know when I'd be back as I was about to return to the jungle for further diets. We were drunk, not in our right minds, and the answer didn't come easy. We looked at each other blankly for a while then my blank stare took on a focus as I noticed for the first time the woman in front of me. She was pretty and there was a chemistry between us which had been building all night. 'Something is going to happen' I thought, 'right about... now'.

I'm not sure who made the first move, who kissed who. She said I did. I thought it was her. In any case we met somewhere in the middle and that kiss, in a seamless movement, turned into an embrace, the removal of clothes, and then we were fucking on the wooden floor of an empty bar, with the Amazon swelling beneath us, carrying its mysteries out to sea while the lights of Iquitos – blue, white and yellow – played on the water around us.

Fucking. I'm using the word deliberately because this was not 'making love'. Nothing as subtle as that. The jungle is raw, primal, sweaty, wet and dripping, the cauldron of potential, and you cannot help being effected when you spend time with it. All around us, in the forests and rivers, other animals – and we were no different from them - were also fucking, killing and eating each other, giving birth, creating and taking life. Sweat dripping down our faces and gluing our bodies together, it felt entirely natural to begin an affair this way. It wasn't wining and dining as TV etiquette tells us it should be, but it was real: a basic truth that the rainforest knows. She became a shadow; I could have been fucking the trees and the river.

When we stood up to dress we couldn't find our clothes. Then I saw Forest. He'd made a nest of them and was cuddled there, his face turned politely away. Maybe he was used to this. Maybe he was shocked to the core. In any case he followed us halfway down the road, licking us as we walked back to town, obviously not too traumatised.

Inevitably, Jane and I shared a hotel room and a bed that night. I woke up at about 5am to find her quietly dressing and leaving without a word. That was interesting, I thought, vaguely, half-asleep. After what we'd been through together just a few hours before, nothing at all was being said. No explanations, excuses, embarrassment, intentions for any kind of future or consignment of this to the past. It felt like a business deal had been concluded and now the meeting was over. Then I fell back to sleep.

I awoke again much later, with a bad head and a single thought: I'm number three. In approximately three months of being in Peru she had slept with three different men: one married, one in a long-term relationship, and me, who she believed at the time (mistakenly) to be in a sexual rather than a purely business relationship with Trudy, my co-owner at our Centre. If I wasn't aware of it before (which I was) I couldn't help but see a pattern now in her behaviour. I was part of it. All three of us (in her mind) were unavailable, promised to others and therefore, I suppose, no threat. Functional.

Despite this realisation, a second thought began quickly to form, gather power and bubble up to the surface, trampling all over the first: *I really like her*. My instincts said run but my spirit said wait, there is something important in this. Which is how and why I decided to fall in love with Jungle Jane.

MEETING THE SHEPHERDESS

'This is a sacred place' moaned the shepherd
'So much the better. The silence will make the bullet even louder'
Silver Kane, *No Habra Tiros!* (*There Will Be No Gunshots!*)

2010. July/August

The Aztecs called it *pipiltzintzintli* – apparently[21]: 'the noblest little prince'. The hummingbird – the guardian spirit of San Pedro, of curanderos and of those who wish to be healed - is its only pollinator. The plant is Salvia divinorum, also known as The Shepherdess, ska Maria, La Pastora, and she has the ability to dismantle reality, facilitate travel through time and take you to other dimensions. This was my next plant diet.

Salvia is a member of the *lamiaceae* or mint family. Its genus name, Salvia, comes from the Latin *salvare*, to heal or to save, while its complete botanical name, also translated from Latin, is understood as 'sage of the seers'. The Mazatec shamans of Oaxaca, Mexico, where Salvia grows, use the plant for divination, visionary and healing purposes.

In traditional shamanic use the fresh leaves are rolled and chewed as a quid or made into a tea and drunk. When taken in this way the effects are usually mild. But not always, as the anthropologist Bret Blosser discovered in the mid-1980s:

I never noticed the transition. I was not aware that I had eaten an entheogenic plant, was in Mexico, was with friends, or had ever had a body. I was engulfed in a complex, fluctuating environment...I remember very little of this first plunge into the world of the hojas, but towards the end I recall an intricate, neon-pastel, slick-lit, all encompassing, non-Euclidian topography. This sense of a distinctive topography has characterized each of my Mazatec Salvia experiences. Of course, what I can describe begs the question of what I cannot describe: being out of the three dimensions and linear time.

When the active ingredient, salvinorin A, is extracted and smoked (the more frequent way of working with Salvia these days) it becomes even more potent.

Salvinorin was isolated from Salvia in 1993 by Daniel Siebert who, in the spirit of all psychedelic pioneers, was also the first to explore its effects on a human being - himself. 'I found myself in a confused, fast moving state of consciousness with absolutely no idea where my body or for that matter my universe had gone' he said later.

I tried to remember what my body felt like. Anything, just something to reconnect me with the 'normal' world. But the more I looked for some little thread of 'normality' to get a hold of, the more it showed me something else. At some point I realized that what I was trying to get back to did not exist. It was just an ephemeral dream. I suddenly realized that I had no actual memory of ever having lived in any other state of consciousness but the disembodied condition I was now in. So I decided to stop panicking and just relax. After all there was no place to get back to. I was totally convinced that this state of existence was all there ever was...

A little later the physical world all started to work properly again. As the effects began to subside I managed to piece together what had happened... I had stumbled upon the psychedelic essence of Salvia divinorum. I grabbed a pen and tried to write down a few notes while the experience was still fresh.

The first thing I wrote down in BIG letters was:

IT IS TOTAL MADNESS

Then:

TEARING APART THE FABRIC OF REALITY...

I had been shaken to the soul.

He wrote in *The Entheogen Review* the following year that salvinorin is:

An extremely powerful consciousness-altering compound. In fact it is the most potent naturally occurring hallucinogen thus far isolated. But before would-be experimenters get too worked-up about it, it should

*be made clear that the effects are often extremely unnerving and there
is a very real potential for physical danger with its use... the effects can
be very alarming. I have seen several people get up and lunge around
the room falling over furniture, babbling incomprehensible nonsense
and knocking their heads into walls... When the experience is over they
have no memory of any of this. In fact they usually remember very
different events. To an outside observer people in this condition have a
blank look in their eyes as if no-one is present (and perhaps no one is).*

As well as its curious effects when smoked, there are a
number of 'real life' mysteries to Salvia. Firstly, there are no
creation myths which tell of its origin. Unlike Ayahuasca for
example, where shamans have legends to explain the origins of
the plant and its purpose on Earth[22] or San Pedro, where curanderos tell of the hummingbird bringing the secrets of God to
Earth in the form of the cactus[23] with Salvia no such stories have
yet been heard. From this we may conclude that Mazatec
shamans are either extremely secretive about their Salvia myths
and legends - or else they do not have any.

D M Turner, in his book *Salvinorin: The Psychedelic Essence of
Salvia Divinorum* also remarks that:

*The Mazatecs lack an indigenous name for Salvia divinorum, both
the Christian theme of Mary, as well as sheep, having been introduced
to the region during the Spanish conquest. The Mazatecs also list a
method of consuming this plant[24] that does not efficiently utilize its
psychoactive content, and seem to be generally unaware of its
tremendous potency.*

It is not just the shamans who are mystified. Botanists have no
answer for the origins of Salvia either. They have been unable to
determine whether it is a naturally-occurring species or a
cultigen for example. The plant's partial sterility suggests a
hybrid although no likely parent species have been identified -
and if the plant was created it begs the questions why and by
whom? Turner again:

Salvia divinorum... is not known to exist in the wild, and the few patches that are known in the Sierra Mazateca appear to be the result of deliberate planting... the Indians believe the plant is foreign to their region and do not know from where it came. And if Salvia divinorum is a hybrid, there are no commonly held theories on what its prospective parents may be.

A further puzzle is that although salvinorin is by mass the world's most potent natural hallucinogen it has no actions on the 5-HT2A serotonin receptor, the principal molecular target for psychedelics such as mescaline and LSD.

Turner: *Shortly after discovering salvinorin A's effects, Siebert sent a sample to David Nichols who initiated a NovaScreen receptor site screening. The screening results were in contrast to those of all previously tested psychedelics. Salvinorin A did not affect any of the receptor sites tested, which included all of the likely known receptor sites for other psychedelics.*

In 2002 Professor Bryan Roth solved this mystery when he discovered that salvinorin stimulates a single receptor - the kappa opioid – but even that is strange and unique since other psychedelics hit multiple receptor sites (LSD, by comparison, has an effect on 50). In other words, no-one quite knows how or why Salvia works. As with all great entheogenic detective stories, then, the answers must be found by those who work with the plant themselves.

The Amazonian diet for Salvia is the same as for any plant: a cold tea of the leaves is drunk for three days and the rest of the diet continues for a further eleven. I also bathed in the leaves and, to take the experiment further, ordered a 20X concentrate of salvinorin, the Salvia extract which is smoked in a pipe.

Jane didn't diet the plant but she was interested in Salvia as well and decided to smoke it with me. We had hardly spoken since our night in Iquitos, neither of us quite sure what had happened or what it meant, so our initial work with Salvia was an adventure, a journey of discovery on all sorts of levels.

I was excited to have someone to play and explore with. I had always envied those pioneers of psychedelic research who had found their companions, their soulmates, their fellow travellers, and were able to share their love of the journey with the loves of their lives. Gordon Wasson (the Mushroom explorer) had his wife; Alexander Shulgin (the pioneer of MDMA) had his; Marcia Moore (the Ketamine researcher) had her husband Howard Alltrounian to navigate with; even Terence McKenna (the Ayahuasca and Mushroom poet) had his brother Dennis. It seemed to me that there was something special about sharing this sort of deep inner work with someone who knew you and who you knew but who still had their own ideas and direction, their own interests and their own motivations for the journey. You learn more about plants that way too – two heads being better than one, at the very least – but more than that: it gives you the potential to learn more about yourself, since that is what the plants are also showing you, as well as more about the person sitting next to you. And maybe more about human nature or the human condition as well since you have someone else to bounce your ideas and experiences off.

Over the course of the next weeks Jane and I smoked salvinorin extensively but there was no further sexual contact between us. This was pure research. No strings attached.

Drinking the tea produces, in general, an increased yet strangely detached connection to the emotions, a sense of alert stillness, a paradoxical blend of 'relaxed anxiety' as well as greater empathy for others, as if seeing into – no, not really seeing, more feeling – their souls and becoming aware of their life stories, wounds, issues and patterns: whatever hurts they are carrying with them. Whenever I speak with Jane or even look at her I have the sense of a child, alone and frightened. Feelings of betrayal and insecurity radiate from her. Is that child who she still is? Is that where 'Jungle' Jane – tough, competitive and defended - came from: to protect her from whatever she went through then? It reminded me of something the artist

Leonora Carrington said of herself as a result of her own childhood experiences: 'How could I give, for nothing was really mine? If the world did not desire me how could it receive my love? I had only learned to desire myself, which split me into two – or more': Jane the woman and Jane, the Jungle variety.

I have just read a book by Carl Calleman (The Mayan Calendar and the Transformation of Consciousness) and something he said resonated with me too when I gave my attention to Jane. It was about what he called 'An illusory sense of freedom': 'How can you fully accept and love someone else, let alone yourself, with a dualistic mind that was designed to be separate and cause separation? Can a person who is only half love herself fully?' – or anyone else for that matter?

Smoking the extract is different to drinking the leaves. The first time I tried the smoke, space curved around me and seemed to flow backwards, as if I was being rolled or sucked into a tunnel or vortex of some kind. When I passed through it and landed on the other side I found myself in a scene from my childhood. I had the idea that I was about five years of age and my mother was pulling me along a road by the hand – I could see it all and felt it clearly. It was like being pulled backwards in time as well as physically. I also had the sense that I could be an insignificant object from the story of my life, like a brick in a wall in the street that my mother and I were in, or a leaf (or even a cell in a leaf) and watching myself pass by (although 'I' was also present as 'me', experiencing all perspectives at once) – so that every object in my life was also me; like our realities were interchangeable. I could look at myself from the point-of-view of everything and anything in that street and feel its connection to me – and me to it. Jane also felt the importance of her childhood but couldn't connect with its meaning any more than I could with mine.

A few nights later I smoked again, this time immediately after an

Ayahuasca ceremony – I wanted to see what effect the two plants had together and whether the impact of the experience was amplified. You bet it was! I suddenly felt myself physically pulled by my shoulders and knew that I was not human at all but a bedspread being laid on a bed. My body slithered upwards by itself (or was pulled by unseen hands) and there was nothing I could do to prevent it. The last remnant of 'me' knew that I didn't want to be a bedspread – I didn't like my pattern![25] *– and I panicked and grabbed Trudy as I was pulled up and over her bed. She held onto me to prevent further movement and to stop 'me' being lost to the world. All of my humanity was slipping away.* I was a bedspread and always had been. *I abandoned the attempt to be anything else and became just an item in a room, with no thoughts or judgements. It took me some minutes to fully shake off the bedspread consciousness, with Trudy holding me down until I returned to human awareness. Then I literally ran (stumbled) out onto the balcony overlooking our jungle and shouted for joy at being human again. Having a head, two arms and two legs, even if they weren't working so well, had never felt this good before.*

I had read the accounts of other Salvia users who had turned into objects when they smoked the extract – it always seemed silly: one had reported being a wardrobe, another said he was a suitcase under a stairway at an airport – but it didn't seem so silly now. In those accounts I'd always assumed that the writers meant that they "thought" or "felt" or "had a vision of being" whatever they turned into, as it is with Ayahuasca for example. But it isn't like that with Salvia. I was *a bedspread just as they* were *wardrobes or suitcases and the sense of losing all human consciousness was alarming.*

When I recovered I smoked again and this time the experience was deeper. I am not sure where I was but certainly not in a jungle; an urban street somewhere. It felt similar to my first time with Salvia where I could have been a brick in a wall I passed by in childhood.

At one point the entire room became a wall and I was part of it.
Extract from my San Pedro journal during the Salvia diet

On the last day of drinking the tea and bathing in the leaves I spent the evening with Jane in the moloka, smoking the extract again. This time we decided on three sessions – three pipes of Saliva each - one of us after the other, taking it in turns.

It turned out to be a pivotal ceremony. The first time I smoked I became another object - or aspect of myself. I was chewing gum stuck to the wheel of a pram which was being pushed along a street. I even knew when and where it was: Birmingham UK in the 1960s. The pram was a Silvercross. I was the baby in it (and also the gum and the wheel) and my mother was pushing it. Again it was like viewing myself from several different perspectives and feeling that I had made some sort of agreement with everything that was a part of my life before I was even born (no matter how seemingly insignificant – a brick, a bedspread or a piece of gum) that this was a journey we would take together and a consciousness we would share. It was as if these things were my soul companions and there was a contract of some kind between us. Every time the pram wheel turned I turned and felt myself rolling around the floor of the moloka. I was ground into the earth repeatedly so that my body (or my consciousness of even having a body) disappeared into it and only when the wheel rotated upwards did I have any remotely residual sense of 'me'. I surfaced one time and had an awareness of Jane sitting close to me and, just as I had with Trudy, I grabbed her and was grabbed to stop myself being pushed into the earth again. She held me as I returned to a sense of myself.

Jane smoked next and found herself in a variety of landscapes with people around her and was told by them that she "belonged" in their world and could stay if she wanted. It was an invitation for her to embark on a new adventure in a new world but, always the paradox, an invitation for her to escape the 'real' world too.

She smoked again and found herself in the body of a machine in an alien factory; a giant multi-levelled conveyor, each layer a different scene – a beach, stars, country fields, a wall, standing stones, each of which was a vast self-contained world which she was a part of, like a character drawn onto rolls of living wallpaper. A blue creature turned a handle and each of these worlds rolled forward until it folded in on itself. The people in these worlds panicked and ran as their reality slipped off the conveyor and ended. The creature controlling it was stoically amused at their reactions and their fear of annihilation, as if they/we really should have evolved beyond that.

Jane's 'reality' was actually multiple realities and it was all just a play, maybe literally rolls of wallpaper each with a pattern which contained its own consciousness, all of it coming to an end, controlled by something bigger than us (the blue creature) which we in our dreaming might, I suppose, call God and project all sorts of illusions onto but who is actually ambivalent, uninterested and just a functionary in a factory of universes. The world – or these multiple worlds around us – meant little in the whole scheme of things and nor did 'God' or the factory he occupied because 'He' and we are all just cogs in a wheel.[26]

On day nine of the diet it was my birthday and La Bruja had sent me a bottle of San Pedro to celebrate. It was the best I've ever had – still is - intense and beautiful, like an all-day all-over sensual massage for the mind, body and soul. I drank a glass and was out for the day. I still had a lot of Salvia in me from all the journeys I'd taken with it and I could feel the sage and the cactus meet in me. They got on well and seemed to have much in common. Both of them are philosopher's plants which raise questions in us that at some point we all must all find answers to.

They reminded me again for example that reality is pliable and there are whole other worlds or dimensions within us which we can choose from to create the circumstances of our lives; that the world is a construct – a game that we are part of or choose to play - that nothing is *really* real and that nothing much matters apart from those things we give our attention to. And, even then, not much, because where do those choices we make come from? They arise from our experiences, our conditioning, our responses to childhood dramas and the roles we have played or the personas we have adopted along the way - so are we ever – *really* - free? Are our choices ever *really* our own?

> *Long ago your naked footprints already sketched out the labyrinth in front of you, which is your path. Listen: By absolute necessity I rediscovered my mother... she gave me her web to dress my shadow and yours*
> Leonora Carrington, artist

> *What was your first face – the one you had before you were born?*
> Classic Zen koan

And yet who we are is still a choice we *are* making. We are free and not-free all at once. As the philosopher Rousseau put it: 'Man is free and everywhere in chains'; an observation answered, just as validly, by Voltaire: 'Man is free the moment he wishes to be'.

I spent the next day with Jane, sharing the remainder of my San Pedro with her, from noon till around 6am the next morning. San Pedro is the medicine of love and La Bruja's is filled with it. On top of that I was with a woman I felt drawn to emotionally and intellectually, as an enigma, a healer's puzzle. It was perhaps inevitable therefore that we would fall in love that day.

We spent hours holding each other and gazing into one another's eyes, trying to fathom the mysteries that lay behind them. It became a compulsion, something we couldn't drag ourselves – whatever our 'selves' were – away from: the connection between us and the knowledge of each other's souls.

We kissed of course but, deeper than that, we breathed together, exchanging air – the nourishment of God, the healing of San Pedro – feeding each other with spirit. With each inhalation I understood more of her and with each exhalation I told her who I was. There was no way that we could not be absolutely honest with each other. San Pedro is also the medicine of truth. We hardly said a word the entire day but we didn't need to. At the end of it we knew each other perfectly.

My Salvia diet ended in four days and we decided to go back into town so we could spend time with each other away from the Centre and my own rules about 'fraternisation'. Before that however there was another Ayahuasca ceremony.

I smoked Salvia again before it and found myself in a street – no, not *in* it exactly; it moved towards me like a film or a hologram projected into the room. On one side of it I was in the moloka watching it march towards me; on the other side, when I stepped through it, I was in New York in the 1950s: a typical street scene, with a father, dressed appropriately for the times – tan suit, brown brogues, hat – leading his daughter by the hand from a subway, walking up the steps towards me. She was dressed in a pink duffel coat, white socks and shiny black shoes. I had a sense that, in some other dimension, this was Jane as a child. During my first experience with Salvia I had been a young boy led by his mother; on this journey Jane was a young girl led by her father. I wondered what that might mean.

I found that I could walk through this 'street screen' and become part of the scene – seeing it from the perspective of a child who had fallen – or walk back through it and be a standing adult observing this new wave of reality as it moved through the room. There was a tingling, like jolts of electricity as I passed through the membrane between worlds. At one point I reached for Jane (who hadn't smoked yet) and placed her hand on the 'screen' to see if she could feel it too. She could, although she couldn't see the street in front of her. Taking the experiment further, I entered the scene again and became part of it, wrapping my arm around the shoulder of a man that I saw there and walking with him through the moloka. I asked Jane what she saw. She said she could see me with someone – or something. It was smoky, undefined, but it had a human shape and was a definite presence in the room. She was observing what should have been my hallucination - a reality personal only to me – and seeing something that only I should have been able to see.

There was something not entirely 'correct' about this other reality though. When the Salvia effects wore off I was left with the impression that it was more like a computer construct; as if we are all characters in a game being played by some other being; as if we are not really human at all in the sense that we have come to understand humanity, but programmes which have been written by an alien intelligence and that 'enlightenment' simply means waking up to this fact. I have given Salvia to many others in ceremonies since then and a similar idea often emerges for them. Some have described us as being part of an alien experiment or a game controlled by forces that cannot be seen or understood. Even Jane's 'blue God' was something like this, creating and destroying landscapes that we thought were intrinsically ours, that we belonged in or owned, where we thought that our lives were secure, real and mattered.[27]

Selva was ill so I had to run the Ayahuasca ceremony tonight. I had wanted to spend the evening with the vine exploring Salvia more deeply and, at the close of the diet, to connect with the spirit of the plant, but that wasn't possible now. I did catch a glimpse of Salvia though. She appeared to me as a woman dressed in white, although I could have been imagining that. It didn't feel like a solid connection. She had a message for us: that human beings 'must change their shapes' if they want to heal, get through this current world crisis and evolve to their full potential. She showed me an image of pyramids and it seemed to me that everything in the world

is also triangular; that everything comes in threes: problem-reaction-solution, thesis-antithesis-synthesis, or the past and the future linked by a present moment of choice.
Extract from my San Pedro journal during the Salvia diet

A few days later Jane and I were back in Iquitos. We hadn't drawn attention to ourselves at the Centre and never acted like a couple (a word we didn't even use about ourselves yet) but I suspected that most people there could sense what was happening between us. We stayed at the Safari that weekend, one of the town's more modern and convenient hotels, close to the river and the boulevard. One of our staff, Matt, drove us and went into the hotel to book our rooms while we waited in the motocarro. He came out to say that the hotel was full apart from one matrimonial suite, would that be OK? We took it of course. He told me later that there were actually plenty of rooms but he knew without us saying a word that whatever he booked we'd end up sharing a room. I like to think that there was just a glow to us but perhaps he had an idea of Jane as well from what his brother had told him.

The weekend turned into three days and we didn't leave the room for most of it, we were so wrapped up in each other. She told me again that her aim with the plant work she was doing was to become more open, less defended and more 'vulnerable'. I had little doubt that she would make it too; I was impressed by what I had seen of her dedication to healing and her willingness to face whatever came up. Sometimes it is not easy or pleasant. When working with teacher plants old memories may resurface - some simply forgotten, some repressed for good reasons – along with new realisations and connections: a joining of the dots of our experiences so we can see who we truly are. This is one of the greatest blessings of the plants and one of their hardest lessons: to see ourselves for the first time in all our horror and beauty and, of course, when we lay our souls on the line, the things that haunt us are rarely pretty. That is the point of a wound: to make our ghosts visible so we can face them – or, if we are of a different persuasion, to at least know where they are so we can continue to run from them.

She told me about her childhood, a subject we had never spoken about before, although her story was much as I expected, given what I knew of her and the way she presented herself to the world. She had been bullied at school (and later at work; a pattern that repeated itself) and had problems at home, she said: violence of an emotional and physical kind - perhaps in other ways too - and had been slapped so hard that her eardrum was permanently damaged. She had watched her mother and sister being hit too. She left home as soon as she could, at age 17, and sought freedom in parties, 'free love' and travel. 'I went off the rails in my 20s' she said. A little girl acting like a big girl in a grown-up scary world.

I have noticed with some clients that sex can become a form of escapism, stress relief or self-defence when pressure, instability or abuse has been a factor in their childhoods. It becomes a mechanical act, a form of trance, a way of removing themselves from the scene so they are not fully present to suffer; a sort of wilful soul loss, I suppose.

There is often a paradox, contradiction and sometimes uncon-scious self-harm in their sexual choices however. A female client once told me how she had lost her virginity at the age of 14. She planned it and deliberately set out to entice the man she wanted but the act, when it happened, was more like rape than a loving encounter. She didn't mention it to anybody but wrote about it in her private diary, later discovering that her intrusive and controlling father (who she felt may also have had a sexual interest in her although she couldn't swear that he had acted upon it) had read through it and against that entry had written the single word 'slut', an expression of jealousy, I supposed, and of his need to control and possess the object of his own desires.

Almost in defiance of her father, she quickly set out on a quest for independence through parties, drugs and sex. By her early 30s she couldn't remember how many men and women she had slept with, but well in excess of 50, sometimes with more than one at once. It took her some years to realise that, rather than freedom, much of her life had been dictated by her father and that word he wrote in her diary; that she had become the embodiment of his judgement, almost a cliché of a self-fulfilling prophecy. She had set out to punish her father through her defiance but the person she hurt most was herself, some of the consequences being a string of abortions, where she wept not for the children she killed but for the damage she had done to her body, and a case of cervical cancer, perhaps brought on deliberately, although unconsciously, as a form of self-harm for the shame she felt at staging her own rape (something that was now an enduring sexual fantasy for her) and the discovery of it by her prying and manipulative father. She seemed unable, however, to stop herself.

I do not understand my own actions for I do not do what I want but the very thing I hate
Romans 7:15

My client, like Jane, was a traveller but her memories of all she had seen never went further than sex. In Australia she had worked on oyster boats, a romantic occupation, at sea and part of the vast horizon, but her most vivid recollection was of having sex in an engine room next to another couple. In New Zealand she worked as a topless waitress in a biker bar because she was 'ashamed of her body' and wanted everyone to see it (whether to overcome her shame or reinforce it was never made clear). In London, a city of history and new discoveries, she had sex with two men she'd just met in a bar. From the way she described it she saw it as an act of power on her part although I am sure that the men who used her thought exactly the opposite. On another occasion, a woman she had an affair with, knowing that her lover was emotionally defended and could not be easily spoken to, had written a note that said 'I love you' and slipped it between her thighs so when her girlfriend went down on her she would see it. Her girlfriend - my client - read it and left the same day. And now she was here for healing because, having had half of her cervix removed, she had a lump in her left breast, almost directly over her heart.

I remembered something I had read about a woman with breast cancer who visited the Mexican curandera Pachita, and Hermanito, the spirit which possessed her when she conducted her healings. Immediately, Pachita held up a knife in front of her patient's face, using it like a hypnotist's crystal to induce a state of trance. 'Why do you want them to cut off your breasts?' she asked. 'To not be a mother' the patient replied.

'And now [next] my dear girl, what do you want them to cut?'

'The glands that swell in my neck... to not have to speak to people... [then] the glands that swell under my arms... to not have to work... [then] those that swell near my sex so I can be alone with myself... [then] the glands in my legs so they cannot force me to go anywhere.'

'And then what do you want?' asked Pachita.

'To die'.

'Very well, my little daughter' Pachita answered. 'You know the path your illness will take. Choose: follow this path or heal yourself'.

Valerie Trumblay, who relates this story, comments that the patient, a stubborn woman who thought she knew better than anyone else, decided not to follow the treatment her healer specified and returned instead to her home in Paris. 'She died two weeks later. When I told Pachita the sad news she replied, "El Hermanito does not come only to heal. He also helps those who desire it to die. Cancer and other grave illnesses present themselves like warriors following a path of precise conquest. When you show an ill patient, who seeks to wipe himself out, the path the illness takes, he will hurry to follow it. For this reason the French woman... quit fighting. She yielded to the illness and helped it realise its plan in two weeks". Before this I had believed that it was enough to make someone conscious of self-destructive impulses in order to save them. From this case I learned the lesson that such knowledge could also accelerate a person's death.'[28]

The situation for my client was similar. Driven by the word her father had used against her, her body and her psyche became little more than a number of holes to be filled, reflecting the bigger hole – the inability to give or receive love - at her centre, and even when her behaviour resulted in cancer she was unwilling or unable to stop because at her core she wanted to die. She was 33 when she came for healing. I believe she was dead by the age of 40. We cannot live without love.

I left her in that world, her world without faith and without love, a victim of herself.
Alejandro Jodorowsky, Zen Master

Karl Jansen MD writes about a similar process in his book *Ketamine: Dreams and Realities* (MAPS, 2004): 'One view is that "excessive penetration by outside forces" in childhood is a possible means by which different parts of the self become separated from each other. This "penetration" is often by words.

'In this particular model a child is seen as being born with an inner archetype of self. "Outside forces" (parents, school, society etc) may then fill the child with their ideas about who that child is. In some cases this may trigger a process of separation from the "true self", especially if those outside forces are strident, loud, manipulative, heavily opinionated and determined to win the child to their cause... The more extensive the penetration by others has been, the greater will be the problems with selfhood...

'Sometimes excessive appetites... are an expression of hatred for the persona that is the end result of this process... "Persona-hatred" is often a better term than "self-hatred" [since] those who say that they hate themselves may only have a limited knowledge of who they are'.

And if The Fool spoke [he would say]: 'Did you know that transformation of consciousness is possible at any moment, that you can suddenly change the perception you have of yourself?'

'... If you wish to act in the world you must explode that perception of the ego that has been imposed and imbedded since childhood and which refuses to change'
Alejandro Jodorowsky and Marianne Costa

Most of Jane's relationships, according to her, had also been casual and she left if they became at all serious. Her longest-lasting had been three years. I asked how she felt when she ended it; whether there was any pain or regret. 'Relieved' she said.

He killed himself a year or so after they separated and since then she had marked the anniversary of his death by putting his picture up on her Facebook page as what she called an 'homage'. It was in a way, I guess, the perfect relationship for anyone afraid of commitment: a risk-free way to express love because it could never be real or meaningful and would never involve true, reciprocal or dangerous feelings since at least one of the partners was dead. And all of this had gone into the making of Jungle Jane. *Uriah hit the crapper.* The soul protects itself.

I felt sorry for her. All of her travels and experiences felt motivated not by the excitement of exploration but an absolute need to escape, and now I knew what she was running from. I doubt that she'd actually seen anything of the world.

Your history acts as your gravity
Joseph Arthur, musician and artist

The suicide of her boyfriend was disturbing too. No-one ever said that the act was committed over her. Those words could never be spoken but they were implied of course and if that was the case it made her a powerful witch, one with control over life and death - and the worst kind of sorceress because she didn't know her own power. Her annual 'homage' was the sort of link that brujas forge in order to manipulate souls.

The journey she had chosen however was about finding that power and controlling it through the courage to be vulnerable and unshielded, and that gave us both hope that something more positive might come from this than was the case for Pachita's client.

Jane's quest for healing was also a battle to forgive. That weekend she changed her surname from her mother's to her father's, which she saw as a sort of breakthrough, although she soon changed it back, and our stories became one.

JUNGLE POLITICS

Gravity is always a two-way street – just as the Moon raises tides on Earth so Earth must cause tides to sweep across the surface of the Moon
Dr Brian Cox, physicist

2010. August/September

Mucura is another protective plant. It has been used in the Amazon for millennia as a pain reliever, a remedy for skin problems, to cure colds and fevers, relieve headaches and, more recently has been shown to kill cancer and leukemia cells, prevent tumours, enhance immunity, destroy viruses and reduce anxiety. The spiritual intention of Mucura is to expel 'bad spirits': whatever may infect us and which does not serve us.

As I began my diet with it I had a group of people staying with me in the rainforest who had come to Peru to attend my Magical Earth programme where they would drink Ayahuasca, diet plants, and work with jungle shamans to learn more about their medicine. Some of them dieted Mucura with me.

I fasted for two days before the diet and drank the brew on the third day, before bedtime. The night was filled with strange dreams. I was trying to heal a group of children in a rundown crèche but their scumbag crack addict parents kept feeding them Ayahuasca from a bottle, trying to make them addicts too. (Ayahuasca is non-addictive and is certainly not crack cocaine but they seemed unaware of that or, if they were, they didn't care). They tried to prevent me helping and when that didn't work they destroyed their children rather than have them healed. As their babies screamed, they cut slices from their faces and fried and ate them in front of me.

The message, when I considered it later, was about family relation-

ships and patterns: how some parents feed their dramas and addictions to their children, hoping to create new versions of themselves in the next generation – whether consciously or not – so that something of them survives. 'They fuck you up, your mom and dad/ They may not mean to but they do/ They pass on all the faults they had/ And add some new ones just for you' *as Philip Larkin wrote in his poem* This Be The Verse. *At the same time they devour their children, taking power from them, moulding and shaping them until their unique personalities are all but forgotten and they become reflections of their parents, with the same issues of power loss and fear although they may manifest them in different ways. In its most extreme form some shamans call this process soul theft: the stealing of another person's spirit.*

In my dream I couldn't trust anyone, even June. By now our relationship was known and Trudy wasn't happy about it. We thought we had been discrete, staying away from each other in camp but of course that was dumb since our first sexual encounter had taken place in a bar overlooked by the whole of Iquitos.

'So you're fucking her now as well then?' Trudy had stated rather than asked. 'That's everyone in the camp now isn't it?' She accused me of breaking my own rules (no fraternisation) – which I denied since my meetings with Jane had all been outside the Centre - and called me a hypocrite, then added pointedly, 'You know she's just using you to get to Cusco (where my next course, The Cactus of Vision, *would be held) and that she doesn't want you as a lover? She says you remind her more of her father than a boyfriend!'*

A heated (and so less than useful) 'clinical' discussion followed about whether or not Jane might be a sex addict or a (less flattering term) given her history so far at the camp. I had wondered the same thing myself but I was bored with the anger at that point so my final comment was that it would be amusing if she were since Trudy's specialty was addiction cures and Jane had come to the jungle because of her own interest in the use of Ayahuasca to helps addicts so for neither of them to have noticed that small detail would be curious, but I supposed it could be possible.

That was the moment though when I knew that I would be leaving. There are too many politics at the Centre now, and too much ill-will – not just towards Jane and I but between the other personalities here as well, and too many contradictions in how things are being run[29] – and I knew that I had a choice: to remain in a 'system' that I wasn't happy with or take a chance on Jane and explore what this connection between us was, where this intensity of feeling came from - and where it might lead. There is another healing Centre, in the Andes, where the work is more exclusively with San Pedro, and I am interested in investing in that. I have already suggested to Jane that I would like to go travelling with her to see more of Peru and three or four months on the road means that I will be away from my own Centre anyway. It has been tense between all of us – Trudy and Jane, Trudy and I; even Jane and I – since all of this has come out and now I don't know who to trust or where any of this is leading except, at the moment at least, to more problems.

Finally in my dream I had an image of a fat naked woman – a blonde with peroxide hair – who was applying metal tips to her nipples. The nipple: the place of nourishment for the baby, now shielded by cold metal to prevent the child from suckling. I didn't recognise the woman nor, as a symbol, do I know who or what she stood for but before I could process it further I woke up to the sound of laughter in my room. It was hysterical, slightly mocking and very real but when I opened my eyes and lit the lantern no-one was there.

The shamans say that Mucura is for the removal of witchcraft and negative energy and shows you things you can't trust in yourself or others. It reveals in dreams the people who mean you harm or who *are using you or lying to you for their own ends.*

Extract from my San Pedro journal during the Mucura diet

I had been drinking San Pedro steadily throughout the whole dieting process, now for a period of some months, and Jane and I had also been working a lot with Salvia. Both plants had been teaching me about healing and seemed amazingly compatible, although they came from different countries and different ends of the spectrum in terms of their healing approach. The feeling they both gave was one of *empathy* – of seeing into people and understanding their intricate manoeuvres, their scripts and dramas, their resistances and avoidances as well as the hopes and fears they bring to the healing process, most of which they are also quite unaware of. The focus of San Pedro however is to bring love and compassion to this understanding – your heart goes out to them as you see that they are no different to you; that we are all frail humans dwarfed by the immensity of night – while Salvia is direct and clinical. She speaks in mathematics and science – a doctor more than a healer – and her instructions for healing are clear and concise: 'Do *this*, do *that*, then walk away' - a sense of deep connection to the problem and knowledge of what to do about it but no real sense of love, at least not in the way that we believe we know what that means.

The shamans say that the way to understand any plant and put its healing into practice is to drink Ayahuasca and there is another ceremony tonight. Compared to our recent run of action-packed rituals filled with possessions and exorcisms it is a relatively quiet affair. Relatively.

We have a client – Dick – with an addiction to prescription drugs and his own paranoia. He believes that he was kidnapped and tortured by Middle Eastern terrorists and that they and the CIA are now stalking him. Even our moloka may be bugged. (It is – but not in the way he means; we had to kill a tarantula we found in there today.) It sounds to me like another parent drama.

Symbolically, to be held against one's will and tortured is the experience of every abused child. To have a 'higher power' spying on one's every move suggests the internalisation of a parent's critical voice and since all of the characters in Dick's story are male I would say that the abuse came from his father. That is my hypothesis anyway. I am not ruling out his view of things either but, objectively, we have not seen any men wearing black suits and shades wiring up our moloka for some weeks now or, in fact, ever.

Selva and I discussed our approach to the healing before the ceremony, as we always did, and our plan was for me to sit next to Dick while Selva handled the ceremony. At an appropriate time I would begin the healing work for our client.

When I began to do so what I saw does not need to be repeated here. I was reminded of a comment by the Mayan shaman Martin Prechtel: 'I don't know why anyone wants to become a shaman – we just see the ugly things; monsters and darkness'. It took a while to get rid of what I saw, all the time advised by San Pedro and Salvia; the former repeating its mantra of faith: *Do not believe in it. See something new and better* and the latter offering a more matter-of-fact, step-by-step approach: *Use the chacapa here, blow Tobacco smoke there.*

I also had a sense of Mucura joining the healing, its spirit appearing in a tall, spindly plant/human form with many arms, each lined with spines and suckers with which to grab intrusive energies. In the wild the plant does look something like this, growing to about a metre in height, with dark leathery leaves close to the ground and taller spikes lined with small white flowers. It has a strong garlic smell – often a sign of a plant which removes toxins and purifies the soul - and is sometimes called 'garlic weed'. I felt the beginnings of a new icaro from it, at this stage really just one line repeated over: *Mucura con Rah, Mucura con Rah* which I sang into my client's body. In time this song would evolve (it is still evolving), becoming a liturgy which enumerates the many different plants 'con RAH' and acts as a talisman or *arkana* (a magical shield of protection) when sung for someone. Some minutes later I returned to my seat and Dick began throwing up, purging his demons. The night passed quietly after that.

What was interesting during our circle meeting next day was what he chose to say or, rather, who he chose to thank for his healing: me of course, since I had carried it out, but also Jane because of her 'wise words' and the advice she had given him after the ceremony. I don't know what she said to him (I didn't even know she'd said anything) but I had a sense, not for the first time, of the potential we had together. It wouldn't be the last time either that I heard clients and participants comment that together we produced an energy that was healing in itself. One of them even referred to us as 'the Living Tao'. It all fed into the myth of who 'we' were becoming.

That wasn't the end of the healing for Dick. He also spent time with Trudy, our addictions expert, and benefited from her counsel. At the end of his three-week stay with us he had cut his drug dependency by more than 75% and was no longer convinced of CIA involvement in his life. He was so grateful for the help that Jane and I, in particular, had given him that he said he would send us a cheque every month for the rest of our lives. I am still awaiting the first.

Mucura is a plant of dreaming as well as protection; that is how it best communicates its wisdom. At our circle meetings I would discuss with the others on the Mucura diet the dreams and insights they had received. Dashiel said he had dreams where he was defended and wrapped in barbed wire, Paula that she had an armoury of guns that she could use against those who wished her harm. During the Ayahuasca ceremony I had received an image of the plant as a male spirit made of leaves (later this changed to a giant clothed in a tunic of leaves and carrying a club of stone). Dashiel saw the same as I had while

Paula (who is Irish) saw the spirit of Mucura as a leprechaun dressed in a suit of leaves. What was common in our descriptions was more pronounced than our differences.

I broke the diet in town with Jane. It was our first time out since being 'out' and it should have been a celebration, not only of closing the diet but of our freedom. It didn't go well though. She was angry at something Trudy had said to her and projected her anger towards me. 'Whatever you say to me I will hold you to' she said with venom in her voice, like a real 5'4" dictator. On another occasion I tried to bring up the perception that Matt, our Centre employee had of her since her affair with his brother, and to suggest that some healing might be needed between them. 'I couldn't' give a shit' she said. A lot of our time was spent in strained silence.

Anger can be a mask for fear and it seemed to me that now our relationship was known and 'real', Jungle Jane was making her return, bringing her familiar childhood terrors with her and an old pattern of putting barriers and distance between her and her feelings. Above all it was sad – two steps forward and one step back for the 'new Jane' and her attempts to become softer and more open. It felt as if the love or connection between us was diminished by the time we were ready to return to the Centre, and I had a sense of 'Uh oh, I've been here before. This is the Jane I heard about before I ever met her: the troubled one who brought trouble'. I wondered whether I should just bail: pull away from this relationship and take my power back before it went any further. Maybe I should apologise and tell her I'd made a mistake, then go travelling alone. I am sure that Mucura wants to protect me and is raising these questions as well so I can prepare for whatever I may need to do.

But 'a promise is a part of the soul' – that is what San Pedro had said – so I thought about it again and realised that, especially when I was younger, in my 20s and 30s, and life went on forever, a million choices still available, I had often quit relationships at the first sign of trouble, believing that they could never be saved or, since they were no longer 100% 'perfect' – whatever that really means – they were not worth the effort at all, even though they were still 99% amazing. Age has brought greater maturity in that respect and the understanding that nothing is perfect and nor does it need to be. This time I'm not going to quit. I want to change my patterns – which is, after all, the point of this work – and become more open and vulnerable too. So let's see how Jane's healing goes and whether she can shake off more of the Jungle before I make any hasty decisions...

On the way back from town the skies opened – a tropical rainforest deluge where the raindrops are larger than coins and slam into you sideways like a wall of water. In an open motocarro we were drenched to the skin and there was nowhere for us to hide. The car couldn't make it up the dirt track to our Centre, which was completely washed out and, after getting bogged down several times, careering dangerously on the mud towards ditches and rivers, and us pushing it more than riding it, we sent it back and walked the rest of the way calf-deep in sludge, falling into puddles with lightening crashing around us.

The anger of the skies somehow lifted the mood between us – maybe it gave vent to the tensions I had been carrying and washed away some of Jane's own anger – and we kissed, held hands and walked the rest of the way laughing at the absurdity of the Amazon: one moment 90% humidity, sun and heat, the next a damburst of rain.

Back at the Centre however something shifted again and we simply said goodnight, went to our respective rooms and didn't speak much to each other for most of the next week apart from nods and polite hellos.

Extract from my San Pedro journal during the Mucura diet

It was the last night of my Magical Earth group and almost everyone was at the final ceremony: all of the participants, along with Jane and the other volunteers, Trudy, Selva of course, and his fiancée, Nora. It should have been a party to reward our participants for all of the work they had done on themselves and it certainly started out that way.

I wasn't drinking that night. The Magical Earth is a 14-day programme with seven Ayahuasca ceremonies and during it we had dealt with the usual round of spirit possessions and exorcisms, balancing of energies, retrievals of power and soul, negotiations with spirits, and everything else that goes into an event like this. I was tired and I had also picked up a slight cold – amazingly, only slight – from being caught in that two-hour rain storm coming back from Iquitos on the night when I had broken my diet with Mucura. I was hoping for a quiet ceremony and it looked like I'd got it. Selva was in charge and everything was calm. It felt like a beautiful night, a really lovely way to finish the programme, so an hour or so into it I slipped away to walk back to my room and catch up on some sleep. With no-one around the jungle was peaceful, just the sound of the insects and my own breathing, and I drifted off quickly.

It didn't last.

Sometime later – 30 minutes? An hour? – I was woken by frantic knocking at my door and Nora's voice calling my name and babbling in panic and broken English. 'Roos' (hardly anyone in Peru can pronounce my name correctly) 'You must come quick. It is Selva. El Diablo! El Diablo!'

I have always been open to the idea of myself as strange – weird might be a better word and one which is certainly frequently used - because my responses are rarely those of other people. I imagine that a cold steel shudder of dread could fairly be expected to dance along the spine of another person hearing that their shaman has been possessed, and not just by some random entity but quite deliberately by the Devil himself – which is what Nora's babble had meant to communicate - and that now they are expected to do something about it. What I thought was 'Ah crap. I was having a lovely sleep'.

Still, I dressed quickly and pulled on my boots. On the walk back to the moloka I had another inappropriate thought: that our ceremonies were becoming a fucking cabaret. Which is not to say that we put on a performance. We didn't. Or that the healings we performed were staged. They weren't. They were quite genuine and people benefited from them. In these last several weeks we had seen people healed of M.E., phobias, chronic pain, ovarian problems, addictions and mental and emotional issues, and all of them leaving the Centre feeling more whole and powerful than when they arrived. But in my head I could also just imagine the voice of the m.c. at The Ayahuasca Comedy Club: 'Ladies and Gentlemen...... In the last few weeks we have given you a levitating woman possessed by a prehistoric dog, a giant tarantula, an ill wind that blew no good, a malevolent insect that tried to steal our shaman's voice – and many other curiosities and freaks of nature. And now, for our *grande finale* and the last night of our show, may we proudly present... the Devil himself!' I suppose it is good to keep a sense of humour about these things.

I hadn't drunk so the first thing I did on entering the moloka was take a swig of Ayahuasca, to 'get on the same page' as everyone else. Then I took in the scene. The participants were quiet, shell-shocked it seemed to me, and watching our shaman who was on his knees, groaning and sweating. He didn't look himself – but then I suppose you wouldn't if you were possessed by Satan. Humour again. I had to put a lid on that.

He was being ministered to by Sarah, the wife of his shamanic mentor don Luis and a curandera herself, who was singing her strange haunting icaros to him that always reduced me to an egoless mess as a result of their eerie and poignant beauty. She had arrived after I'd left, making the three-hour journey from her healing Centre to ours, she said, because she'd had a vision that something would happen that night and that Selva would need her help. Not long after her arrival Selva had been singing and then something happened: he froze, became rigid and his voice changed to a growl. Then he fell on the floor and his eyes began to glow red. 'These are all the signs of El Diablo' she said, 'and Selva is in his 33rd year, the time of trials for Jesus and all healers'.

If you are meditating and the Devil appears, make the Devil meditate too
Ejo Takata, Zen Master

Where do you start when you have to fight the Devil? I had no idea; it's not something I do every day. But I had to start somewhere so I began singing.

Plantas con Rah
Plantas con Rah
Mucura – shhhhhhaaaaa
Plantas con Rah
Ajo Sacha - shhhhhhaaaaa
Plantas con Rah
Chiric Sanango - shhhhhhaaaaa
Plantas con Rah
Guayusa - shhhhhhaaaaa
Plantas con RahTobacco - shhhhhhaaaaa
Plantas con Rah...

It was the icaro for Mucura that had planted its seeds in me some nights before during the healing for Dick, but now it had become something more: an enumeration of all of the plants I had ever dieted and whose powers I could draw from and direct. Every one of those *shhhhhhaaaaa* sounds was the direction of that plant's energy into Selva's body to strengthen him and weaken whatever was inside him. And all the time San Pedro's voice was there too, telling me not to believe, not to give power to the Devil.

Selva writhed, spat and growled back at me as I hit him with the chacapa, blew smoke into him and kept up the song for 30 minutes, throwing every plant at him that I had worked with and knew. As Dashiel, one of our participants, put it later: 'You sang the shit out of it'. I guess I must have because at some point anyway Selva became Selva again. He collapsed on the floor and began to shiver as his wife-to-be gathered him up and held him. Sarah and I looked at each other over the body and nodded – 'It is done' - then I began to walk the room and calm things down with gentler and quieter songs. Half an hour after that Selva had regained enough strength to bring the ceremony to a close, as the shaman in charge should do, and our participants went back to their rooms.

I spent a little time with Selva in the quiet of the moloka to make sure he was OK but it was clear that he was being well looked after by Sarah and Nora so after a while I walked back to the casa grande to get my head together. It was dark when I reached it, illuminated by just an oil lamp or two, and Jane and Dashiel were the only people there. I made a drink and sat down on the sofa, the opposite end to Jane, leaving some space between us. I wasn't quite sure where we were following our time in Iquitos as we had hardly spoken to each other since then and now wasn't the time to get into that.

We chatted for a while, dissecting the evening and making light of it, and then Dashiel left for bed. Jane moved closer to me then and lay with her head in my lap, looking up at me. 'I love you' she said.

It felt as if I had exorcised two demons that night: whatever was in Selva and the more virulent spirit of Jungle Jane. The latter would not return, except in flashes, for months. As for Selva's Devil, I don't know.

Jane and I wanted to sleep together. We would be moving on in the morning, to Cusco for my Cactus of Vision group, to San

Pedro and to greater adventures so it was our last night in the camp and despite my own rules we decided to walk down to the moloka and find a space there. Only Selva and Nora remained when we arrived, having decided to sleep there too. We didn't speak, just acknowledged each other and then Jane and I found our own part of the room. It felt good, the Centre's two healers and the women they loved sharing a space together on this, our final night, like a silent goodbye and a nod to all we'd been through together. I never saw Selva again and I never returned to the Centre.

MOUNTAIN SPIRITS
(THESIS)[30]

Satori may be defined as intuitive insight into the nature of things, as opposed to logical or analytical understanding. In practice, it signifies the discovery of a new world... When we experience satori, everything around us is seen with a kind of perception that has never before been known...
DT Suzuki, *Essays on Zen*

2010. September/October

Cusco is a beautiful little town, highly influenced by the colonial Spanish style but retaining its earthy and Earth-honouring roots; the ones the Catholic conquerors tried to eradicate but never really could. I'd visited it many times but Jane had never seen it. I loved it and I knew she'd love it too. And of course she did because she was, in a sense, me - or rather, we were each other.

By now we had recognised a unique and magical bond between us, something that neither of us had expected or experienced before. We knew each other's thoughts and feelings; we almost didn't need to speak because we knew what we each had to say. The rest – laughing at the same jokes, liking the same music, food, books and films and having the same approach to life and adventure – the little things that 'ordinary' couples look for to prove their togetherness – seemed mundane in comparison to what we had, although we shared those too. It had come together for us in days. No more fear, no more resistance to love. We didn't question it: we were soulmates, the loves of each other's lives, thinking ourselves blessed that we had found each other again in this lifetime after surely spending so many others together. I loved – love - Cusco and she loved it too. Of course.

The next time we drank San Pedro was at the Temple of the Moon, an ancient ritual site next to the walled garden where La

Bruja holds her ceremonies. There were around 20 participants in my group and La Bruja, who I trust completely, assured me that they were in safe hands with her and her assistants, so Jane and I slipped away to walk in the hills. I visited the garden a few times that day to check on people and hear their stories or add healing where I could but mostly I spent time with Jane, so entwined with her that there was no separation between us.

Just as we had in the moloka when we first drank San Pedro together, we gazed at each other for hours and felt the flow of love between us, and every time it got too intense and we had to look away, we had the most amazing view of mountains and valleys and clouds which overwhelmed us almost as much. We were locked in beauty – the beauty of each other, of our surroundings, and of the soul in flow – bathed in the unrelenting ecstasy of San Pedro. We breathed into each other, exchanging and mingling our life forces, becoming one with each other and with the clouds and the air around us. Love became formless and was everywhere, like a force of nature, as if bliss was carried by the warm mountain breeze that blew through us.

One of the mysteries of San Pedro is its use in sexual magic at Chavin de Huantar and other sacred sites. Almost nothing is written about this and almost no-one knows the true practice or why these ceremonies were performed. There is no denying the sexual power of San Pedro though, or the energy it stirs within you which is so strong that, properly directed, it could, I imagine, be used to achieve almost anything.

Ancient alchemical practices weren't uppermost in our minds that day but we were so close to each other and surrounded by so many miracles, both in the world around us and in the deepest truths of ourselves, that eventually this 'orgasm of the soul' had to find its physical expression and so, on our wild and amazing mountain, we made love.

Jane climbed on top of me and her long hair fell around me like a curtain. Every time it opened I saw a new her. One moment

I was with an 80-year-old wise and happy woman who was content to be at the end of her life; a possible life that we might spend together and which held promises of total fulfillment. Her hair was grey, her cheeks soft and leathery but her eyes were shining with love. The next I was with a child – wide-eyed and innocent, before all those family dramas she had told me about. When I looked again she was a wild woman, the next a gentle lover. The visions were so real that I kept shaking my head to get a sense of which Jane was real. I suppose they all were. At some point I just closed my eyes and went with sensation.

Mouth wide open like a baby, I allowed her to feed me without limit, like the Earth become woman, all women, all things, while I contentedly devoured the universe
Alejandro Jodorowsky

When I opened my eyes again the Jane I knew – or thought I knew (how can anyone tell when there are so many faces to the person you love?) – had her head thrown back, her hair cascading around her and she was deep in orgasm. My own soon followed, ripping me into splinters of light; a creative impulse exploding into the universe. It was one of the most powerful times of our lives and I know that if that energy were harnessed all sorts of miracles would not only be possible but inevitable, even required of us by God. Perhaps that was the secret of Chavin.

We gathered ourselves and lit a Mapacho. I made her a promise that day that I would always be there to feed her smoke and water, two of the three essentials of life as I saw them, the third being love. And I promised her that too. *Fumar, agua y amor.*

When we returned to our lodgings that evening I told her that I loved her 'from the inside out', that I was first in love with her soul. She said that she wanted to spend the rest of her life with me. Then I put a question to her: 'Have you any idea what I'm thinking?' She did of course but pretended not to. 'No, tell me' she said and I told her that Andean shamans make beautiful weddings.

She told me to ask her again in the morning when I was no longer under the influence of San Pedro. I did and she said yes. Of course. We had been together for just a few months but to both of us getting married was the most obvious and natural thing in the world.

And so the first time we drank San Pedro together – La Bruja's 'medicine of love' - our own love story began, the second time we got engaged and the third significant time we drank – about a week later – was at our wedding.

Our shaman, the priest for our union, was Jaguar. He is also a diviner who uses coca leaves to make his predictions about possible futures. Most of my Cactus of Vision group consulted him and he gave meaningful answers about their lives and the paths of the soul they should follow. I suggested to my wife-to-be however that during her consultation she didn't ask questions about our future together since a marriage is what you make of it and readings like this, while helpful, can sometimes become a sort of *fait accompli* to the mind if we allow it. I think it is better to give our lovers the space to change and grow and to support them in that while recognising that in all relationships there will be ups and downs but with love everything is possible. Even 'flaws' or 'failings' are opportunities for healing and growth and for lovers to support each other.

The Western mind tends to be more fatalistic about divination than the Andean. While we regard it as a certainty that the events foreseen *will* and *must* happen as we have been shown them, Peruvians treat the information given as a chance to embrace some outcomes or avoid others now that they have the data they need. As one of my teachers once put it: 'Destiny is the inter-section of fate and intention'. In other words: anything is possible since fate is a wind that blows from all directions but what we choose to hold on to as that wind passes is what we make of ourselves, the destiny we create from all of the possibilities offered to us.

Jane, my stubborn, beautiful bride-to-be was not going to be persuaded by that however and among other questions, she asked Jaguar what our marriage would be like. He cast the leaves and laughed at what he saw. 'It begins in love and it ends in love' he said, and before another question could be asked which might create destiny from fate, he added 'And that's all you need to know'.

And it was. We were blessed and wrapped in love. Nothing could ever go wrong.

The day of our wedding was glorious. Jaguar took us to the Temple of the Condor Heart, a mountain shrine close to the Temple of the Moon. It is so called because the natural rock formation looks like a condor, a bird which in Peru represents spiritual union. Near its Centre is a hollow space with one solitary rock in the shape of a heart. An altar fashioned from a slab of stone is at the other end of the formation. Jaguar made us a throne of it and invited us to sit there.

He had told La Bruja some days before to bring San Pedro for us because we would have to drink five glasses each during the ceremony. La Bruja had been horrified. Her San Pedro is strong and she replied that five glasses would probably kill us. We knew the dangers too and were apprehensive but we trusted Jaguar and were committed to drinking it if that was what it took for us to be married. I would rather have died than not marry her.

In fact Jaguar has a sense of humour and we drank only two glasses during the ceremony. We poured and served them to each other, offering them with promises and words of love. She said that she'd be my wife forever. I said she always had been and that this ceremony was just an expression of that. *Something* had drawn us together across space and time. That much was clear.

A promise is a part of the soul...
A vow is a sacred contract and we must live it or lose a part of
ourselves

We gave each other rings, which we had previously blessed in San Pedro. They arrived fortuitously (are there ever really any accidents?) as a friend of La Bruja is a jewellery artist and had sent samples to her a few days before. They were silver and inscribed in Sanskrit with the words "A thousand blessings". There just happened to be two with the same message in our perfect sizes.

As we gave the rings to each other Jaguar spoke: 'You are not coming together for the first time here today' he said, 'because you have always been together. You came from one place to this Earth – Heaven – so you have always known each other. You have merely found each other again. You belong to each other. You always have and always will.

'In Quechua we have a single word for two different activities. That word means to dance and to fight – because every fight is also an opportunity to dance! It means to support each other. In every marriage there will be disagreements but don't set limits; remember that you love each other - that's why you are here! So dance!

'A fight is a limitation. Moving through it is to dance, to see the flow and movement of life and to be graceful with it so that you grow together. Remember the journey you are on and give each other every opportunity to dance.'

We kissed then, both tasting and smelling of San Pedro and a warm mountain day. Then we and our wedding party – a ramshackle gathering of Q'ero friends, shamans and brothers, and guests from among our participants who had stayed on as witnesses – walked back to La Bruja's garden for the reception.

Jane looked beautiful that day. We had found her the perfect wedding dress in one of Cusco's tucked-away shops: brown and green, rags and lace, a silky peasant dress. She is only a size eight and 5'4" tall and there are not many Peruvian women who match that description – in height yes, but not in shape - so there was no reason for that dress to have even been in that shop or for us to have found it. But there are no accidents. She wore hand-made boots of brown and rust, and ribbons in her hair. A perfect gypsy bride.

We were blessed with the reception too. Our impromptu chef, who just happened to be assisting our ceremonies that year, had previously worked at La Rosa Nautica, one of the best restaurants in Lima – and one I'd never been allowed into because it has a dress code and whenever I have visited it I have just emerged from a jungle so never looked the part. Instead when I've dined there I have been invited to do so at a table outside – which is actually no hardship since La Rosa Nautica is on a pier and it is wonderful to have the ocean beneath you as you eat. This time however, one of its chefs had come to us! We were served with 20 courses, accompanied by strawberry daiquiris and passionfruit cocktails.

We had been given a dispensation by Jaguar to eat at our reception since normally when San Pedro is drunk no food can be consumed. Jane, who loves food, was mortified at the idea of not eating and delighted at the permission to do so. Not knowing how many courses would be presented she fell upon the first (popcorn chicken with sweet chilli and honey sauce – 'so tasty!') but could barely manage the last (chocolate-dipped strawberries) and I had to feed one to her against her not-so-convincing protestations so she could say she'd tried everything.

La Bruja gave us a wedding present of a night's stay at Andean Wings, the boutique hotel she owns in Cusco, where rooms cost anything up to $500 a night, and which is frequented by rock stars like Bono and actresses including Lucy Liu. After a day of excitement, San Pedro and cocktails we were both a little dizzy when we got there and we really didn't need a trip to the bar. But we visited it anyway to drink a toast to each other and our great good fortune at finding one another again and now belonging to each other through marriage. When we got back to our room the hotel had provided us with roses and champagne. Then my wife fell asleep on the bed, drunk and no doubt as amazed as I was at what had just happened between us. It was as if our souls had recognised something in each other that we had been driven to act on but our minds hadn't quite caught up yet.

She awoke in the morning surrounded by roses, each of which I had stripped the thorns from.

LUNA DE MIEL

Who knows how it could be tomorrow?
I've been waiting for you and you've been coming for me for such
a long time now
Pixies, *I've Been Waiting for You*

2010. October – late December

Our honeymoon was a semi-planned tour of Peru. I'd been
taking groups there for years to drink Ayahuasca and San Pedro
so I knew the jungles and mountains but had never done the
tourist route. Jane had never visited the country at all so it
sounded a great idea to us both. It began in Lima where,
remarkably this time, we did get a table at La Rosa Nautica
(although we didn't take it, preferring the balcony) and from
there we flew to Arequipa to visit Colca Canyon (deeper than the
Grand and more beautiful), then to Nazca to fly over the famous
lines and try to decode their meanings; Titicaca and the floating
islands, each handcrafted from reeds, where individual families
now lived, and the nearby town of Puno, a place dismissed as
uninteresting by some travellers but in its own way pretty. Pisaq
and the Sacred Valley too, to drink San Pedro in ceremonies with
two new shamans: Javier Rodriguez and Michael Simon. We
were so high during the first ceremony – on ourselves as much
as San Pedro - that we laughed non-stop for three hours, until we
were literally blue in the face. At some point in the day though
our laughter stopped and, looking up at the ruins of Pisaq and
the Temple of the Sun on the 'grandfather mountain' above us,
we felt our ancestors gather around us. 'It is your time now' they
said. 'Your chance to find love for yourselves and for all of us; to
allow love to heal the wounds we left behind. We couldn't make
it, but perhaps you...?' I had the sense from San Pedro that we
are here not only to deal with our own concerns, as painful as

they sometimes are, but have a role to play in history and evolution and that this is our true purpose: to *try* at least to right the wrongs of the past through a commitment to love now and through this to create future generations of love, like a wave that ripples through time. On our second ceremony we found new friends in the huachumero Michael and his partner Maggie, who are doing just that.

Most of our travels were by bus, sometimes overnight, where we got to flop sleepily on each other or write love notes to one another in the frosting on the windows that our breaths made. At other times I read to her – *Sarah's Key*, a book about personal discovery and family secrets. We were ecstatic. It was amazing. We had found our soulmates.

We found something else out too. Part way though our honeymoon we discovered that we were pregnant.

Perhaps we should have been delighted to be blessed with a child so quickly but Jane was terrified. She had never wanted children, for reasons she never explained and didn't have to, although I found her attitude towards children surprising – not because anyone *has* to have a child or because they are 'required' in a marriage but because most people are open to the possibility or at least not terrified that it might happen. Her fear seemed to stem from the idea that a baby would limit her freedom but in practical terms that didn't make sense since a child will adapt to any lifestyle you provide for it. In the Andes women (and men) simply put their child in a papoose – a shawl tied around their shoulders – and go about their day. We had even had babies and toddlers at the San Pedro ceremonies we attended, brought by Q'ero families who had come along to assist, and they just played quietly or slept, content and well-adapted to the way of life their parents gave them.

I guessed that her fear might be more deep-seated. At our healing Centre in Iquitos I had met a woman who had never wanted children because her own childhood had been difficult, especially with her father who had caused her so much pain and distress that she had become addicted – in her case to drugs and alcohol - as a way of escaping from him and from life. Her decision not to have children was at least partly motivated by her desire to punish her father for what he had done to her – 'I didn't want to make him a grandfather so he could damage somebody else's life' – but by doing so she also hurt herself. Her father died when she was 50 and by then it was too late for her to conceive. It was then that she realised she would have loved a child of her own and, through her son or daughter, might also have healed the wounds of her past. While I was ambivalent about having another child myself since I am already the father of three, I didn't want Jane to make the same mistake as that woman from Iquitos.

In the end we decided to keep our child, not because Jane's fears subsided (I would wake up in our hotel room sometimes and find her crying at the thought of a baby) but because it was *our* child, a special San Pedro baby conceived in love by two people who were absolutely meant to be together.

We called it Prawn, having discovered on a website that a foetus of that age looked sort of like one, and found ourselves a fridge magnet in that shape from a local market. From then on, wherever we visited we took a photograph of our prawn in that location so that our child would have a record of all the places it had visited *in utero*. We called our photo-file *Prawn in Peru* and put it up on Facebook without telling anyone else what it meant, a secret code and a silly joke between the love-struck teenagers we had somehow turned into.

One place that Prawn (and we) definitely had to visit was Chavin de Huantar, the birthplace of San Pedro. Like Machu Picchu or the Nazca lines, Peru's other great conundrums, Chavin is a mystery. This large ceremonial site was a gathering place for people to worship, take part in rituals and consult oracles, with occupation there carbon-dated to at least 3000 BC.

The initiations of San Pedro shamans also took place there, according to anthropologists. These rituals were conducted in underground chambers with only rudimentary light entering through small "windows" (actually thin channels dug out of the rock) and mirrors placed strategically to direct this light and create a disorientating otherworldly feel. Other channels were made for running water, its sound creating an odd, echoing eeriness. The initiate, led into this chamber of darkness, would not expect any of this, and having drunk San Pedro would be totally unprepared and unable to comprehend this other world he had been brought to. In this way the familiar landscape of reality would vanish and he would be face-to-face with the spirits, emerging reborn as a healer from the womb of the earth.

The temple at Chavin is a large flat-topped pyramid surrounded by lower platforms. Its inside walls are decorated with sculptures and carvings and outside it is adorned with stone heads depicting men under the influence of San Pedro and narcotic snuffs, shapeshifting from human to animal form, often feline in nature. I became wolf-like when I conducted healings on San Pedro; they became pumas and jaguars. Obelisks stand at various places in the grounds, some carved with alien heads radiating lines of energy to suggest the consciousness-changing power of San Pedro. In the very centre of the temple is another obelisk, a sculpture of the Lanzon, the supreme deity of Chavin. The figure is anthropomorphic, with the head of a jaguar (one of the guardian spirits of San Pedro) and a human body.

The architecture of Chavin changed over time and a new temple was built between 500 and 200 BC. The Lanzon is again present, holding a strombus shell in his right hand while the left holds a spondylus. The spirals these shells represent suggest the San Pedro experience – the 'dizziness' that the cactus provokes - and are also depicted in textile art from this and other regions.

Two rivers converge there, a phenomenon known as *tinkuy*: the harmonious meeting of forces, making the temple a cosmic centre of considerable power.

But then something happened. Some sort of social upheaval took place between 500 and 300 BC and Chavin started to decline. Ceremonial sites were abandoned, some unfinished, and local people pillaged their stones and carvings to use as building materials while the land was put to agricultural use. No priests were left to defy them.

What happened? No-one knows; that is one of the mysteries of Chavin. But tuning into the site Jane and I both felt a sense of gloom and darkness. Trying to find an explanation for our feelings it seemed to us that the old shamanic ways had become too institutionalised and filled with rules and dogma by priests who then proceeded to abuse their power, a process that has been repeated many times over in most religions of the world. If sexual magic was practiced there it felt more like a violation than an act of love and wilful creation. Eventually the people left, abandoning the priests to their excesses. With that the Chavin culture died but the 'cult' of San Pedro was born as the initiates and the faithful spread throughout Peru taking their knowledge with them.

It was a depressing day, overcast and drizzling with rain, even without the sadness and disappointment of Chavin. What had begun as a sort of pilgrimage to the birthplace of San Pedro and was meant to be a highlight of our tour had become a wash-out, revealing not beauty and light as the origins of my ally, but abuse and corruption. San Pedro had told me at the start of my diet that it would be revealing its warrior face – a harder, more destructive side which was quite capable of delivering 'tough love' - and this was part of it. My challenge was to find beauty, soul and compassion even when it seemed lacking in all that I saw around me.

The challenges continued when, having climbed back onboard our bus and made the three hour journey to Huaraz, the town in which we were staying, we found a full-blown riot in progress. A foreign mining company had bought rights to one of the sacred lakes in the area so they could drain it and search for gold – outsiders with no conception of what was holy still searching for El Dorado even after all these years. Because of the processes involved, even if the company restored the lake to its original condition after their work was done (which they had no plans for) the water would remain polluted.

Not surprisingly the townspeople were up in arms. Literally. There were daily protests, most of them violent, and windows were smashed all over town while rubbish piled up in the streets. Protestors as well as police were killed and from day two all roads into and out of Huaraz were blocked, which also meant that supplies couldn't get in and local people were suffering. Just as importantly for us, it meant that we couldn't get out.

With our honeymoon in ruins and blood on the streets we were more or less confined to our room for a week with nothing to do except watch pirate movies, drink warm beer and go slowly but surely insane.

It had to happen – and after five days of this it did. It was probably an accumulation of things: the tensions of those last few weeks in the jungle, the whirlwind of our marriage, discovering that we were pregnant, then the disappointment of Chavin and now the depression and anger of Huaraz; on top of which, we had been in each other's company 24/7 for weeks. Whatever the final straw was it resulted in our first ever argument, a shabby little affair which was nothing to be proud of. It didn't even have the balls to call itself a row. Instead it was whiny and sneering.

At some point, probably wisely, Jane left the room while I continued to mope. She returned some hours later to say that she'd found a way out of town with a couple of American tourists who had hired a taxi at a hugely inflated price to run the blockades and drive them over the mountains.

'Good', I said, 'go'. I was still angry and had no intention of going with her and I advised her not to go either – people were getting killed out there – but I may as well have been talking to a wall. Jungle Jane packed up and left.

I woke up in the morning miserable from our argument and worried for my wife. I checked with the hotel and was relieved to find that her taxi had made it to the coast. There had been problems – rocks had been thrown at the car and at one point it looked as if they would have to turn back – but the driver, a friend of the hotel owner, had carried on and reported that all were OK. As far as it went that was good news but I still had no idea where Jane was now. I spent the next two days trying to reach her and finally got a response: she was in Lima and safe.

The roadblocks were lifted two days later and I caught the first bus out of town to be with her. We met at a café. I was hoping for a loving reunion and was ready to own my part in our argument; I just wanted it behind us and our familiar passion and loving intensity back. But instead of my wife Jungle Jane showed up. 'I was thinking about us all the way back to Lima' she said. 'And by the time I arrived here I was sure of two things: that I love you and I want to be with you - and that I don't want this baby. I don't know if that's a deal-breaker for you?'

A 'deal-breaker'? Wow. Was that really how she saw our marriage and the life of our child? If I said I wanted to keep it was she going to pack up and run, 'deal' off? My choice, such as it was, was to lose our baby or lose them both.

We spent the next few days in Lima, me in a sombre mood, trying to come to terms with things – grieving for the loss of our child, our 'special San Pedro baby', and for something that had died in our relationship too – and she happier than I'd seen her in weeks. Relieved. On the night before she left she fell asleep on our bed and I lay with my head on her stomach, saying goodbye to the son or daughter she had carried so briefly for us. In some shamanic traditions a child cannot even be conceived unless a shaman journeys first to the Tree of Life where the unborn grow like fruit, and makes prayers for one of those souls to incarnate.

Maybe I hadn't prayed hard enough or Jane's prayers had countered mine.

The next day she boarded a plane for England to arrange what she called her 'procedure' and I booked a flight to Spain where I would spend Christmas alone.

ANOTHER MOUNTAIN

*Those who travel to mountain-tops are half in love with themselves
and half in love with oblivion*
Robert Macfarlane, *Mountains Of The Mind: A History Of A
Fascination*

2011. January - July

My house in Andalucia is really two houses: the casa grande, the
big house, which has six large bedrooms that will easily sleep 15.
It is where participants stay when they join me for courses. And
the cottage, which has three bedrooms, a lounge, bathroom and
a separate kitchen. It is where I live. There are a range of
outbuildings in the grounds – the workroom where courses and
ceremonies are held, a massage and therapy room and a
bedroom for workshop leaders or the housekeeper and cook I
employ during courses. There is a shower room too, a relaxation
room that we call The Hermitage and, of course, the obligatory
pool because summers in Spain are *hot* and can last from April (a
beautiful time of year when wild flowers cover the fields in
colour) right through to October.

The gardens are an acre or two. I did a lot of work on them
during my first year here, creating winding paths, a spiral
garden to grow vegetables, an outside teaching area in the form
of a pagoda we called The Temple, a poolside bar, and I planted
a number of trees – plum, apple, lemon, orange, fig, quince,
almond, magnolia and cherry. In season you can start at one end
of the garden and pick fresh fruit from every tree, eating your
way back to the casa grande. And of course, this being Spain,
there are olives and grapes. Tohay grows here too, as does the
San Pedro I planted.

I called the house The Hummingbird, in honour of San Pedro,

and it does have that energy to it. Probably two or three hundred years old, it is in the mountains and standing in the garden the hills surround you, holding you in their arms as you gaze out over uninterrupted views for perhaps a hundred miles on a clear day, to the Sierra Nevadas which even during the Spanish summer are covered in snow, merging with the clouds as if separate from the earth. We used to call them The Floating Islands. At night, with no light pollution and miles from anywhere, the skies are so big that they arc around you and are filled with stars, like diamonds laid out on velvet.

The house is haunted of course, but by happy ghosts. The whole area where we live was once a revolutionary stronghold, a mountain retreat against Franco's forces during the Civil War, and there are gravesites dotted around the hills of those who fought and fell for freedom. We would lie awake at night sometimes and listen to our ghosts. It always sounded like a joyful reunion – conversation and laughter – and I imagined one of those revolutionary heroes returning from battle to be with the woman he loved.

Our nearest towns are Montefrio ('cold mountain') and Algarinejo, in opposite directions, both about 10 kilometres away. The former has two churches, one of them round: one of Spain's few remaining mosques, a remnant from when the Moors held power in this area, and a more traditional Christian church, built high on a rock overlooking the town, a symbol of victory from when the earlier revolutionaries of Montefrio purged the Moors and took back their Catholic culture.

Algarinejo, meanwhile, is nestled in a valley between mountains. You approach it via the high road (a *real* high road, unlike the one which supposedly enters Iquitos) and looking down on it, especially at night when it is lit by hearth fires and the lights of cottages and cortijos, it always reminds me for some reason of the 'little town of Bethlehem': *How still we see thee lie.* It is a tiny town but it has one of the finest restaurants in Spain and gourmets from all over the country visit Algarinejo to dine there.

My mountain is a beautiful place and I love it. I really wanted Jane to love it too as it would be our first home together – and I knew that she would because we had always been so similar, so *simpatico*, that if I loved something it was inevitable that she would too. Of course.

She arrived in Spain on January 10. We had last seen each other on December 22 and those three weeks apart had felt like a lifetime. I collected her from the airport. She was drunk from the plane and excited to start her new life, and once again we were so deeply in love that it was sometimes difficult to separate one of us from the other, as if we had one heart and soul that we shared. We never once mentioned our child.

It seemed to me that she was really making an effort to blend in, to become part of the laid back Spanish lifestyle and to go deeper into her mission to become more open and vulnerable. That was the side of her I loved best.

When she had met up with them in England her friends were amazed that she was married – the 'wild child', the 'littlest hobo' who escaped her home at every opportunity, married and settling down? Unthinkable. They would have been even more amazed to see her now as she happily took on the role of *alma del casa*[31] and began to put her mark on our home.

It would have been unreasonable of me to expect that Jungle Jane wouldn't come with her at all of course, and she did show up on occasions. Like the time when we took some visitors to our local bar and she got angry with me for something I'd said. She stormed out and walked the four or five kilometres home instead of getting in the car to ride back with me and once there, after a lot of door-slamming and shouting, she started packing to leave. Or the time when she got angry again during a workshop I was running and I suggested that she take time out to stay in town for a few days. I returned from ceremony that night to find that she'd packed everything except a few poignant reminders of her, such as her wedding dress and a love note I'd written her, neatly laid out on our bed, then vanished without saying where she'd gone. She returned a week later.

She knew she had a 'storming out' problem. It was one of the things she wanted to work on and she was always personally disappointed when it happened again because she hoped she'd outgrown it years ago. But, quick to recognise 'anger issues' in others and to diagnose an appropriate treatment for clients and participants, when she was possessed by Jungle Jane she just didn't seem able to join the dots and recognise that her door-slamming and hasty packing also had its origin somewhere. Shamans: the wounded healers – and wives: a pain in the arse sometimes.

But we always forgave each other. In fact, I didn't even see her behaviour as anything *to* forgive; I simply accepted it as part of the woman I loved. Our morning mantra became:

'I love you.'
'I love you.'
'What shall we do today?'
'Anything we want…'

And it really was like that: effortless and flowing. In the last few years I had felt myself moving increasingly into a state of flow – that way of being where things simply work without effort – and with Jane here now it was perfect. Whatever we imagined or wished for came true and the world left us alone.

Sometimes we would get up and paint our visions or the plants we were dieting, sitting in the garden under the blue skies and Spanish sun. Or we might drink San Pedro and lie by the pool, building mountains of fruit and bread and lakes of amaretto and olive oil to charm the ants she'd taken a shine to. Or drive into town for coffee and *tostadas* (toasted bread and tomatoes with garlic oil), or visit the coast for sea trips and tapas or Granada for Moroccan food and Turkish baths. On other days I drove her to our local waterfall where we coated ourselves in mud and lay in the cool waters, or to the megalithic site not far from us where we wandered through ancient stones, explored caves and learned more about healing plants.

With fresh mountain air, sunshine, freedom and healthy food we were fitter and happier than we'd ever been and we loved our life. Jane even began teaching a little, running journeys on my Shamanic Practitioner course, and one night took over as 'lead shaman' in an Ayahuasca ceremony for 12 participants, singing icaros she had learned from the plants. She began research for a book she would like to write too, on Salvia, one of the plants we had explored together in Peru. Life was changing for her, opening up in line with her intention, and Jungle Jane became less of a driving force as Spain worked its magic on her.

Our work with the plants continued too; in particular with Salvia. I had dieted it in Peru, although I didn't feel that I'd made a firm connection to its spirit, and Jane and I had smoked several pipes of the 20X concentrate together. That had produced profound psychedelic effects but we felt now that experimentation with different strengths would be beneficial.

Most of the literature we had read on the contemporary exploration of Salvia (such as J D Arthur's book, *Salvia Divinorum*) used lighter concentrates of 5X strength although some reports on the web used 10X or higher. We decided on a range – from 5X to 100X, the strongest then available – in order to test the outcomes of each. Our idea was to start with the extremes, first 100X then 5X, then explore the grades in between until we arrived at the best for us. While we waited for the new extracts to arrive we continued with 20X concentrate.

In Peru our experiments had been informal but at our home in Spain we decided to introduce ritual procedures which are more common when working with teacher plants. In particular we thought it important to work with the mesa.

The mesa (the word literally means 'table') is the most important part of South American shamanism. It is an altar comprised of a single piece of cloth woven with symbols and patterns which is charged with spiritual power and becomes a gateway to the soul of the universe. The Peruvian curandero Eduardo Calderon described it as 'the important part of a curing session for the simple reason that it is the panel where all the elemental forces are computed.'[32] On it are placed ritual objects which are rich with healing intent. These *artes* (or 'arts') hold spiritual energy in the form of artefacts from archaeological or ritual sites to represent the power of the ancestors, herbs and perfumes in ornate or antique bottles to bring good luck and healing, swords and statues or stones from cemeteries and sacred sites which stand as emblems for the powers conferred on the shaman by his guides and allies in the Land of the Dead. Other objects might include hardwood staffs, bones, quartz crystals, knives, deer antlers and boar tusks (for strength in the face of challenges), shells and lithographs or paintings of the saints[33].

Jane had begun to create her mesa while we travelled Peru on our honeymoon. I had got her an antique cloth from Cusco, hand-woven by one of my brothers in the Q'ero community. The Q'ero are the first people of Peru who live at high altitudes and in such rugged conditions that they were never conquered by the Spanish who never even knew of their existence. Indeed, most people in Peru were unaware of them until a few decades ago when these wisdom-keepers arrived in Cusco from the mountains to deliver prophecies for mankind which they had safeguarded for thousands of years. In 2008 I had become friends with Juan, a member of this community, and became a godfather to his daughter. It was a mesa cloth he had made which I had given to Jane.

On our travels around Peru she had collected various artes for it such as stones from Machu Picchu, the 'crystal city' of the Incas, and gifts I had given her including an antique key (the emblem of San Pedro), a seguro (a talisman in the form of a bottle containing magical plants for luck and protection), crystals and other items.

Our first Salvia ceremony in Spain had four participants: our friends Jorge and Gail who were staying with us for a few weeks, and Jane and I. Jane began them in darkness as is traditional when working with Salvia by laying out her mesa and offering a prayer to God, the saints, the elements and artes on her altar and to the spirit of ska Maria. She then loaded our pipe with Salvia leaves and a pinch of the 20X concentrate.

A pinch is literally all you need. Many people, especially if they have experience with other psychedelics, are surprised at how little is required to create an effect. As the writer Diaz remarks: 'Because the dose is so small and insignificant looking, there is a tendency for people to think they need more... I have seen more than one intelligent, careful and experienced person accidentally do too large a dose because of this. Fortunately they had sitters and managed to get through the experience safely.'

Because of our research in Peru however, Jane had become practiced at measuring by eye. She smoked first while I watched over her journey. I took the pipe from her after she had taken a few draws on it and she lay down quietly on her back with her eyes closed. She was 'away' for about five minutes and when she returned, still somewhat under the influence of Salvia, she spoke of her experience.

I had noticed that Salvia seemed to be taking me on a progressive journey through its world, familiarising me with the territory, a sort of initiation where my experiences got deeper but always included a linking theme of some kind. The theme for me, so far as I was aware of it then, was related to issues from childhood which were affecting my relationships now – 'patterns that I didn't like'.

Something similar was happening for Jane. In a previous

journey she had found herself in a landscape – a country field – that seemed to be moving. Being present in the landscape itself she hadn't noticed the movement at first but became aware of it when she saw that the scene had an end to it; that as she looked forwards the field disappeared and was replaced by blackness. As she explored this she realised that she was on a conveyor belt on which this landscape rested like a product on a factory line that would eventually roll off the end. It was as if reality folded as it reached the end of the line and that stage of the process concluded.

From a wider perspective – standing back from the scene – she was able to see that there were actually several conveyor lines, one on top of the other, which each contained a different slice of reality, on this world or another, each stacked horizontally and each being propelled forward from existence to annihilation. Her 'blue God' turned a handle in order to move these layers on. This 'reality- machine' itself was mechanically very simple: the handle connected to cogs which caught on zippers beneath each layer of reality and pulled it towards its end. Jane was not frightened by this imagery of annihilation and endings – the 'Jungle' in her would never allow her to be scared or, at least, to admit to it – but she was puzzled by it and reflective. She had no idea what it meant.

Our other Salvia extracts arrived in February and we decided to begin with 100X strength, the idea being to then work with 5X and from these extremes to find our preferred level.

I had read very few accounts from people who had smoked 100X concentrate but those I did were not reassuring. In general the headlines were along the lines of 'Nightmare', 'Madness' or 'To Hell and - I think - back'.

The two of us alone now, Jane was again the officiating 'shaman' and smoked first while I sat for her. From the outside it looked a very different journey to those I had seen her take before. She sank backwards and lay down on her back (normal for her) but was then immediately on her knees, staring into the darkness of the room and evidently in conversation with someone in front of her who I couldn't see. She put her arms out before her, beseechingly, and asked 'Really? What do you mean? How does it work then?' There was a pause as she waited for answers. I sensed that she was asking questions about her reality-ending 'Armageddon machine' or the nature of reality itself from the spirits of SalviaWorld or perhaps her blue God. She seemed to understand the answers given. Then she went into a child pose with her head on the floor, then turned and fell against the wall, clawing at it as if she wanted to merge with it or break through it and escape any connection with childhood. It was the most agitated I'd seen her on any journey. Finally she lay down on her back with her eyes closed and was 'away' for what seemed like a further five minutes.

We recorded this session and played it back almost hoping and believing that we may have captured the voices of the spirits she was talking to - Salvia is so strong that this might even be possible – but there was nothing like that on the tape. Jane could not remember anything of the journey either and had no recollection of talking to anyone or, disappointingly, the answers given.

I smoked next and, as I felt the onset of the journey, I stumbled to the door. I didn't get very far though before I was on my knees on the flagstones outside. That is not entirely accurate however as from my perspective I was not 'on' anything; I *was* the flagstones just as I *was* a bedspread or a wheel in Peru. I sank into them and my body was comprised of them. The residual part of me that could still remember 'me' was amazed once again at how easy it is to forget SalviaWorld – its potency and how real it is compared to the world we think we know. Jane followed me out and I looked up at her and said 'I remember this, I've been here before'. Exactly what I remembered I can't say; maybe a feeling or the sense that nothing is real, or rather that

SalviaWorld is as real – or more real – than the one I am used to.

There are gaps in my memory then but when I came back to a sense of myself I had moved again and was lying next to our pool. I also remember standing and looking over our fence but instead of seeing the familiar olive groves and mountains I saw a car park, London, and a housing estate in the 1970s and had a feeling that some sort of criminal activity was taking place. Then I was lying on my back again, staring into the night sky. The stars were pinpricks in velvet, beyond which there might be anything. I had a sense of someone near me, a woman looking down at me. 'Jane' I said. It was a statement but also a question: 'Are you Jane?' which meant 'Am I coming back now?' She took my hand and helped me up and I hugged her. *She* is what is real. I had been away for about 20 minutes. It felt like another life.

Our next ceremony was with 5X concentrate and for me there felt little difference between this and 100X except for the duration of the experience and the ability to remember more. The intensity was the same, the themes were similar but the journey lasted around five minutes rather than 25.

I was back in the housing estate by the car park I had seen on the 100X journey. It was more specific than that in fact. I was a brick again, as I had also been on one of my first Salvia journeys in Peru, but now in a wall on one side of an alleyway on that estate in my recent vision. Jane was standing in front of me and my consciousness was equally between brick and human. From this perspective I looked at her and thought 'I love you so much'. Then my human consciousness began to fade as I withdrew more and more into brickness. My vision and awareness of Jane narrowed and my last thought was that I had always been a brick but I had loved this woman so much and dreamed so hard about being human that I had convinced myself that I was and that I could love and be loved by her. But I had deluded myself and 'got above my station'. I was a brick and nothing more. I could never be human and didn't deserve Jane or her love for how could she

– a beautiful and perfect human being - be expected to love a brick?

I never felt that I connected with the spirit of Salvia during these journeys any more than I had in Peru – that would come later and bring surprises and revelations of its own – but I learned a lot about the message of the plant. Salvia speaks of time travel, of seeing the future and of other dimensions. She is straightforward and direct and she wants us to understand that anything is possible, even – literally – journeys to other worlds outside of our known space-time – *if* we commit our hearts and minds to it.

We dieted other plants too, usually during ceremonial courses which took place at The Hummingbird. An important one for Jane was Poppy, while I worked with Rosa Blanca (White Rose).

Beautiful white Roses grew by our storeroom, alongside Tohay, next to the place where Jane had built a garden altar, covering it with mosaics and objects she had found and painted, while Poppies grew all around our teaching area. Flowers are more delicate than roots or leaves so the process for dieting both plants was simply to add their petals to cold water and let them infuse overnight, then drink the water in the morning.

The spirit of Rose came easily and quickly to me. During an Ayahuasca ceremony we held for a workshop group, my visions took me to a cold mountain landscape beneath a pale sky filled with drifting snow. Pyramid-shaped blocks of ice were stacked there, each containing one human being – or one human soul, at least – frozen and unable to move. Watching over this scene, dressed in white, with long dark hair, was the spirit of Rose. She had white flowers in her hair, their centres red and yellow, the only colours in this landscape; everything else was pale and grey.

Dark. Cold. Dead. Forever.
Everything would be like... black ice.
The whole universe just burnt out

Theodore Roszak, *Flicker*

The purpose of Rose, I gathered, is to watch over and heal the souls of those who had become emotionally frozen in grief and isolation; those who had forgotten that life is a game without purpose or meaning apart from that which we give it, and who had begun to take things too seriously, finding themselves locked in a timeless moment of pain and despair. When they were ready and the spirit of Rose had healed them she would also free them, liberating their souls from the cold futility they felt and bringing them back to life.

A song began in me, the icaro for White Rose:

Call me back from cold stars
I have a heart
I have a path
I have a home… and its here
Because I was forged here on the anvils of angels
And there is a fire in me that cannot die
Spread your warmth here, sweet Rosa Blanca
And thaw the hearts of God's sad frozen people…

Roses have been important since ancient times in ritual and medicine and, as I subsequently discovered, were once known as "the gift of angels". They have aromatic, astringent and tonic properties which control bacterial infections, promote healing and improve emotional states such as depression and lethargy, as well as colds and breathing problems. Oil of Rose is used in aromatherapy for countering anxiety, grief and negative feelings. All of this I discovered from later research but I knew it anyway from my vision of Rosa Blanca.

Jane didn't talk much about her experiences with Poppy, saying only that she found it a useful ally in her own healing mission to become softer and more open, and that its blood-red colour suggested that it would be effective for healing emotional issues connected to family history or ancestry (the 'bloodline') and for conception or menstrual problems.

Lynne, a psychotherapist and participant on the course who also dieted Poppy, had more to say about it however.

May 2011. Spain, with San Pedro
"What do you stand for?"
Lying on the decking in the sun, looking at all the life around me. The Poppies here are in various stages of growth, budding, pre-flowering, flowering, seeding with petals falling off, some covered in aphids, farmed by ants, various insects crawling over the stems. Poppy noticed my admiration and invited me to share a breath. I focussed on the centre of a living flowering plant – no need to pick her/him – and simply absorbed the essence on the inbreath and gave Poppy who I was on the outbreath. Red infused my mind and body. Powerful and life-enhancing. Incredible joy too. Poppy dances and says "Here I am, stand and be noticed".

Q: What do you stand for Poppy?

A: "Life and love".

Poppy asks me what I stand for and I cannot answer. I ask for help to find out. Poppy can stand its ground in the midst of thousands of competing plants and animals. Sympathetic to bees, tolerant of aphids and ants, Poppy doesn't mind being touched or shaken by the wind but flinches if its leaves are broken or chewed.

May/June 2011. Poppy tea
One cup for 7 days in the mornings, increased to 3 cups a day for 2 weeks. I asked Poppy how to begin. "[Drink] my petals" [she said]. Each petal is unique, some rounder than others, splodges of black on some but not all. I started with 25 fresh petals infused in off-the-boil

water for 15 minutes. Increased to 100 petals per cup. Pale pink, meadow floral smell and taste. Peaceful, light and gentle. More calming in the morning for me. Helps me to focus my intention for the day. Smooth to the throat.

May/June 2011. Poppy tea
"An easy breath creates power"
20 to 40 chopped leaves per cup. Once the taste goes, it is soothing to the throat. I can take a deeper breath – there is a difference in my asthma. More pronounced effects in the evening. Menstrual flow increased on days 1 and 2.

July 2011. Poppy tea
"Create space for remembering your dreams"
Used green pods, not dried. Cut with a plastic knife and preserved the sap. Removed the seeds. Honoured Poppy by promising to scatter seeds from the plants I have left later in the season. Boiled up to 3 pods per cup. Acrid taste makes me retch. Soporific. Used during trancing too and got more vivid images. By 3rd week of use there is a definite change in my recall of dream material. I focus on a picture of Poppy as a "dream gate". I ask Poppy to help me remember buried material and the door opens.

July 2011/ongoing. Poppy seed/seed oil meditation
1 teaspoon of dried seeds crushed. Drain off oil and rub on chakra points. Seeds smeared on bread and eaten (a ritual thanks to Poppy). Still exploring this method of dieting.

Effects on the chakras:

Base/Sacral – [Helps with] Loyalty to friends, faithfulness to lovers, grounding, connections to past relationships. The qualities of what I remember. How much do I cause my own suffering? Does what I stand for limit or grow me? What sustains me? Connection to *changing fertility and cycle of life. Not just a woman's plant though – both anima and animus respond. Working with Poppy through menopause. The flower is a hermaphrodite, suitable for work with both sexes.*

Heart – *Opens feelings, helps heal hurts. Inner child work potentially. Dancing imagery particularly powerful. Poppy has its own heartbeat.*

Throat – *Soothing, clearing. Speaking up for the self and beliefs. Notice how this works with the breath. Later, focus on the subtleties of having a calm voice.*

'The herb is Lunar, and of the juice of it is made opium; only for lucre of money they cheat you, and tell you it is a kind of tear, or some such like thing, that drops from Poppies when they weep, and that is somewhere beyond the seas, I know not where beyond the Moon. The garden Poppy heads with seeds made into a syrup, is frequently, and to good effect used to procure rest and sleep in the sick and weak and to stay catarrhs and defluxions of thin rheums from the head into the stomach and lungs, causing a continual cough, the fore-runner of a consumption; it helps also hoarseness of the throat, and when one have lost their voice, which the oil of the seed doth likewise. The black seed boiled in wine and drank is said also to dry the flux of the belly and women's courses. The empty shells, or Poppy heads, are usually boiled in water and given to procure rest and sleep: so doth the leaves in the same manner.' Nicholas Culpeper, 1653*

Extract from Lynne's journal during her Poppy diet

Poppy has a long history as a plant teacher in Spain. At one site, the Cueva de los Murciélagos (or Bat Cave) in Zuheros, not far from my home, large numbers of Poppy seed capsules were found distributed around the body of a woman, thought to be an ancient shaman, sitting in a meditative ritual pose. The remains were carbon-dated to 4200 BC. Zuheros, I decided, was a place that Jane and I should visit. Another thing to add to our 'To Do' list.

When the course ended we celebrated with a meal at the restaurant in Algarinejo then settled back into our easy routine of days by the pool and nights exploring Salvia. A few days later Michael, the shaman we had met on our honeymoon in Peru, and his partner, Maggie, came to stay with us. He brought me a gift of San Pedro: his 'Three Wise Men' mixture of three different types of cactus, and also five different San Pedro batches, separated by the numbers of their ribs. The next phase of my diet with this plant could now begin: to drink the medicine every day for a month and to explore the effects of the ribs, as San Pedro had suggested to me back in the jungle.

It would have to wait a little while though as we had an appointment before then, to attend Jane's sister's wedding in the UK, immediately after which we had arranged to visit Ireland, the place of my wife's ancestry, then take a few months off to go travelling to Morocco and Mexico in search of Peyote and Salvia.

It wasn't that we were rich but that life in Spain is cheap and we had dedicated ours to our marriage, to each other and our work with the plants. I would drive our old jeep down to the coast where we could get a low-cost ferry to Morocco. Our trip to Mexico would be funded from my savings and in any case was a research adventure that would go into writing a new book. We loved our life, the plants we were forming relationships with and all they were teaching us. Through them we were learning how to love each other more deeply.

DO YOU TAKE THIS MAN?

Outside there's a box car waiting
Outside the family stew
Pixies, *Here Comes Your Man*

2011. July

Her sister's wedding was on July 1. We had been looking forward to it for almost a year but now something was up.

Jane had been gone for a week as she had flown to the UK earlier than me to help with preparations and, alone on my mountain, I had begun to have feelings of dread. It was a nameless foreboding which had no shape or form, just a sense that something was wrong. Salvia is a plant of divination, of seeing the future, and this felt like a message from it, but with all plants you need to know their language and understand how they are communicating with you so you know what that message is and can act upon it. But I had not yet met the spirit of Salvia despite my diet in the jungle and my research with it in Spain so to me it felt like the diviner's sage (as it is also known) was trying desperately to warn me of something but I had no clue what, only that it was connected to the wedding.

In my experience, when plants have something to tell you they begin with a whisper and this ominous sense of something undefined but dreadful was the first whisper from Salvia. I ignored it. I didn't really have much choice (as I saw it then) as I had to be at the wedding to support my wife and share the occasion with her sister.

Again, in my experience, if we ignore what a plant has to say, the volume of its voice becomes steadily raised until it is screaming at you. Salvia started screaming on the morning of the wedding itself. I unpacked the things I'd brought with me: a new suit and 'proper' shoes – the first I'd bought or worn in more than 10 years – a tie, shirt, cufflinks, some gifts for my wife and her sister, and a new silver earring for me in the shape of a heart. Kitsch, I thought, but appropriate and amusing. It was still in its box but even so, when I took it out it was somehow broken in two. A pretty blunt and obvious message, especially as nothing else was damaged.

The excitement I felt at being in England and about to see my wife again gave way once more to the feeling of dread I had carried here with me. I sat down on the bed, not even wanting to know what that broken heart might mean when, suddenly and out of nowhere, the clearest image entered my head, so real that I had to shake myself to be rid of it. I was lying on the ground at the wedding dressed in my new suit, but I was screaming and my wife was standing over me looking down in anger and disgust. I knew right then that I wanted to be anywhere but at that ceremony. And yet still there was nothing I felt that I could do about that. I was expected, I had accepted the invitation and Jane wanted me there.

And so I went - and nothing unusual happened. Jane and I were so delighted to be together again that the other guests would have been forgiven for believing it was our wedding. We hugged, kissed and rewrapped ourselves in love. Jane gave a speech and mentioned me in it – the first formal public acknowledgement of our own marriage to her family and friends. When I hung back she insisted that I be part of the official photographs because I 'was family now too'. Her relatives told me she looked the happiest they'd ever seen her. One of them gave us a wedding gift of our own. In the late afternoon we left the reception and found a quiet spot in the garden where we could be alone and make love, both in our wedding clothes, getting grass stains all over them, not that it mattered. So what had that Salvia vision and all those warnings been about? It was business as usual for us and I began to relax.

At the end of the day we took a taxi back to our hotel and went up to our room. And that is more or less all I remember except waking up some time later to find my wife throwing her belongings into her bag and telling me our marriage was over. 'You will never hear from me again' she said. I followed her downstairs, completely confused, and watched as she left in a taxi.

So, despite everything else that had taken place that day and the familiar closeness between us, the dreadful *had* happened, just as Salvia warned me it would. For two days I emailed and phoned her but there was no reply so when I ran out of options I cancelled our flight to Ireland and for the second time in our marriage I flew back to Spain alone.

Nobody in Andalucia was particularly surprised. A number of them had seen her storm out before or been at our house when she had packed everything and vanished for a week and they assumed she'd just come back when she was ready.

And in fact she did. She arrived early on Monday morning. I had received no message from her so I was surprised and relieved when she walked in. But she said she had just come to collect her things and that her father was with her, waiting outside in the car. I wondered what on Earth she was doing with him after all that she and her mother had told me about him but my first words were only a sort of exasperated 'Oh Jane, no' (the two I didn't add were 'not again'). But then it dawned on me that this time was different. It was serious. She had planned her arrival in Spain for the time when we – and, for all she knew, I alone – should have been flying to Ireland, and she had brought him with her. Clearly, it seemed to me, she had intended to be gone, probably leaving no note again and just a few more poignant reminders, when I got back from Ireland. I felt myself go into shock. *Why?* What was going on now?

We talked for a while as she packed, but there was madness in the room that day, no clear answers and nothing made sense – until I remembered who (or rather, what) I had married: *Jungle Jane*. Hard, competitive and defended. Then I knew exactly what had happened and that there was no way back for us now – not because I didn't want it or that she didn't either, but because she could never allow it.

She had left our hotel room in anger, that much was clear. Had we been in Spain it might have amounted to another of her stormings out for an hour, a day or a week, but we were in England where she had family and friends so this time she went to them and, still angry, no doubt told them about all the problems she had in her marriage – problems which, if they existed, she had never discussed with me. When her anger subsided she must also have realised that she had stormed out this time on the day of her sister's wedding and in so doing stolen the occasion from her in the worst possible way. A divorce trumps a marriage for drama and high emotion, but you better follow through with it because melodrama and histrionics from an older sister on a wedding day is in extremely poor taste.

Jungle Jane, proud, competitive and tough had backed herself into a corner she couldn't escape from and rather than lose face she just had to win now, even if she defeated herself in the process.

She talked about her 'principles' and said that she had two rules when she got married: that there should be no other people in our marriage (no infidelity) and that she would not tolerate any attempt to control her. It was the first I'd heard of these principles but they were irrelevant anyway. There could have been no infidelity even if I'd wanted it (which I didn't); we were together every hour of the day on our mountain.

But then, what of that girl from the jungle, I wondered? The one who saw no problem at all in an affair with a married man, followed by another with a man who she knew had a long-term girlfriend, and then with me when she thought that I was with someone else? Three relationships, one after the other, all with men who she knew or believed were unavailable. How did her principle of fidelity apply then? As for control, wasn't she the one who told me that she was 'bossy' and controlling even then? The competitive one who wanted things her own way and always had to win? The one who was controlling our relationship now?

These are my principles and if you don't like them...well, I have others
Groucho Marx, comedian

She said she felt dependent on me – but the truth is *she was*. We lived 10km from anywhere and she didn't own a car; she couldn't even drive. She had no job, no income, and in her desire for 'freedom' she had never owned a property or had assets of her own, so I had taken care of everything. There was no alternative and it didn't matter anyway. Now she wanted independence and to take it she had enlisted the help of a man who, from what she had told me about him, didn't score highly according to her own rules of anything. It would have been amusing if it wasn't so tragic.

'This is the hardest thing I've ever done, but I have to do this' she said as she was packing. I had no idea what to say. I knew why she was going – or at least I thought I did – but I had to ask anyway.
    'But you love it here' I said.
    'I love it here *with you*'.
    'Then stay and we'll work this out'.
    'I can't' she said. Her voice sounded almost pleading, as if she wanted me to save her from her own choices and actions. 'If I stay I will become a shell'.

To know ourselves we must empty out, become a shell. When we get rid of who we've become we have a sense of who we are...
Extract from my San Pedro diary during early work with the plant

'I have to go now to start grieving for my marriage' she added dramatically. And then she was gone. Her father had been busy that weekend, giving one of his daughters away and taking the other one back. It was July 4, Independence Day, the day that Jane gave up independence to return to the life she had been running away from since she was 17.

She was gone but the madness continued. I saw it as a process of her trying to make sense of what she'd done. A few days after she left she sent me an email thanking me for giving her the 'best two years and eight months' of her life. Within days the story had changed and instead of me giving her anything I had 'taken everything' from her. Finally, her story became 'I gave *you* everything' (followed by the rather grandiose statement: 'I gave you *me*'): a not-so subtle shift from the Jane she was becoming back to the Jungle variety.

Following that there was usually silence between us but occasionally she might email me again with other angry or grandiose statements ('What you want and what you need is what you once had [meaning her]. That is not the case now' or 'I want to be left alone'), which I recognised as the voice of 'JJ', as I had started calling her. Then, a few days later she phoned me – the first time she had called since she left and curiously enough on the day that I took off my wedding ring and decided that we were over; that I didn't want her back, not as who she was now. 'It's so hard not seeing you or talking to you anymore' she said, but she had promised herself that I would never hear from her again and, despite whatever pain she was going through, she was sticking to that. 'Never compromise, even in the face of Armageddon' in the words of Rorschach, a character she liked in *The Watchmen* novel we had read together. A pretty stupid philosophy I thought, especially given what happened to him next.

But it was pointless to argue with her or to even try to remind her that she'd made a bigger promise to herself and to me on a mountain in the Andes not so long ago. It just wasn't worth arguing with JJ, especially at long-distance. At close quarters it often led to another storming out but at least she returned. With a thousand miles between us a confrontation was going nowhere. Which is exactly where it did go. Talking to her on Facebook one day she told me that she felt a 'big black hole' where her heart used to be and that it was hard for her not to 'lay down in traffic' each day - then she deleted me from her friends and that was the last I heard from her.

In her final Facebook notice she dismissed what she had once called the 'love of my life' and 'my ideal life in Spain' as 'so much for that' and added, without any sense of irony, 'onwards and upwards, never backwards!' She was *back* in the town she grew up in, *back* in her mother's house, *back* in her childhood bedroom, *back* in her old job, *back* with the friends she had said just a few months ago bored her because they never moved on – *back* in the life she had tried so hard to escape from. I couldn't see how much further back she could go without regressing to the womb and the fact that she couldn't see it at all meant she was also fully back in the role of JJ, who had to be in control and win, despite the losses it brought her. As Guy remarked when he first met her in the rainforest, it looked as if she had always been running from something. *Take me away to nowhere plains.* There was nothing more I could do to help her.

The realisation of who she was, what I had really been sharing a bed with, and at what she had chosen to return to made me sick – in a literal and physical way, not just in my soul. *Dark. Cold. Dead. Forever… The whole universe just burnt out.*

LOVE-SICK: ADDICTION AND ADORATION (ANTITHESIS)

I began to understand that life goes on, that I must accept the pain instead of struggling against it or searching for consolation. When you eat, you eat. When you sleep, you sleep. When it hurts, it hurts. *Beyond all that there is the unity of the impersonal life. Our ashes must merge with the ashes of the world*
Alejandro Jodorowsky, Zen Master

2011. July/August

Shock – known in Peru as *manchare* or *susto* – is one of the classic causes of soul loss: the feeling that you are no longer whole, that you are bewildered and lost, which can also give rise to mental, emotional and physical problems. I had them all. I felt spaced-out, dizzy, confused and my mind was racing – 'ruminating' as psychologists call it – going round in circles, trying to understand something – anything - but getting nowhere and finding nothing.

I felt grief, of course – like my heart was missing and the void it left had been filled with a nausea that just wouldn't leave - but also failure and guilt. For all I had learned from the shamans and the plants and my own work as a healer, I had not been able to save the person in the world who mattered most to me. But then, was it ever my job to 'save' her? She was my wife not a client. Can a healer really 'save' anyone anyway? Our job is to give people the tools to save themselves. And if they don't want to be saved? What then?

There was a sense of panic too. I didn't understand how I could have got this so wrong. The connection between us had been empathic, so how had I so badly misjudged where she was at or how she really felt about us? Perhaps 'our' dream and our belief that 'we can do anything we want' hadn't been shared at all. Perhaps it was only *my* dream, which of course, made it my delusion. And if that was true – that something I was so certain of was based on wishful thinking and lies – could I trust *anything*: my relationships with others, for example, the world I had created around me - or even myself?

I began to lose faith even in God. Things are always changing and we are on a journey - that much is true - which gives us the opportunity for new experiences, for growth and new choices. But then, isn't it remarkable just how often the same issues and life patterns keep re-emerging and how the experiences we choose and our interactions with others are driven and dictated by them – and we don't even see it until we stumble into their dead ends and blind alleys again? Then we realise, too late, 'Ah, here I am again. I know this place. I've been here before'. Is that how limited God's script is – just these one or two dramatic arcs punctuated by a few good times as a distraction from the fact that we are clichés in a cosmic soap opera and that the writer of our scripts is unimaginative and dull?

> *What if a Demon crept after you one day or night in your loneliest solitude and said to you: 'This life, as you live it now and have lived it, you will have to live again and again, times without number, and there will be nothing new in it but every pain and every joy and every thought and sigh and all the unspeakably small and great events in your life must return to you, and everything in the same series and sequence'?*

Friedrich Nietzsche, philosopher

It was the same feeling and the same realisation I had had back in the jungle with Salvia and San Pedro, but now on a visceral instead of an intellectual level: the sense that of course we have freewill and can make any choices we wish, but only within the given framework of our lives and this framework is so vast and powerful and unconscious that the decisions we *do* make are more or less predetermined. Nietzsche called it the law of Eternal Recurrence and I felt stuck in it.

I knew what I was doing: wallowing, as a few shamans told me I had a tendency to do: analysing, intellectualising, seeking answers where none existed – or if they did they were both too complicated *and* too simple to yield any meaning. Jane and I had found each other in *this* lifetime, created *this* relationship and it ended in *this* way because of all the influences upon us throughout the whole of our lives but even so, we – or, rather, she – had taken a decision that it should end. So what did all that tell me? A big fat nothing. I might as well have said 'it ended because it began' or 'it ended because we're alive'.

Faced with the unanswerable, I finally stopped wallowing and decided that I had been presented with a learning experience, a sort of koan that San Pedro was asking me to solve. I remembered an exchange between Jodorowsky and his Zen Master, Ejo Takata where Jodorowsky is offered the following puzzle: 'Why is there a cat in the painting in Kyoto of the Buddha entering Nirvana?'

Jodorowsky, then just a young student, goes off on one in response: 'Because the cat has a Buddha nature? Because the cat is a symbol of the moon and female energy and the Buddha is therefore telling us to unite the masculine and feminine sides of our natures? Because the moon appears at night so the Buddha is saying that we must enter the dark night of our own souls in order to find enlightenment? Because the cat and the Buddha are one?'

I'm paraphrasing of course, but it really did go something like this, until Takata had finally heard enough of this rambling and picked up his *kwatsu* stick to hit Jodorowsky unceremoniously over the head with it. A bonk that echoed throughout eternity, like the sound of one hand clapping. Then he calmly pointed out the obvious: 'No, there is a cat in the painting in Kyoto of the Buddha entering Nirvana because the artist painted a cat'.

In the final analysis my answer to the greatest koan of all –

Why? - was just as simple: *she left because she chose to.* Her choice may have been based on a thousand childhood experiences, conditions and coping strategies arrived at over more than 30 years but in the end *it was just a choice.* She made it. As simple as that.

Knowing that didn't help my physical symptoms however. For days (it felt like weeks and it may have been) I had headaches, cramps in my legs so severe that I had to go for long walks to unfreeze my muscles, cold sweats, heart pains and I found it hard to breathe or to get my mind into any kind of survival shape. Alone on our mountain I thought I was dying. I wondered whether I would get an annual 'homage' on her web page as well if I did, as another testament to perfect and risk-free love.

I finally called Elizabeth, a friend and therapist in Ireland who has experience in situations like this. She has been through the emotional wringer herself and emerged intact. She was an alcoholic from a young age, then joined Alcoholics Anonymous and has been clean for 20 years. During her time at AA she realised that alcohol had been a way for her to avoid dealing with deeper emotional issues so she joined Sex and Love Addicts Anonymous and Co-Dependents Anonymous. She is now a counsellor for all three. I explained the situation to her, the plant work we had been doing and the physical pains I was experiencing. She recognised them all.

'I had to crawl from my bed even to get to the toilet whenever I left [my boyfriend] - and I left seven times!' she said. 'With relationship addiction losing your lover is like heroin withdrawal. The pain – physical and emotional – is the same. I know a woman, bright, pretty, confident, who slit her throat because of feelings like these.'

'I follow the SLAA steps to recovery more than AA these days because the booze only masked my inability to relate to people but I didn't understand that and had to wait a few years for the alcoholic fog to clear. I guess San Pedro just wants you to cut to the chase. Awareness is the first step but it's a spiritual journey.'

'Hurt people hurt people' she added. 'What San Pedro wants is for you both to find the root of your wounds so you can heal them. You can either run from them when they surface or go through the pain and solve them. It's up to you what you choose but only by facing them can you have any hope of really being free'.

Through Elizabeth I discovered that relationship addiction is a condition that affects 5% of the population (15.5 million people) in America and 0.5% of the population in the UK (300,000 people) and that it could also explain how I was feeling. Helen Fisher, professor of anthropology at Rutgers University made brain scans of compulsive lovers looking at photographs of their partners and found that the areas of the brain that light up are the same as for drug addicts. 'The properties of infatuation [have] some of the same elements as a cocaine high: sleeplessness, loss of a sense of time, absolute focus on love to the detriment of all around you' she said in *Psychology Today*.

Loss of a sense of time certainly sounded like us. We could – and did – lose whole days by doing little else but loving each other and playing in our garden. We barely saw another soul and we were happy with that: an absolute focus on love.

Dr Thomas Timmreck writes about the process of falling into love addiction. 'After going through an initially innocent moment of attraction [addictive personalities] idealise the other person to the point of divinity. The individual is then blindly attached to the other, becoming incapable of making a realistic assessment of the relationship they are in. They begin to project all kinds of illusions onto the other person… and the process can be very fast.'

'[They] commonly and repeatedly form a relationship with avoidant partners. The avoidant is compulsively counter-dependent – they fear being engulfed, drowned or smothered by their partner. They enter relationships closed-off emotionally and let nothing and no-one in... [These relationships] inevitably lead to unhealthy patterns of dependency, distance, chaos... where each is attracted to the other because of the familiar traits that the other exhibits which, although painful, come from childhood.'

There are patterns to our lives in other words, and themes that run through them from our earliest days. (Addictive) lovers come together to fulfil (or hopefully heal) their childhood wounds but until these are made conscious and faced the relationship itself is likely to deepen them by continuing the pattern. Perhaps we remind each other in some intangible way of our fathers or mothers, for example, with whom we have had difficult experiences which we now try to heal through the love we have for our partners. We end up however with the same relationship playing itself out unless we recognise that there is even a wound to be healed.

The Ketamine explorer, Marcia Moore, may have been an example of this process in action. She married Howard Alltounian within a few weeks of meeting him, in a whirlwind romance that was in some ways similar to the one between Jane and I. In his book *Ketamine: Dreams and Realities*, Karl Jansen remarks that this suggests 'a high level of "projections" in the relationship, as they did not seem at this early stage to really "know" each other at all. Their perception of having met in "past lives" may be (at one level) another way of saying that each recognised an aspect of their own being, which they knew in childhood but had forgotten, in the other (i.e. they "projected" what they wanted to see onto the other)... There are sometimes hidden (or not so hidden) elements of sadomasochism in relationships where people do not really "see" the other person but are caught up in a fantasy'.

'Until this need [process] is made conscious', Timmreck continues, 'this cycle can only give rise to a push-pull dance of emotional highs and lows [where] healthy intimacy is replaced with melodrama and negative intensity... With this comes inevitable negative consequences [which are] most revealed as the love addict experiences withdrawal when a relationship ends. When a break-up occurs an addictive lover longs for the attachment and loving feelings of the lost relationship as much as a heroin user craves heroin when the drug is no longer available...'

As for 'avoidants', Dr Susan Peabody writes that 'Ambivalent love addicts... suffer from avoidant personality disorder... They don't have a hard time letting go, they have a hard time moving forward. They crave love but at the same time are terrified of losing themselves to true intimacy. Ambivalents end relationships when they start to get serious or when their fear of intimacy comes up.'

She left because she chose to...

Love addicts see what they want to see and not what's actually there, which is why the initial phase of their relationship is often extremely passionate and romantic. It feels glorious, magnificent, like all their dreams have come true. It's a high temperature, sexual, romantic furnace. As they begin to feel safer in the relationship they naturally show more and more of their neediness and that's the cue for their partner, the intimacy avoider, to start withdrawing faster and faster...

Intimacy avoiders tend to avoid any kind of intensity within their relationship by creating intensity in activities or addictions outside of the relationship (think of porn addiction here: it's controllable, unlike a real person). They don't allow themselves to be known within the relationship so they can protect themselves from involvement and emotional control or manipulation by the other... As a child, being enmeshed in somebody else's emotional needs can create a deeply ingrained conviction that intimacy brings misery. And yet, at the same time, intimacy avoiders fear abandonment at some level, usually unconsciously. It's a fear which comes from being abandoned as a child by their caregiver. Here's how that works: when a child is forced to nurture a parent the parent is actually abandoning the child's needs to be looked after. And so although abandonment is a less obvious experience for intimacy avoiders than emotional enmeshment with another, it's certainly real.

Rod Boothroyd, *Are You A Love Addict Or An Intimacy Avoider?*[34]

I talked all of this over with Bobby, another therapist friend in Spain, and she lent me a book by Oliver James. I had never read it but recognised it because, in another synchronicity, some years ago his girlfriend had asked me to give her a healing, which I did at their London flat. She was a journalist and later wrote up her experiences in the Daily Express newspaper. Her partner Oliver, a psychologist, was writing his book at the time, *They Fuck You Up*[35]– the one I was now holding - about family dramas and the damage they cause. It fell open at page 166. I know that sounds 'shamanic' but I swear it is true. It literally fell open in my hands.

Scripting the Avoidant Pattern

One fifth of us have this allergy to intense involvement with others, wanting self-sufficiency, neither to depend nor to be depended upon. The Avoidant assumes that others will be hostile and rejecting. Anticipating this, we get our retaliation in first by being spiky and stubborn and if we are nonetheless forced to become involved we employ a domineering, intrusive style.

Not surprisingly, given our misanthropy, we were the kind of person who did not want to settle down and have children in our early twenties and may still not have done so by our thirties ['I don't know if this is a deal-breaker for you']... If we do overcome our reluctance to tie the knot and marry, half of us are divorced by our mid-forties compared with only one quarter of secure people. On splitting up we appear not to care, often actually expressing relief and dwelling neither on what has been lost nor on what might have been ['So much for that']. *Physical measures, such as heart rate or the amount of palm sweating prove that we are deeply upset on the inside, we simply don't show it...* [The Avoidant] *has a penchant for one-night stands, sex without love and with partners who are already spoken for...*

If we are Avoidants we prefer work to love, maintaining that success in the former creates happiness in the latter. Yet work is a constant source of annoyance because our fellow workers are so incompetent and noncompliant. Highly critical of them, we prefer to work alone and to concentrate on solitary processes, like computing, which protect us from the stress of having to deal with infuriating peers...

Avoidants are more likely than other types to be agnostic, but if pressured to picture a god we imagine him to be a distant figure who is inaccessible and highly controlling [a blue 'God' with a reality-annihilation machine?]. *He is rejecting and we think it unlikely that he cares for us very much. This turns out to be a strong clue to our Avoidant pattern of attachment. We have, like our view of the supreme deity, an image of our mother as rejecting, controlling and negative – an image which developed because, on the whole, that is what she was actually like... She was controlling and intrusive, determined to interrupt our flow and redirect it in her own desired direction...This rejecting pattern of care does not end in infancy. Avoidants are liable to have been the object of insensitivity for the remainder of their childhoods, with rash, critical and unsympathetic reactions to the travails of adolescence. The end result is that as Avoidant adults we expect rejection in relationships and put the boot in first – we reject before being rejected.*

I turned over to page 168 and found more to think about.

Scripting the Clinger Pattern

... found in about one tenth of us. We want to be completely emotionally intimate but no one is ever quite as close as we would like. We feel uncomfortable and lonely without intense emotional involvement. Despite the fact that we constantly give of ourselves, the recipients of our emotional largesse don't seem to value us as much as we value them. Our relationships are prone to highs and lows, to jealousy, conflict and dissatisfaction. We are liable to mother our partners, protecting, feeding, sympathising, smothering. We are looking for unqualified closeness, keen to move in with new partners and to share their life as soon as possible... We are at greater risk of divorce than those who are secure.

As a child we were liable to be a victim, especially of Avoidants, with whom we may none the less have become friends and in later life choose as partners. At first sight odd, this marriage of opposites has a certain logic. The Clinger's vulnerability and insistence on showing emotion forces the Avoidant out of his shell and engages him with another human...the mutual difficulties of the two patterns make for something that works...

We are likely to believe in the existence of God, who has the distinct advantage over people of not letting us down and not making us feel like an insignificant failure. His love is unconditional and predictable and it is possible to be worthy of it by following reliable procedures: prayer, ritual, doing good works.

Whereas the parental cause of Avoidance is rejection, with Clinging it is inconsistent, unreliable care. Mothers of babies who are subsequently discovered to be Clingers are confusing... For much of the time there was a strong sense that she was not very involved – not filled with passion for us. She initiated little and was a passive, emotionally absent presence. It may be that depression caused a flat, empty mood which even our beguiling infant smiles could not penetrate...The Clinger's mother was not as averse as the Avoidant's to picking her infant up but she did so with little warmth, unaccompanied by kisses or loving words...

At the heart of the Clinger is a fear of abandonment. It causes the clinging but at the same time we wriggled and resisted attempts to hold us because... we also felt furious at having been left before...

I have always resisted imposing labels on others or giving names to their 'conditions'. Labels detract from the humanity we share with each other. It makes the person in front of me something 'other': I am a healer, she is a client; my life is in order, hers is in chaos – whereas to my mind we are all just human beings trying to make the best sense we can of the world. But in this instance I saw a value in James' labels (although I can't say I particularly liked being described as a clinger) and it had a 'shamanic' resonance too as I remembered the first plant that Jane and I had dieted together, what it was used for and what it led to between us. It gave me somewhere to start at least if I was going to heal this, know myself better and avoid in future whatever it was in me that had contributed to the end of our marriage.

With something to hold on to my universe finally stopped spinning but I knew that this was only a starting point. I had begun this journey wanting to learn from San Pedro and to understand the nature of love and healing. He told me at the outset that he would be revealing his warrior face – and he had. Tough love followed. Along the way I had also found Salvia, a plant which speaks of love and destiny in a different but somehow similar way. It was time for me to consult these plants again to see what lessons I should be taking from this. I began a diet with serious intent.

SAN PEDRO IN THE GARDEN
OF GHOSTS
(SYNTHESIS)

On this rock I will build my church and the gates of Hell will not overcome it.
I will give you the keys of the kingdom of heaven
Christ addressing Saint Peter (Matthew 16:17-20)

2011. August/September

When I first began work with San Pedro the plant asked me to drink it daily for a month and explore the effects of its different ribs. Lack of time, a marriage and other commitments prevented me from doing so then but now I had all the time in the world. I also had a supply of La Bruja's 'love medicine' and Michael's 'Three Wise Men' mixture as well as the blends of the ribs he had made for me. I had a quantity of Salvia too, in various levels of concentrate. It was everything I needed.

Before I started, however, I wanted to take advice from La Bruja, whose San Pedro Jane and I had drunk when we first fell in love and drank again at our wedding. San Pedro had in a way brought us together and fashioned our marriage. With Jane now gone I had the uncomfortable feeling that either we had betrayed the spirit of San Pedro and the gift of love that he gave us or else he had abandoned us and if either of those possibilities was true, it seemed to me that if I drank the cactus now I was going to get my arse kicked all over the universe.

La Bruja reassured me. 'Ross, you know better than anyone that it's not San Pedro's fault or a "punishment" that this has happened. You were brought together for a good reason and sometimes we need to understand and get the lesson of why we were put together. There is always a perfect reason. Learn from it and know you have grown from this. There is perfection in everything so don't dwell on the negative, get past it my dear friend, as hard as it may be'. Then she added, 'We shamans are not intended for marriage. We are lone wolves', a stunning use of words under the circumstances since Joy, one of my participants on the Cactus of Vision journey – a hilarious elderly drama queen - had used exactly the same ones when, under the influence of San Pedro she offered Jane some Bronx-style advice for our married life: 'He is a lone wolf and you are a fierce squaw! Don't forget that – and never piss where he pisses'.

'Don't be sad' La Bruja continued. 'There is something great and glorious coming for you so be grateful and go back to your heart and ask to be guided on your journey. Of course you must drink [San Pedro] again. Whatever comes up will be a great relief to you, even if you go through some pain. I held ceremony today and I put you in there with love. You will heal my friend. I send you much love and may peace and understanding and more love be with you'.

Michael's advice was more or less the same: 'Yes, absolutely drink! Even if your ass gets a friendly kick it can only be for the better. Or maybe you just get a few hints and new perspectives on the situation. I would say drink a decent dose of four full spoons of the powder [about four times the normal dose] so you put your mind to rest for a few hours.'

And so I drank. I wanted the ceremony to send healing to my wife as well and to return any power she had given me during our relationship, as well as taking back my own so that the break between us was clean and our souls could disentangle. And so it began in love and it would end in love, just as Jaguar, the diviner and priest for our wedding, foresaw.

The days of San Pedro and nights of Salvia which followed taught me about life and its processes and the nature of love and healing. My physical pains eased a little but did not leave completely (it takes three months or so for an addictive substance to fully exit the body – even if that substance is one's wife). There was some sickness because of the diet as well and on top of it all, loneliness. It was like our garden had another ghost now because everywhere I looked I saw her shadow – tending the patch she had made, making mosaics and decorating her altar, by the pool, laughing – and every clear-sky day and night filled with stars I wished she was here to share it so that she could experience again the beauty of the home she had loved and let go of the anger which was damaging her so much.[36]

The effect of San Pedro, when drunk over a prolonged period of time, is to create a state of relaxation and acceptance. You may be dealing with difficult emotional issues and San Pedro does not absolve you from the responsibility of exploring them but it adds an element of objectivity and places a little distance between you and the subject you wish to examine. If not that, then it is like going into those dark places with the support of a strong and protective friend, a guide or a counsellor. The cactus does, however, require that we *do* enter those places in order to understand them and take back the power we have given to them and lost from ourselves in the process. Again, like an exorcism of sorts.

Three years ago in Peru I watched as one of my participants went through this. As a teenager Alexia had met and fallen in love with a young man who had turned out to be anything but what she expected. When she moved in with him he effectively kept her prisoner and controlled her every action. She was subjected to sexual and emotional abuse and he also gave her a heroin habit. She had several breakdowns during their time together and became a *real* shell, a shadow of herself.

When she escaped she was in therapy for years and eventually became a therapist herself, learning techniques for dealing with the terror and trauma of her past until it was, she said, fully packed away, forgotten and forgiven and she had moved on to a successful and happy life.

San Pedro thought differently.

She drank the cactus with us and spent almost an entire day lying in a ditch outside the Temple of the Moon, crying, screaming and vomiting. The most painful experience of her life, she said later, and also the most liberating. She realised that in fact she had dealt with nothing. Instead she had learned ways to suppress it, trapping her memories and pain in a corner of her mind which she never visited so that her trauma was contained but not conquered and its energy continued to infect her soul, her emotions and the way she engaged with life. San Pedro puked, screamed and cried it out of her until, eight exhausting hours later, she could say that *now* she was finally free. She drank San Pedro again two days later and had one of the most blissful experiences of her life. Then she knew without doubt that she was healed[37].

Back in the jungle, when Ayahuasca had told me the story of its origins it also said that San Pedro was the guardian of the Earth and of all things on it, including human beings, and this is another way in which it heals: by revealing nature as spirit-filled, intelligent, aware and an expression of love and God. When we understand that the world itself is alive and can see it with our own eyes we cannot feel alone and abandoned, the underlying cause of so much sickness and despair.

On my mountain in Spain the trees were breathing, whispering to each other and to me; the hills were shining, filled with life and magic; the entire world was crackling with potential, excitement and joy at its own presence and the love of existence. Every feature of the land was art, painted by an artist greater and more talented than us – and yet we are this artist too. Our senses interpret what God has drawn for us and *we* create beauty from it but, more than that, there is only one energy to the universe and it fills us all, we just as much as God.

I was reminded of a story La Bruja told of one of her early encounters with San Pedro when she was training to be a huachumera. She was walking with her shaman in her own mountains, having drunk San Pedro, when she glanced up and saw what she took to be a stairway carved into the hillside; a stairway comprised entirely of light. It appeared real but she knew it must be a vision, a hallucination, a communication of some kind from her soul or her unconscious given to her in symbolic form just as Ayahuasca might do, so she asked her shaman to explain what it meant.

'There is no meaning and nothing to explain' he said. 'It is a stairway of light.'

'You mean you see it too?' she asked.

'Of course' he said. 'San Pedro simply shows you what is real and always there. It is just that we can't see it most of the time because our minds get in the way.'

She wasn't entirely convinced by this, still believing that it was a trick of the mind or her unconscious feeding her symbols since this is the Western way of interpreting such things, so her shaman told her to take a photograph if she didn't believe it was there. She took the photo, not expecting much from it, and carried on with her day.

Later she had it developed and if you ever visit her hostel in Cusco or look in my book, *The Hummingbird's Journey to God*, you will see what came out. It is a stairway of light carved into the hillside in the mountains near the Temple of the Moon.

How do we explain this? We can either accept what that shaman told her: that the world is ensouled and we are a part of its spiritual community or, if you are more of a scientific persuasion you might consider the work of Henri Bergson.

When Aldous Huxley was given mescaline in 1953 and wrote later that it allowed man access to mystical states by overriding the brain's 'reducing valve' he was quoting the French philosopher Henri Bergson who in the previous century had proposed that the brain acts as a kind of filter for memory and experience so that our conscious awareness is not overwhelmed with a mass of largely useless information, irrelevant to our survival.

Bergson suggested that if these filters were bypassed we would be capable of remembering everything we have ever experienced as well as knowing everything that is happening anywhere in the universe right know or, indeed, is yet to happen, so that states such as clairvoyance and precognition are entirely possible. Huxley applied this theory to mescaline, suggesting that it could override this valve in the brain, bypassing the filters that stop us from perceiving and knowing everything and feeling ourselves a part of it. He paraphrased this by quoting the poet and mystic William Blake: 'If the doors of perception were cleansed everything would appear to man as it is, infinite.'

There is more to the world than our minds allow us to see but plants like San Pedro, by relaxing us, by lightening our moods and expanding our awareness, let us explore the world in a new way; a way where *anything* is possible based only on our choices and willingness to believe in a new state of being.

THE EFFECTS OF THE RIBS

No matter how many ribs the cactus has, San Pedro remains San Pedro, concerned with love and power. Within this overall healing perspective however, the number of ribs gives different frequencies and qualities to the plant. This is its subtle medicine.

Even-numbered cactuses are gentler and work on the physical body and denser energy levels: those bits of us that have become stuck in our stories, while cactuses with odd-numbered ribs contain more active energy and give more visual sensations.

Even numbers also bring balance (a sense of completeness in the 'squaring off' of ourselves) whereas odd numbers lead to movement, progress and evolution. In mystical numerology and sacred geometry it is the same: odd numbers seek to become even for the sake of wholeness but by doing so they also become fixed and no further progress is possible. In order to *evolve* we must also *revolve*, moving forward from odd to even to odd again so that resolution is sought but never quite found, not in the sense that we can apply a once-and-for-all formula to things or operate according to rules and principles because every situation is unique. *If man is five then the Devil is six and if the Devil is six then God is seven.* In psychological terms, an even number of ribs guides you to look at your personal history and see all that you are now as a result of that story, while an odd number shows you your potential and who you may still become.

Six ribs. The six-ribbed cactus contains the four directions – the four winds of East, South, West and North, along with two others: Heaven and Earth. The person who drinks it stands at the centre, the place of harmony and balance, and is able to expand in all directions, exploring the medicine wheel of themselves to heal their various needs and conditions: East for the body, South for the emotions, West for the mind and North for the spirit. Bringing all of these points into alignment leads to wholeness and an opening of the heart.

Dieting the six-rib eased my physical pains and helped me stay open to love instead of closing myself off and allowing it to harden into the sort of anger that is typical in break-ups as a form of self-defence; a survival mechanism for the ego. Michael says of the six-rib that it 'is primarily for balancing the masculine and feminine energy within ourselves. It helps couples to connect on a deeper level as they surrender to their true essences. The six-pointed star[38] is good medicine to find equilibrium and the centre within. Its affirmation is: "I am a divine expression of unity, I am whole".'

Seven ribs. According to Michael the seven-rib is a good "all-round" medicine. Reconnection with the heart is its main property and it brings vivid visual sensations and insights. While dieting it, unsurprisingly, I had a dream about my relationship with Jane. We were living in London, in a luxurious apartment of glass, chrome and bleached wood – a 'dream home' (in both senses of the term). She had been sitting alone in her room for a few days after some disagreement between us (something she had also done in 'real life' in Spain) and now she emerged with a suitcase, leaving again. She sat down with me on our sofa, handing me notes she had written. I thought she had been locked away in self-pity and self-indulgence but instead (or as well) she had been busy dissecting our relationship. What she gave me looked like a typewritten marriage contract on which she had scribbled her accusations and feelings. The pages were littered with them. Next to a clause which said that I promised to love and respect her she had scribbled 'At 7.16am on February 11 you did not love or respect me'. Alongside another clause where I promised to protect and care for her she had written 'At 2.28pm on March 6 I did not feel protected or cared for'. It was precise and nit-picking. I was reminded of something she said to me on that difficult weekend back in Iquitos before we became fully involved with each other, when I nearly left her before the skies opened and washed away the discomfort between us: 'Whatever you say to me I will hold you to'. Another of her mysterious principles. Then, in my dream, she walked down our marble stairs to the door of our apartment and left without once looking back. *Never compromise, even in the face of Armageddon.*

The dream message of San Pedro was that no matter how glorious and rich a façade of love is, no matter how full of shining glass, chrome and opulence, it is not *true* love – not in San Pedro's terms and his requirements for love – unless the stuff at its heart is also brilliant, rich and honest. When pain is withheld and issues from the past are not allowed to see light their shadows grow deeper and longer, and that is not love but darkness.

Eight ribs. The eight-ribbed cactus, because of the number of directions it has, is more balanced than others. The journey with it is mellow and supportive although the medicine is single-minded in purpose, connecting the mind with the body to heal and balance physical or material problems.

Nine ribs. The nine-rib is a detoxifying medicine which enables the body to release the pains and poisons arising from trauma and shock. 'It is good for when we are standing at thresholds in the passage of life and an aid for changing destructive life patterns' says Michael. 'It opens the gates to the upper world and can allow you to see beyond your physical body, to observe life from above, as if through the eyes of the condor.'

The lessons of the Devil:
Met El Diablo again. Not Selva's this time but mine. I suspect there are as many devils as there are gods and we each have our own.

The one that the nine-ribbed cactus showed me was a crackling being made of an energy that comes from beyond logic; a thoughtform or a 'bad idea' created from all the confusions of the world. In my mind's eye he looked exactly like tarot depictions of him. He said that he is looking for men and women who are 'not 50-50'.

He meant that human beings have a normal equilibrium (50/50) where they are neither 'good' nor 'bad', 'filled' nor 'empty', 'light' nor 'dark' but part of the natural order. When someone is 'not 50-50' they are unbalanced and, because of this, they invite their personal disasters.

It doesn't matter in which direction this imbalance occurs. If we are 'less than 50%' there is a vacuum in our souls where we are so lacking in power that we are open to all sorts of energies and influences and, by and large, these will be of a negative kind. Imagine someone so poor for example ('less than 50%' in terms of economic power) that they cannot afford to feed themselves. Would he or she kill to stay alive? Of course. We see stories like this all the time, and not just in 'third world' countries. Michael Moore's documentary, Fahrenheit 9/11, has a section about the American town of Flint, where poverty is now so widespread that the military concentrates its efforts there to enlist young men and women who are then sent to war zones to kill other poor men and women in order not to starve themselves. Dogs of war eating dogs of war.

It is the same with spiritual power: when you are below 50% and your soul is starving you will do whatever it takes, including taking power from others because you are too desperate to care about the forces that motivate you as long as they provide what you need to survive. Needy husbands take power from their wives and those wives take power from their daughters until, in the typical family dynamic, the last victim in line ends up kicking the cat. And so it goes and so it goes.

And the book says 'You may be finished with the past but the past ain't finished with you'[39]

Too much power, on the other hand, is difficult to carry unless the soul which bears it is pure. 'Power corrupts and absolute power corrupts absolutely'. This is why the focus of shamans and healers is always to return their patients to balance, *not to improve them or make them 'better'.*

Relating this to the idea of flow I could see that over the last few years I had come to a place of easy relationship with life, a state of grace where I was happy and had all that I needed, but this had also made me complacent and unaware of the problems of others around me who were not in the same position. I was concerned for the difficulties of my friends, Gail and her boyfriend, for example; I sympathised with them, I gave them money when they needed it, never expecting it back (which is just as well since I never got it back) but I couldn't identify *or connect with them at a heart level because I just didn't recognise their problems beyond offering a material solution. Without meaning to I had, as Salvia warned me, 'got above my station'.*

San Pedro wanted me to experience the effect of this from Jane's point of view. Her comment as she left was that she felt dependent on me - 'owned' - and that she didn't want to become 'a shell'. From a literal perspective it was ludicrous. How could she not feel dependent when she had organised her life that way? From an emotional perspective however I felt what it was like now to be in her position. It made me uncomfortable too and I understood how words and gestures have power, how anything I did or said could have been interpreted (or misinterpreted) when seen or heard from the perspective of someone who felt powerless to begin with.

Little things: I had offered to buy her driving lessons and a car, thinking it might give her more independence and freedom, but she never acted on it and I never really knew why. I understood now that it would not have given her the true freedom she wanted because it would all still have come from me. For it to be meaningful she would have had to buy those things herself – but she had no money. Catch 22.

I felt her frustration. She could only ever be free within her own paradigm of freedom – by working as a volunteer at a healing Centre for example, where she was still dependent on others to feed and house her but could justify it with a few hours of service a day. In such an environment she might even believe that she was giving to others. In our marriage, on the other hand, nothing was asked of her and she had nothing to give, so there was no way around the truth. For someone who needed freedom so badly, she must have felt trapped; 'owned' as she put it. Even a meal out became another debt she could never repay and, on some level, she must have resented it. Now that I saw it, there was more that I could have done, but I hadn't understood how she felt until now.

The lesson in this for me was one of humility and to learn it, it looked like I would have to lose everything – a karmic turnaround where I became her for a while, with nothing to my name – and only earn it back by 'cleaning up my act'. Certainly, I was not in the flow of anything anymore.

Once I was a god
And like a god I died
Jack Parsons, scientist, poet and OTO magician

To achieve that state of grace again I was going to have to work my way back into God's good books and, next time, take care to handle the power it gave me and never lose sight of my emotional impact on others. Ironically (or perhaps not, since this is all about balance) it was a lesson I received from the Devil. Even 'Satan' is an ally sometimes.

Extract from my journal during the San Pedro mountain diet

Ten ribs. The ten-ribbed cactus raises the vibration of the body to a higher level. According to Michael it provides 'a good platform to connect with the Creator... [its affirmation would be]: "I am co-creating with God".'

In my musings about freewill and what choices we really have I had come to two paradoxical and seemingly contradictory conclusions: that 'our history acts as our gravity' and the stories we have woven from it control our actions and reactions in the world; that our thoughts and behaviours are subtly and unconsciously determined by factors beyond our awareness and therefore beyond our control – and that for all this we still make choices. Nothing can truly be known – that is one of the frustrations of life: like those experiments of quantum physicists who seek the law of everything but find that their own presence in the experiment determines the outcome; that light is a particle *or* a wave depending on how we look at it but since *we are looking* it can never be both and we can therefore never really know *light*, or that Schrodinger's cat is both alive and dead inside its box of poison gas and it is *we* who free it or kill it when we open the box to check its state. Faced with such knowledge we can get lost in the mystery and contradiction of life and fall into despair at having so little control over our fates – or into optimism at our mastery and power to create worlds.

The effect of the ten-rib is to point us in the direction of the latter: to give us a focus on power and to soothe us in the face of uncertainty; to reassure us that life is an adventure and that its ups and downs, given a long enough timewave, will all balance out. Either that or (and) we die, so what does it matter anyway? *Life* is the point of living.

SALVIA TEACHINGS

In September I was joined on the diet by a young man from America who had asked for a private healing retreat because of relationship issues he was facing and feelings of anxiety and depression as a result. He had broken up a little while ago with a woman he loved but who was unwilling or unable to commit to their relationship, even though she loved him too. Eventually and almost inevitably, he said, she had cheated on him and returned to her life of drugs and parties. He didn't know what to believe any more and felt lost and anxious.

The similarities to my own situation were obvious and this, I am sure, is never by accident but deliberate on the part of the universe. It is why shamans are called wounded healers – we are not expected to be perfect human beings, fully evolved and trauma-free; on the contrary, we are supposed to know pain so we can heal. As the Lakota Sioux shaman, John Lame Deer, put it: 'A medicine man shouldn't be a saint. He should experience and feel all the ups and downs, all the despair and joy, the magic and the reality, the courage and fear of his people. He should be able to sink as low as a bug and soar like an eagle. You have to be God *and* the Devil, both of them. Being a good medicine man means being right in the midst of the turmoil not shielding yourself from it.' The only real difference between a 'healer' and a 'client' is that we explore our suffering and learn as we go through it so we can heal our sickness and teach others what worked for us.

We decided on a Salvia diet for John, one I would do with him. It would be my second with this strange plant which opens doors to other dimensions, to a new form of engagement with what we take to be 'reality', and increases our powers of precognition and the ability to see into the souls of others.

There is little point in going into all that this second diet revealed to me or to John because that story is told in my book *Shamanic Quest for the Spirit of Salvia*, along with the findings of subsequent workshops where Salvia was smoked. It was during this diet, however, that I finally met the spirit of Salvia, the essence and intelligence of the plant which had eluded me before, and that is worth mentioning because her nature and form were anything but expected.

Salvia is referred to by shamans in terms which invoke a sense of the Virgin Mary – *La Pastora* (The Shepherdess), *hojas de Maria* (the leaves of Mary), *ska* (or *xka*) *Maria* (Mary's plant) – and create an image of a supportive, caring mother figure. The anthropologists who have studied Mazatec usage of Salvia have therefore made an association between the qualities of the plant and the virginal Holy Mother, but this may be a fundamental – and profound – error. The clue to this comes from Albert Hoffman who remarks in his book *LSD: My Problem Child* on a ceremony he attended in Mexico where Salvia was handed to him by a young girl, a virgin dressed in white. From this we get an idea that it is the *ceremonial attendant*, the shaman's assistant, who is expected to be pure so that she may handle the plant and leave it untainted rather than Salvia itself because, in my experience, the plant is anything but virginal or motherly.

My encounter with Salvia came midway through the diet on a night when John and I drank Ayahuasca to connect with its spirit.

First I was shown the birth of ska Maria. Her mother was a bride of God, a nun – but unlike any other. She stood, open-robed and naked before a wooden altar entwined with snakes, on fire from the candles which sat upon it, a mirror recessed into an arch above it reflecting flame into the room and casting a crazy impassioned glow onto the whitewashed, dirty and peeling walls in the rundown church where she stood. She was holding a bottle of mescal in her right hand and others littered the floor. She was drunk and reeling, laughing at God – and giving birth. A cold steel chain around her waist dangled down between the lips of her vagina and attached to it was a human skull flecked with brass, copper and bronze.

The stone floor between her legs opened to reveal a pit into which the skull was lowered. The same flames illuminated it, as if the skull was being dropped into Hell, and at its centre stood a large black cauldron of bubbling ice where the skull was finally immersed. When it was raised from the icy waters it had been transformed into a human girl-child but one from which owl feathers also grew, and this was ska Maria.

A slut-nun with a mescal flask
in a Mexican brothel-church
birthed you ska Maria
before an altar of snakes and flame...
A skull-baby boiled in permafrost,
a daemon/demon owl-child,
dark-haired, pale and naked,
spitting smoke and holy water

My image of The Shepherdess had nothing virginal about it. Instead, it was holy-unholy, Catholic-profane, madness and wisdom. Born of a skull and coming from grief, she carried life and hope inside her. A paradox. A girl-child becoming an owl-child, the guardian of curanderos.

Her image was reminiscent of Santa Muerte, the saint venerated in Mexico whose name translates as "Holy Death" or "Saint Death", although she is referred to by other names too, including Señora de las Sombras (Lady of the Shadows), Señora Negra (Black Lady), Señora Blanca (White Lady), Niña Santa (Holy Girl) and La Flaca (The Skinny One). Santa Muerte appears in a long robe which covers her skeletal figure, with a scythe in her right hand and a globe in the left. The scythe symbolises the cutting away of negative energies or influences and, as a harvesting tool, represents hope and prosperity. But it can also mean death, the moment at which the silver thread is cut. The globe represents the Land of the Dead and can be seen as a tomb to which we all return. Having the world in her hand also means power.

Other objects that can appear with her include scales, an hourglass, an owl and an oil lamp. The scales allude to equity, justice and impartiality as well as divine will. The hourglass denotes her relationship with time and suggests our short stay on Earth as well as the knowledge that death is not the end but the beginning of something new as the hourglass can be turned over to start again. The owl symbolises Santa Muerte's ability to navigate the darkness and also her wisdom. The lamp is for the power of the soul to light our way through the darkness of ignorance.

An icaro began to form itself from this image. Melancholy and plaintive, it sounded like a lullaby or a song of mourning for all the sadness in the world, for all that John and Jane and I had lost and for all that everyone loses and gains in reaching out to another, in being part of the human journey.

When you were born the stars hung sickly,
your three wise men were uninspired
Your mother's voice sang too thickly
lullabies of smoke and wine...

Salvia: La Pastora
Ska Maria: Salvia

Next I found myself in a dark wood and the grown child, a brunette standing on a low rock, was looking down at me while leaves and shooting stars skittered across a midnight sky. She was earthy, primal, elemental. She was holding the skull and chain which had been her placenta, swinging it above me like the pendulum of a clock. The message was 'Focus on what's important; there is no time...' Salvia speaks in double meanings and paradox. In this case the message that 'there is no time' could be taken in two ways: that we are running out of time or, more literally, that time does not exist. Though they seem to oppose each other, within the vision both statements felt true and not at all contradictory. I had the sense that she herself was between time and beyond life and death but embodying both in the symbol of the skull-baby chain-placenta.

There was an air of sadness about her too, as if she also had wounds and was trapped by the role she had taken on. It made me want to hold and protect her and, as I thought that, the wind blew her long white dress against her, revealing the tight body of a young woman naked beneath silk. It was a sexless sexuality though - although it felt like temptation or a promise: that man can have sex with the gods again as we once did in forests like these - but I had no doubt that she would be wild, that making love with her would be a dissolution of the soul.

I told her that it was a seductress not a Goddess
Howard Alltounian, in a warning to his wife, Marcia Moore, about Ketamine (similar in effect to Salvia), just before her Ketamine-related death

She was a shapeshifter too and in my vision took many forms, all of them fleeting; just enough to give a sense of her as an infant, a crone, a grinning corpse; all things at once – just as I had seen my wife while making love on our Andean mountain. All of her many faces were in some way impure or perverse. The Living Tao.

The path into light seems dark...
True power seems weak...
True purity seems tarnished...
True clarity seems obscure...
The greatest love seems indifferent

And that was ska Maria: protective, direct and very matter-of-fact. It had taken me more than a year, two Salvia diets, two continents, and many pipes of salvinorin but I had finally met The Shepherdess. That is the initiation, what she expects from us and what we must be prepared to give. She can be elusive and shy as the shamans say but she is also fascinating, demanding, beautiful, unflinchingly honest, sad-eyed, crazy and very, very dangerous.

Having met the spirit of Salvia she began to teach me. The lessons she has to impart are in many ways similar to those of San Pedro although her style is wholly different. Again, there is little point in going into all of these here as that story is told in my book on Salvia but it is worth mentioning some of them since so little is known about this plant or its purpose.

Augury: Salvia is a plant of divination and there were a few occasions during the diet when I did get a sense of the future, although the circumstances were sometimes more immediate, mundane and 'earthy' than matters of great spiritual consequence. One was when I had driven to town to pick up supplies for John and I and took a few minutes to sit and relax in the park. In fact I couldn't relax at all because my attention, for no apparent reason, was continually drawn to my car instead of my surroundings. Twenty minutes later I returned to it and discovered that I had been given a parking ticket, even though my eyes had been on it all the time so I had no idea where the parking officer came from. It seemed to me that through hints of foreboding Salvia had alerted me to something that was about to happen, just as it had in the week before the wedding I had attended with Jane. There is also another meaning to the word divination however which stems from its linguistic origin *divinare* ("to be inspired by a god") which may be closer to the truth with Salvia: that the ally gives us to power to become 'divine-rs' – more aware of our divinity as creators of reality so we can rise above our limitations. Perhaps the plant is not literally (or only) about foretelling the future therefore, but a means of connecting with or knowing 'the mind of God', as Ronolfo described it when he visited my rainforest Centre during the first Salvia diet. More alarmingly even than *seeing* the future, what this means is that we *generate* that future through our thoughts and the attention we give to specifics. In my case, perhaps I had somehow *willed* that parking ticket into existence, or the loss of my wife, by even unconsciously allowing those possibilities. We need to be very, very careful then about how we use our minds because thoughts become real.

Identity. Who am I? Who are you? These are common questions during encounters with Salvia and San Pedro. (In fact, almost all of my later ceremonial participants have used the word "Who" in the context of a statement or question relating to identity after they had smoked Salvia with me). It is one of the most important questions we can ask: Who do I *think* I am? Beyond age, roles, life experiences, how others perceive me or I perceive myself; beyond principles, pride and patterns - knowing that only love is real and my time on Earth is finite - how do I want to live? In love or fear? Choose the former and anything is possible; choose the latter and we limit ourselves.

And, after all, what is personal history but a dream?
Ram Dass, philosopher-poet

If we clarify our identity we might also see the future more clearly and diviner's sage may live up to its name because if we have a greater sense of ourselves and know where our beliefs and patterns come from and lead us to, we can predict their outcomes as well and then do something to change them. Knowing the future by knowing ourselves is a different sense again of the word divination but it may be more helpful than augury because it offers us a choice not just a destination.

Becoming Objects. There are various accounts with Salvia of people losing their boundaries, just as I had done during the diet in Peru and subsequently in Spain, experiencing consciousness from the perspective of wheels, bricks, pavements, bedspreads and other non-human objects. In the language of Salvia there is a message for us in *what* we become which may also help us answer the 'Who am I?' question. One of my later participants had a difficult childhood for example, with parents who belittled her and could never provide the closeness or love that she needed. Smoking Salvia, she became wallpaper stuck to the floor in her parents' house and was trampled all over by them. It is an obvious metaphor for her childhood experience but it is also qualitatively different from a brick in a wall or chewing gum stuck to a wheel. Jane saw only endings in the form of a machine which devoured landscapes and all of the life they contained, and her *grande finale* was to leave Spain and turn her back on all that she loved. By knowing and changing ourselves however we can know and change the future – *if* we wish.

Parallel Universes and Other Dimensions. Salvia is an interdimensional plant which can take us to other worlds. One of my participants, in his Salvia vision, talked about passing through 'interdimensional gateways' opened up by the sage. Others saw reality being 'unzipped' or experienced waves or walls of other realities advancing towards them in a way which felt so real and inexorable that it was more than just a change in perception or consciousness.

We live as film, on a film, the skin of a bubble. What is real lives behind, waiting to push through, swallow us up, reclaim us.
It may not be nice
Theodore Roszak, *Flicker*

It is interesting in this respect to observe the speed of adoption as teachers of the three plants I have worked with most closely – Ayahuasca, San Pedro and Salvia - and to consider where their consciousnesses may be taking us. There has been a growing awareness of Ayahuasca since the 1950s for example but it has taken until now, 60 years or so later, for the plant to become well-known. San Pedro first came to popular attention in the 1980s and it has taken just 30 years for it to become a plant of interest for contemporary shamans and seekers. Salvia meanwhile began to come to prominence in the 1990s but has now been more widely adopted than both, at least as a recreational drug, and that has taken just 20 years.

As a timeline of recent human history then, we became aware of Ayahuasca, the 'plant of the universe', at the time of the space race. It took us to the moon. San Pedro brought us back to Earth and was there at the beginning of the environmental movement. It taught us to care for our planet. Salvia is now leading us away from the Earth and even the known universe. It is fascinating to speculate what its agenda may be at this point in history, as the old theories of science, based on limitations (such as Newtonian physics and Einstein's contention that nothing can move faster than light), are replaced by new ideas based on quantum probabilities. Things are moving faster and in new directions, maybe even to new dimensions, and the plants have been guiding us from the start.

We are forced to confront the idea of other dimensions. It is the only theory which has been able to unify all the laws of physics
Michio Kaku, quantum physicist and hyperspace theorist

Time Travel. Salvia is the Mistress of Time. Daniel Siebert, who first extracted salvinorin from Salvia, referred during his trip with it to the resurfacing of 'past memories, such as revisiting places from childhood'. But 'memory' is not a strong enough word. In his first experiment for example he found himself in his grandparents' living room furnished as it was when he was a child. As he remarks, 'This *was* the real world, *not a memory or a vision.* I was *really* there and it was all just as solid as the room I'm sitting in now... all the points of time in my personal history coexisted. One did not precede the next. Apparently, had I so willed it, I could return to any point in my life and really be there because it was actually happening right now.'

During my first journeys with Salvia I was also taken back to my childhood. I was with my mother in streets I knew 40 years ago. I can't say that these were *memories* though because the events that took place there were not recollections of things I *know* to have happened or significant enough to have been 'issues' which I have repressed. To me, as for Seibert, they were entirely real and happening.

It felt as if Salvia was giving me an opportunity to revisit the past and not exactly relive it but change my view of it and consequently change the future and present by seeing it from a new perspective and adopting new beliefs and behaviours as a consequence. In other words, these were not memories in the way we understand them but a form of time travel: dimensional shifts to a place where, as the scientist Michael Talbot expressed it in his book *The Holographic Universe,* the universe had 'bifurcated' and I had been able to take another of its paths which I had not explored then, simply by perceiving my childhood(s) differently.

Overlapping Realities. 'Every object in my life was also me; like our realities were interchangeable'. That was my experience in Peru and it was apparent again during my diet in Spain: that a sort of pre-birth agreement had been made between me and everything I encountered, even something as seemingly random and insignificant as a brick, a leaf or a bus stop. All of it was conscious and aware and shared a purpose and intelligence with me. Everything therefore has meaning and information for us because whatever shares its existence with us *is* us. It was no accident then that fate had brought Jane and I together because, just as I felt it in Cusco when we were first in love 'she was me or, rather, we were each other'. It was no accident either that our relationship became what it was or ended as it did. Given who we were and the choices we made it could have been no other way. As La Bruja said, we 'were brought together for a good reason'. The important thing is to understand why and to learn from it so we make better choices next time.

Zen. Like San Pedro, but again in a different way, Salvia evokes a Zen sensation – the experience of paradox in the union of opposites: that the void may also be full, that nothing may also be something.

Zen is a word I often hear used by people when they try to explain their Salvia experiences. One workshop participant described his journey with it as 'like a Zen meditation on the "formless field of benefaction"'. Another remarked that 'It felt very Zen - an experience of The Void which was also completely full - a paradox which seemed to be the very essence of Zen... myself and 'God' or 'spirit' were one'. Perhaps for these reasons Salvia might be a useful aid to meditation on the core questions at the heart of our religions. Certainly it is a philosopher's plant, enabling us not just to hear and ponder a koan in our search for enlightenment but to *experience* and *live* it.

Love and Karma. Salvia can feel emotionless, straightforward and direct. J D Arthur in his book on the subject calls it 'almost without feeling'. The passing of information seems sterile and clinical; cold even, and certainly very different to the teachings of San Pedro (fatherly and protective) or Ayahuasca (motherly and supportive). During his diet with it John remarked that 'I didn't feel any personality to Salvia except something metallic not flesh... like pure mathematics with an organic feel'. What is also significant, however, when we return from our journeys into SalviaWorld where we encounter the void and experience no-love and no-thing-ness, is the equal-and-opposite realisation that love is not just significant, *it is all we have*, all that can save us, all that is real, and all that makes us unique as a species. It is part of the Salvia paradox: to be in the place of no-love is to know the importance of true love on our return.

This has ties to another Salvia concept, that of overlapping realities: that we are connected to everything we experience and need therefore to act in an appropriate way towards everyone and everything we encounter *because it is us*. To remain in balance we must be as neutral as Salvia herself; to burn karma or accumulate merit we must behave impeccably and *with Dignity* (another San Pedro message) because if we relate to life in a way which is not in the spirit of love we will attract those same unloving things to ourselves. This is the meaning of karma: that whatever energy we put into the world or whatever form our behaviour takes towards others is exactly and in equal measure what we will get back from them so that we experience life from all perspectives. Coldness begets coldness and anger follows from anger until finally in our quest for salvation we *have* to understand that love is all that matters.

APHORISMS, INSIGHTS AND MUSINGS

My reflections from this San Pedro diet and the themes that ran through it are summarised here. They are personal, of course, given the 'set and setting'[40], but perhaps they are more than that.

Soulmates, love and healing. The world is obsessed with soulmates. We all want to find 'The One' – that special person who completes us. But completes us how? That is a question rarely asked. As San Pedro explained it, the essence of a soulmate relationship is its intensity and the issues it raises because of the passion it generates. The lovers may come together because they have mutual and complementary wounds, most of them stemming from childhood – a desire for closeness, for example, combined with a need to escape.[41] The meeting of soulmates provides the opportunity for an awakening. Because it takes place in love, a healing possibility is provided for issues and their origins to be unveiled and dealt with, each of the lovers reflecting the other and supporting their partner to do so. But both lovers must first acknowledge and accept that they *have* issues, be courageous enough to face them, and honour the promises they made to each other when they embarked on that journey together.

The art of the healer. San Pedro was honest with me from the start. He knew, when I began my apprenticeship, that I had come to learn about love and healing and he told me that he would be showing me a new perspective on this because it is one thing to sit on a beautiful mountain with a woman you love and drink San Pedro on a clear and sunny day and to know without doubt that God exists, that everything is sacred and we are blessed; it is another to hold onto love when your soul is shattered and you feel like God has abandoned you. It is easier then to retreat into fear and anger but love is the warrior's challenge and, as San Pedro expressed it: 'No warrior is ever made without a war to be part of'. That war takes place in our hearts and the battleground is us.

The greatest skill of a healer then is not *what they know* or the techniques they have learned but *who they are* and how they have chosen to live: in love rather than fear. Their courage in this and the faith they hold on to can then be passed to others and that is how healing results: in the certainty that everything is just as it should be, and that, no matter how dark *this* moment may be, across the journey of a lifetime things *will* work out as we intend them.

Circles. Everything wants to be a circle – a process in flow which will naturally complete itself if we allow it. The body, the emotions, the circles of the mind and the spiritual quest we are on will all bring us back to where we began, wiser and more powerful for having made the journey.

Problems begin when we arrest the flow because then we trap ourselves in an event that happened years ago, repeating the same moves endlessly because we have decided that we will always be the person who suffered then. When we cling to a moment like this another process begins: *we struggle,* trying to hold on to who we were or what has gone while knowing that something new has taken place. This tension between opposites is the origin of suffering. The solution is to let go and experience that suffering fully instead of avoiding it, and to learn from it instead of denying it or blaming somebody else for our pain. *When it hurts, it hurts.* To deny a part of our experience is to deny a part of our lives and the journey we are on - and if we do that then the universe will send us the same lesson again, in increasing volume, until we finally get the message. First the spirits whisper, then they roar.

Reflecting on our lives in this way is called 'taking an inventory'. When I made mine I was looking for a first cause, an origin point in my life where my own pattern in relationships might have begun. The plants showed me an image I had first seen back in the jungle while working with Salvia. It seemed insignificant then: a street scene where I was being led as a child along a road by my mother who was pulling me by the hand towards an unknown destination. I had not understood the message then because the image itself seemed trivial. But then I remembered something from a few years later: a time when I got into trouble at school and my father was called to a conference with the head teacher who wanted to expel me. Explaining my behaviour to him, my father had described me as 'easily led' by others.

In my ghost-garden now, I sensed it was true. I have often thrown myself into the dreams of others, wanting not just to help them realise their potential but doing much of the work for them. It was how I had come to Spain in the first place. Some years ago my friends Gail, Doris and I had decided to become business partners and buy a house here where we could run workshops and offer ceremonies. The Hummingbird was the result. Doris and I were putting in cash but Gail would have to take out a Spanish mortgage for her share. I knew from the start that would be a problem since she would have difficulty getting a job in Spain to repay it (she didn't even speak Spanish) but Doris did not want us to invest without Gail and so, trying to make the dream a reality for everyone, I agreed to go along with it. The outcome was that *I* ended up giving Gail a job for the next two years as a housekeeper on my workshops in Spain - which meant that when I began my apprenticeship in Peru she had no income of her own and had to return to England, pulling out of the Centre and leaving Doris and I to pick up her mortgage.

As for Doris, she rarely visited Spain and ran just a few workshops of her own which attracted hardly any interest. I was left to keep the place afloat. She then decided that she didn't want to be involved in the Centre at all and used Gail's departure as an excuse to abandon it too. The implications of this for me now were that I was left alone on the mountain, responsible for everything, although Doris still expected the first share of any money we made.

And then there was Jane. She wanted excitement, travel and adventure so I gave her Iquitos and the jungle, Cusco and the mountains, Spain, the plants, and a home she loved. She went back instead to all that she said she *didn't* want.

> *I gave you everything you ever wanted.*
> *It wasn't what you wanted*
> Paul Hewson, musician

The common theme in all these scenarios – other people's dramas aside – was *me*. How did I keep getting into these situations? By trying too hard to create the dreams of others - to the extent that they had nothing left for themselves to dream.

Maybe a dream should just stay a dream for some people. I will not, in any case, involve myself with others in the same way again and I watch myself now whenever I sense this motif arising in me of being 'easily led' into new situations, so I understand what my own motivations are and what needs in me they are signalling.

Quantum Therapy says something similar to this shamanic philosophy of being-in-flow. In QT, which borrows its ideas from the 'new physics' of quantum theory, a person is seen as a 'particle' with a location and a 'wave' with momentum simultaneously. 'Sometimes there is too much "particle"' says Karl Jansen[42], 'such as when a person is "frozen" with shock, hurt, anger, hate and resentment. Healing and letting go of negative emotions may involve "melting", which itself involves an image of motion: the wave'. One way of achieving this is through the practice of forgiveness which frees us from attachment to a single event and puts us back in flow, allowing the circle to complete itself. 'Thus, the forgiveness is practiced for the benefit of *the person doing the forgiving* rather than out of altruism'.

Addiction. Elizabeth's counselling about love and addiction and James' labels had been useful at first, giving me a reference point by which to understand the processes in my relationship, but ultimately I threw them away. Shamans work without labels. How can love ever really be a 'condition' to be 'treated'? *It is what it is* - although the nature of that love and how we express it may tell us a lot about ourselves.

Doris occurred to me, for example, as a case of addiction which would not even be recognised, although her recent actions would fit the definition we have of it as 'a persistent, compulsive dependence on a behaviour or substance' which is damaging to ourselves and/or others.

The reason for her lack of involvement in our Centre and her departure from it was, she said, because her daughters had started to have children of their own and she wanted to be in England with them. That is understandable and reasonable but a grandmother's doting can become obsessive too, in Doris' case to the extent that she was prepared to throw her own dreams away and allow her business to die. I knew from what she had told me that marriage and motherhood had been difficult for her and it was obvious to me (and, to some extent, her) that her obsession with family now was meant to assuage guilt and salve wounds and she was prepared to sacrifice herself and her identity to it. But society does not recognise such manoeuvres as sickness or disapprove of besotted grandmothers any more than it does workaholics or gym junkies because they are regarded at worst as harmless eccentrics, although any obsession can be damaging.

The word 'addiction' seemed meaningless then because maybe we are all in some way addicted and 'easily led' by our patterns and programmes. If we are aware of them, however, what our more habitual behaviours and our default judgements and feelings provide us with is an opportunity to see and change *any* aspect of ourselves which doesn't serve us by using it to explore what our souls are really trying to tell us: in Doris' case that we can let go of guilt or make amends in a more positive and constructive way instead of nailing ourselves to a cross.

Grief. The pioneer in our understanding of grief is Elisabeth Kübler-Ross, who lists the stages of grieving as *denial* (a conscious or unconscious refusal to accept the reality of a situation), *anger* (with oneself or somebody else; the desire to make someone responsible for the situation you find yourself in), *bargaining* (negotiation, often with a 'higher power', for a positive change in circumstances), *depression* (feelings of sadness, regret or uncertainty) and finally *acceptance* (coming to terms with events and moving on). These stages are not always linear or the same for everyone. It seemed to me, for example, that Jane had dived straight into anger and stayed there before arriving seamlessly at acceptance ('So much for that') whereas my own mood was one of sadness, regret and uncertainty.

San Pedro had different ideas about grief however and a new suggestion for how to deal with it. His was a three-stage process based more on gratitude than on grieving: 'Be grateful for what you had, grateful for what was lost and grateful for what remains'.

I preferred his way of looking at things. Gratitude means that we focus on beauty, positivity and the good things we have instead of imagining that happiness can only be found in the past or in one person or thing. *Active* gratitude became my daily practice. I was grateful for everything I had experienced with Jane and for all that we shared in Spain and Peru. But I was also grateful for her departure and the lessons it taught me. And I was grateful for what I had now: the freedom to explore the world without her, running from nothing and towards everything.

We may all in some way be locked into our patterns, addicted to our pain and still reliving our childhoods but we are also the ones who give meaning to life and it can be any meaning we wish.

Simplicity. Some years ago I decided that I wanted to simplify my life, but I didn't even know what that meant. It is not until you spend time in the jungle without electricity or running water, or on a mountain in Spain, that you realise how little you actually need: just sunlight, fresh air and nature, and the food you pull from the soil. Healing is the same. I have often watched La Bruja sit quietly with someone who is going through a difficult time in ceremony and simply listen to their story. I joke with her now about what I call her 'yoghurt healings' after I watched her sit with a man who had lost faith in God and himself, who screamed for an hour and cried for his life while she calmly ate yoghurt and listened, occasionally wiping away the negative energy as it left him, sometimes offering advice about how he could change, but mostly just listening. And sometimes that is enough.

I have done it myself in San Pedro ceremonies, and often these healings are the most moving. I sat with a man in Peru who needed to re-experience the death of his mother, and listened while we smoked a Mapacho together, knowing that I could do nothing to ease his pain because his grief needed to be felt. But at least I could share the moment with him as he honoured his pain. We can be witnesses for each other and through that we witness ourselves.

Principles. Ideals are stars, guiding us towards a new destination. Even standards have value because they give us balance and maintain what is current. But principles are anchors dragging us backwards into our past, to the time when we first arrived at them, and to the painful experiences which are often at their centre and gave rise to them. As such they do little except link our present to what is long gone and hold us trapped in ancient history. They have no place in our healing or evolution.

Becoming open and vulnerable. This had been Jane's intention and her genuine healing quest, one that I had supported but never interfered with or tried to direct. The more I think about it now though the less convinced I am by her method since, as I observed it, the words were often spoken and her desire expressed but little seemed to change.

To try to understand why, I returned to the notion of opposites and what the Tao has to teach us: 'True power *seems* weak'. In other words, our outward appearance is the mirror of our internal state. By projecting her hard and defended Jungle Jane persona therefore, she was on some level acknowledging to herself and the world that she was *already* vulnerable and afraid. That is why people put up barriers in the first place: to protect the soft spots at their centre.

This being the case, the more strategic healing approach if we wish to become (outwardly) softer is to work on the core of ourselves and make that more solid – not tough and inflexible or rigid and fixed but more filled with power and fluidity; to create ideals instead of principles for ourselves and practices which allow us to live them. Since the human condition is a homeostatic one, seeking balance, the effect is to *make us* more open because we are no longer afraid of the world.

In the end, Jane wrote that her work with the plants now seemed like a 'raw joke' to her so I assume that she abandoned her quest for softness. Plant work is not for everyone. It can be as challenging as it is liberating. But by approaching our issues with a clear and effective method we stand more chance of finding the breakthrough that we are looking for.

Judgements. When we judge someone else we accuse ourselves and stand naked before the world, revealing our own wounds and the quality of our souls. The tendency when we are judged, that is, is to judge back and often we find a legitimate reason to do so: the same reason that we are being judged in the first place. The pot almost always calls the kettle black because the faults that we see in another are our own. A he-says-she-says battle follows where, amusingly and ridiculously, we openly accuse ourselves more than each other: the 'victim' becomes the 'perpetrator' and then the 'victim' again, *ad nauseum.* Neither party can win because they are actually fighting themselves.

The question we must ask, then, is do we *really* want to solve the problem and restore balance or are we more interested in victory and revenge, even if it perpetuates our own suffering? The answer is to love more, not less. This is San Pedro's philosophy. It is also the origin of the Christian idea of turning the other cheek. It was illustrated for me by a man I met during a plant workshop who is a promoter for musicians and artists. Martin's posters were often torn down by his rivals so they could promote their own bands instead. His response was not to tear theirs down in return but to ask if he could help them by putting their posters up when he put up his own. He also invited them free of charge to the events he staged. With no energy to fuel it the 'battle of the bands' ended and what could have turned into a turf war became friendships, with rewards for all, including the bands and their audiences.

Another example of Martin's ability to act counter-intuitively, the opposite of what our wounds and patterns might lead us to, was his behaviour towards his father. A dogmatic and fundamentalist preacher Martin's father abandoned him when he was young and sent him to live with another family because he was embarrassed by his son's 'unchristian' (hippy) attitudes, his work as a musician and his interest in new states of consciousness. He didn't speak to his son for years and prevented his wife from having a relationship with him either. Martin decided not to resent his father or judge him in return but one day instead he set up his musical equipment in his father's church and when his father came in Martin told him to sit down and listen. He then played him some of his songs. When he finished his father and he began to talk, not about the problems in their relationship but about the transformative power of music. Having once condemned his son as a 'sinner' and told him he would go to Hell because of the music he played, his father has now introduced the same music as part of his pastoral duties in outreach programmes for young people.

Acting counter-intuitively and going against our programmes may well be the key to love.

Questions. We waste so much of our lives looking for answers - our sciences and societies are built on it – without thinking that there are none to find or that every one we arrive at simply raises more questions. We were content once, for example, to believe that the world was built of atoms; now we know that the world is made of energy, but the planet didn't stop turning all the time we were 'wrong'. Eventually we will discover that the world is created from nothing but thoughts and choices. It is the questions not the answers that matter, because the moment we stop asking we stagnate and pin everything down to laws that even our gods must follow and then we have no more options. The answer-filled world is a boring place where, like lab rats, we run our mazes for familiar rewards, knowing that the outcomes and pay-offs are always the same. Questions keep us alive; they keep us in the mystery; they allow us to evolve, to make new choices and to learn from the fluidity of life. But they must be asked without any expectation of, or desire for, an answer, just for the joy of asking them.

Impermanence and change. Nothing lasts. But nothing is ever lost if we learn how to love and share it. 'What I give to others I give to myself. What I don't give to others I lose.'[43]

Jane died almost exactly a year to the day of her departure from Spain. San Pedro had told me to 'keep the door open for her', which I did, never expecting her to walk back through it and not wanting her to now either, not as what she had become.

But that wasn't the point – *she* wasn't the point – because I wasn't working for her anymore. I kept the door open – *fumar y agua* - in my heart and mind for a year, because I had promised her and San Pedro I would and I was determined to act from love and live the lessons of the plants. *A promise is a part of the soul.*

During that year she would enter my dreams, always dressed the same and always in the same environment: a sort of nowhere place between worlds, but pleasant enough. She looked content with the life she had made until a final dream in which I found her in her familiar environment but face-down and lifeless, and then the dreams of her ended.

The last one arrived on June 29: Saint Peter's Day. After that I never saw her again. Jane was gone forever. Long live JJ.

BODGE & BODGE

The branches of all trees hold the same moon
Ejo Takata, Zen Master

2011. August/September – July 2012

A few weeks after I took off my wedding ring I met Lily. We found each other in Spain although she was originally from England and returned there with me when I moved back to the UK in October. Neither of us was looking for a relationship and, in the small Spanish-Catholic town of Montefrio and its scarcely-populated mountains, I never expected to find one with anyone even remotely 'on my wavelength'. But the spirits had other ideas.

We met by chance (if there is such a thing) but the similarities between her and Jane were unavoidable. Physically, she was about the same height and size, a year or so younger but roughly the same age. Same colour eyes, same hair. She was a masseuse and a tarot reader. She'd had similar experiences as well, travelled widely and explored herself, but from a calm place; interested in adventure and discovering new things, not trying to avoid the old ones. More remarkably still, she knew my (by now very ex-)wife and of all the places she could have lived in England, her house was a train stop away from Jane's sister. It was hard not to conclude that the plants have an agenda of their own and that some have a preference for working with a certain 'type' of woman, because Lily's interests are also Salvia and San Pedro.

And yet things were moving forward. After my discoveries on the diet and my promises to myself – about not entering the dreams of others, doing the work for them, or having another person dependent on me again – I was happy to discover that Lily had a home and career as well as ideas and interests of her own; that she could and would contribute. She also had a good relationship with her family and appeared – and still does appear – to have no issues with them or any baggage she is carrying with her. The more I got to know her the more I realised that she actually *was* independent and not just using the word.

England, on the other hand, was and is a disaster. With the single exception of America, which it longs to be and to which it defers on most of its political, social and economic decisions, Britain has to be the most fear-filled, conflict-ridden and competitive place on Earth, notwithstanding any of the 'third world' countries I have visited. Grey, overcast and dull, it is expensive to live here, you get little in return, and you are constantly harassed by official – and officious – threats and demands for more money. The houses are small, the gardens tiny, and compared to Spain it is so overcrowded that the natural environment is all but dead. In the last three or four years of living away from it I had forgotten how much I disliked the place and being back here now I could see where some of Jane's anger had come from.

She would have arrived back at the time of the riots, when British people, for a moment at least, made a stand against the greed of our bankers and the unjustness of our policing. The broken windows and houses on fire must have brought it home to her that up until now she *had* been living free – in all senses of the word – and had had the independence she left in order to gain. Now she was living in a box in a nowhere town, dependent on others again and trying to find a job during the worst recession in years. 'You took everything from me' is how she saw it, but I didn't make her choices. I heard from friends that within months of being back she was planning her next great escape to Canada and wanted to save badgers. Exit stage left (again), pursued by a bear (again).

But I had problems of my own. I got back to find that my house had been pretty much wrecked by the tenants I had let it to. They had flooded the basement, destroyed the roof, the boiler was broken and the shower was leaking so badly that a wall collapsed. Everything that was wrong had something to do with water, a not-so subtle reminder from San Pedro that I had to 'get my house in order', beginning with my emotional self and the relationships I was coming back to.

Lily and I began dieting together. In Spain, she had dieted Seaweed, drawn to it by an Ayahuasca vision, while I continued my work with San Pedro.

'Dance with me' were her first words to me. This lady takes having fun very seriously. She is a welcoming hostess spirit with a nurturing, protective side. Beauty, dance, music, love, lust, flamboyance are intrinsic to her nature. Seaweed appears to me as a slim, energetic emerald green lady with a velvet voice. Sometimes she dresses up for the occasion!

In terms of healing she is particularly good for "women's problems" such as menstruation and fertility issues, depression, a loss of joie de vivre, retrieving lost or repressed memories and regaining power. She is also a useful spirit for men who are very feminine, and she has a hermaphrodite aspect. Seaweed can also be called upon to bring wealth and abundance as she has access to the hidden treasure of the seven seas.

Extract from Lily's journal during her Seaweed diet

Now she wanted to diet Cacao, a healing food used by Mexico's pre-Olmec people from as early as 1750 BC. In Mayan mythology, the Plumed Serpent, Quetzalcoatl, gave mankind *kakaw* (Cacao) after humans were created from maize by the goddess Xmucane. A festival was held thereafter in April each year to honour Ek Chuah, the Cacao god, which included the sacrifice of a dog with Cacao-coloured markings, and offerings of feathers and incense. In a similar creation story, Quetzalcoatl discovered Cacao (*cacahuatl*: bitter water) in a mountain cave along with other sacred plants. The *Madrid Codex* depicts priests lancing their ears and covering Cacao with their blood as a sacrifice to the gods. The beverage was traditionally drunk only by men as it was believed to be toxic for women. That, however, was not going to stop Lily.

Both of her diets were food-based (rather than drinking the plants as a tea or smoking them, for example) since that was the advice given to her during Ayahuasca ceremonies (which was lucky for her as she loves food; something else she has in common with my ex). She had eaten Seaweed for a total of 14 days; with Cacao she chewed the nibs and used the powder in her food for 16 days. The outcome is always in the effectiveness of the results and while this is not a standard Amazonian way of proceeding, it produced useful information for Lily.

'I help people to forget their past so they can look forward to a more pleasurable future.'

Cacao has shown me many faces: the lover, the warrior, half beast/half man, a cuddly lovely being and a psychedelic Mayan God.

On a very fundamental level he is about Love. He offers qualities of optimism, enjoying the present whilst also moving forward, looking at all the possibilities available instead of limiting oneself, one's pleasures, psychic abilities and alertness. Cacao gives a strong sense of melting away sorrow and resistance so that you can completely surrender to the sensuous enjoyment of life. His warrior side gives a sense of power, physical prowess and fearlessness. His spirit has a strong connection with the heart so he could be useful for people with heart conditions.

Cacao played a major role in teaching the Mayans their knowledge of the cosmos. It is worth noting that the Aztecs and Mayans occasionally added Cacao to the psilocybin mushroom brews that were drunk during their ceremonies.

'You are a holy communion
A true food of the Gods
An irresistible seed of male sexual potency
To be scattered out into the world...'
Extract from Lily's journal during her Cacao diet

At New Year we made a *pago* together (sometimes called a *despacho*) – an Andean form of offering to the spirits where, paradoxically, we give away all of the things we most want in our lives, in the knowledge that the universe operates by reciprocity and we will receive these gifts back many times over. Into a parcel of Christmas wrapping paper (because life is beautiful and every day is Christmas!) we loaded chocolates, sugar and honey (for the sweet things in life), perfumes and oils (for love and sensuality), money and other goodies – everything that we wanted more of. I had made a similar one for Jane and burnt it on her behalf when I returned her soul to her in our garden during my San Pedro diet, hoping that through it she would find, well, whatever it is that she is really looking for. Lily and I took ours to my local beach and sat with it at midnight as the ships sounded their horns, smoking Mapachos and drinking champagne before giving the pago to the ocean so that the gods of the seas would carry our gifts out into the world. Then we returned to my house and began a new diet with Salvia – the first for her, the third for me.

We meditated for a while before we started, to see how the plant wanted us to work with it. In the past I had drunk the leaf tea and chewed and smoked the leaves as well as the extract; the classical Amazonian or Mexican ways of dieting the plant. This time I asked Salvia how *it* wanted to be dieted. It told me to fast for five days and eat nothing, while drinking the leaves in tequila. It seemed an unusual process, although my research into

Salvia had taught me that the Mazatec shamans who work with it have a different view of diets to those in the Amazon. On their diets, for example, beer is often allowed as it is not regarded as a spirit powerful enough to affect Salvia and during their ceremonies the ritual chewing of leaf quids may be followed by a glass of tequila. Certainly Salvia leaves in tequila is a curious taste (though not hugely unpleasant) – but not as extraordinary as some of the food combinations that Lily came up with when, having meditated on her diet in the same way as me, she was told to eat normally, more or less, but to add Salvia leaves to all of her food. Salvia spaghetti may have been tolerable, but Salvia blanc-mange? Thankfully, I never had to find out what that tasted like because I was fasting.

Salvia is a plant of divination and Lily is a tarot reader. I read cards too, although not in a standard way. My method of reading is to intuit the meanings of the symbols in the context of the question and my own or another person's life instead of following a guidebook procedure – a sort of 'psychomagic' approach. We started a daily practice of reading for each other throughout the diet, allowing the diviner's sage to enhance our insights by speaking through us. The results were often interesting, producing interpretations that I am sure I would not have arrived at alone.

Day 1

Today's 'theme' is about power and the feeling is one of sadness, something I am familiar with from previous Salvia diets, which always seem to start with a sense of melancholy and distance from the world. It is a plant of philosophers and poets, after all, so I suppose that's not too surprising.

The question arising – a familiar one again, with both Salvia and San Pedro - is 'Who am I?' In the context of today's theme what this means is that if we don't know who we are or what our ideals are we can give away a lot of power – even with good intent and a generous spirit, not because it is being 'stolen' from us or we are being 'used', but simply because we don't know our limits or boundaries and/or we don't ask for something in return.

What we do get back we have to recognise for what it is as well. We cannot expect to receive on our own terms, only in the ways that another person knows how to give, but if we don't understand ourselves or what those terms are, we may not know that we have received anything at all and our relationships with others become unbalanced. It comes down to knowing ourselves, what we are prepared to offer someone else, and communicating clearly what we need in return.

For Lily, the whole world has become green tinged and she sees images of spiders. Biologically, spiders are always hungry and so always trying to lure insects into their web in order to consume them. When we lack power we may do the same, calling others to us to fulfil a role that we require of them rather than relating to them in terms of who they are.

In Mexico it was believed that the creation of the world was assisted by Tocotl, the Spider God, who spun a hammock to hold up the Earth. The Mayans believe that after death the soul must wander the dark passages of the underworld until it meets a great river which it cannot cross on its own. Each soul can only get to the other side with the help of a spider person who spins a web raft and accompanies the dead soul across the river, linked in a spiritual bond so that each relies on the other until they reach the far side. And this too is the nature of love: getting someone safely to the other side.

I ask the cards for a prediction of the year ahead. I draw the Lover, the Hierophant and Fortitude. 'By learning how to reconcile the opposites in yourself and to allow them in other people, you will *gain strength in a loving not forceful way'. Like the spider, hungry for life, and the soul ready for death, the opposites cross the river together to arrive at a place of safety.*[44]

Day 2

Lily is pondering the 'Who am I question' today but Salvia tells her to 'Forget who you are'! There is a certain logic to that, I know, in terms of letting go of the past and the habits and patterns we have allowed to become our identities and our destinies, but that only gets us out of the past and into the present so the question still remains: Who am I now? *What are my ideals?*

The answer, according to Lily's Salvia is that 'Perversity is the way to enlightenment': stand everything on its head and turn it upside down, that's how you answer this question. I can believe that of Salvia too.

Day 3

I feel optimistic and good today; a real sense that things in my life are getting better. I had a dream last night of Salvia's home planet (nobody who smokes the extract believes it comes from Earth) as cold and icy, made of crystals that break apart and reform as she walks on them. I also had a sense that there is something beyond Salvia – a new plant ally – which is on its way here and has a new message for us. The modern world has only just discovered Salvia; are things really moving so quickly now that it is already time for another guide to aid our evolution?

Day 4

Woke up with the same optimism, then real Salvia trippiness kicked in – not the visuals but a feeling of not being anyone or anything, that nothing at all is real, with that slight edge of fear that Salvia sometimes brings as a consequence of this realisation, because the flipside of nothing being real is the knowledge that we create every-

thing, and that is a big responsibility. I felt like I had to be very, very careful in my interactions with Lily and others – even with thoughts and words – so as not to create anything carelessly or irresponsibly. The air around me was filled with thoughts from other people, from the world 'out there' and I was conscious that, with a word or a thought of my own, I could change them and have an impact on everything. Until I was absolutely clear in my own intentions, I knew that I had to still my mind and be quiet because after my work with San Pedro I know that thoughtforms are real and that much of our thinking is also based on habits not on clarity or intention. And after my experiences with Jane, I knew that I never again wanted to create anything that I didn't intend or invest faith in someone or something which is not genuine and real – 'shining from the heart' as San Pedro put it.

When Lily got up we did a Salvia leaf reading – a new form of divination we sort of invented on the spot – looking at the patterns that the leaves made on the surface of bath water just before I bathed in the plant, and interpreting the symbols in the designs. My question was about a trip to Mexico that Lily and I were planning; the same journey I had wanted to make with Jane in the summer she decided to leave, in search of Peyote, Salvia and new adventures. The information provided by the leaves was subtle; more of a feeling than a mechanical reading of their shapes on the water, but the sense of it was good: that a journey with Jane would have been marked by our usual intensity and probably have resulted in drama but with Lily it would be a real *exploration, without 'issues' being part of it.*

Even after my bath I was still tripping and panicky over the complexity and meaninglessness of life - and all the power I had over it. I asked Salvia what I should do about these feelings and she suggested I drink hot chocolate – practical and direct! I did and it immediately helped, grounding and calming me. Then I asked about all this power we have as human beings to change our own lives and others' - and the nature of reality itself - just by a thought or a gesture. This time San Pedro answered. 'Simple' he said. 'Think nice thoughts! And do something good for the world'.

Day 5

Lily and I smoked Salvia last night in a ceremony to bring the diet to a close. My intention was to ask for clarity on the new direction of my life and for information on where in the world I should be. I was pretty sure I didn't want to stay in England with all of its fears and depression and Lily and I had discussed moving back to Spain and re-opening my retreat Centre there. But that didn't feel right either, not with Doris interfering from a distance and Jane still haunting its grounds.

Salvia showed me landscapes. They were Spanish-looking and had Gaudi-esque structures on them, organic and made from salvaged materials and mud, like glorious village huts designed by a crazy artist. Waking this morning, I knew where it was: a valley in Spain fringed by the most amazing mountains – over 30 acres of countryside with natural springs and streams and trees with fruits of every kind; the perfect place to build a home like the ones I had seen. I suggested the idea to Lily and she agreed we should live there.
Extract from my San Pedro journal during my third Salvia diet

If ever there was a plant made for Goths I would say Salvia's your lady. She's powerful, no-nonsense, surreal and otherworldly. She has a strong connection with the dead. This may well be because she is a connector of the different dimensions. There are those who say she is not from this planet, which I can very much believe as the visions I have whilst working with her have indeed been very other-worldly and at times reminiscent of the artist Giger's. I frequently see spiders which themselves look like they could be from another planet.

In my experience she works a lot with personal power and strongly encourages you to be within your own centre of power. If you are not it has a destabilising effect on everything else in your life.

Stripping down to what is essential is key with Salvia. Taking an almost ruthless approach to life. Ridding yourself of unnecessary thoughts, emotions, involvement with certain people and actions because these things only bog you down and take your energy. She once stripped me down to my core (after smoking the extract) to show me what is really important: that we are not our bodies or all the things that we identify ourselves with (our job, gender, sexuality, race etc...); what we are is consciousness.

While I was dieting her she managed to completely obliterate my mind. I could see myself talking, full of thoughts, questions, completely incessant. She came into me from the right side and took over my mind and it stopped. Even if I tried to think something I couldn't. Quietness of mind, a meditative state, is a powerful one to be in.

Salvia is associated with divination and seeing into future possibilities. She can give very clear guidance about future decisions. Love and relationships are a strong area for her too; particularly personal responsibilities within relationships.

She has important lessons to teach us about our place in the bigger picture: that we are essentially a small piece of the universe and there are infinite universes beyond ours and, beyond that, a dimension where time and space do not exist at all. We certainly are not the most advanced beings! But we have the potential to shift our attention beyond matter and connect our consciousnesses with that of other beings. She showed me a vision of us destroying the Earth and each other, the Earth destroying us, then coming back and repeating the same cycle over and over... This is what will happen until we collectively raise our consciousness.

Reality is bendable. She often tells me this. In this sense she can be used for magic and healing – if we believe that anything is possible. Often if we wish for something and we do not get it, it is because of a limiting belief that it is either not really possible or that we don't deserve it so we automatically block it. We need to forget about what we believe to be the limiting laws of material reality and look beyond that to tap into dimensions where there is no such thing as illness, unhappiness, material insecurity etc... so we can draw that into our dimension and make it a reality, never forgetting to take the responsibility to make these things happen for ourselves.

There is often a sense of absurdity to Salvia and she has a dark sense of humour. There is a pointlessness in taking things too seriously and sometimes all you can do is laugh at life. Knowledge isn't power; the use of knowledge is power.
Extract from Lily's journal during her Salvia diet

Unless you have the right environment for it, England is probably the last place you would want to drink San Pedro. The cactus cannot be drunk indoors; it requires nature, and its effect on consciousness is to expand it so that you also need to be outside, to have space around you and to be safe in a tranquil place away from noise, pollution and the people we tend to grow here who are by and large so plugged into the 'normal' social dream that they have never questioned anything and would find it curious at best if they should stumble across anyone on San Pedro.

For these reasons I had not drunk it since being back here but I have cactuses in my house and, on at least a weekly basis, I had been meditating with them and journeying to the soul of the plant. One day I asked San Pedro what I should do to continue my apprenticeship. 'There is nothing *to* do' he replied. 'Initiation simply means a beginning; it means you are on path, it doesn't make you the master of it. That takes a lifetime of practice. But you know how to heal, you can make the brew, you know yourself and others better for your experiences and you still believe in love. The student is never ready when the maestro says so, only when the student says he is ready'.

I knew it was true. I have told my own students the same thing: that *being a shaman* is different from *learning about shamanism*; ability comes from doing, not through sitting in a workshop and hearing how others have done it. Skill develops with practice.

There is a fallacy in modern Western shamanism that a healer must be fully healed himself – that he must cure his own soul – before he can heal another. The problem with that is that the only time any of us will be *fully* healed (or, at least, as healed as we are going to get in this lifetime) is at the moment of our deaths. Other than that, we are only ever as perfect as we can be right now – and while we are alive the journey continues.

Some years ago I spoke with Rubén Orellana, an expert on the historical and contemporary aspects of San Pedro shamanism and healing in Peru, and he had said much the same thing. Dr Orellana is a historian who was for many years curator of the Machu Picchu sacred site but he is also a curandero with a practice in the Sacred Valley. As a 'walker between worlds' – an intellectual and a practitioner – he understands both sides of the work.[45] I mentioned to him that a lot of people these days would like to become healers – especially Westerners it seems – and asked him 'What would an apprenticeship with you involve? How long would it take?'

'I cannot say that it will take so many weeks or months or years to become a healer' he replied. 'Linear time does not apply with San Pedro or with healing. After five decades as a healer I am still learning myself. Today we want definitions and definite answers: How long will it take? What will it cost? What is our schedule? We love the instant – instant coffee, instant healing, instant visions... instant shaman! But that is not the way in our tradition... receiving this knowledge is a cycle. It is not linear but requires that you do your own processing however long that takes. For some it is a short while, for others it may take years, so there is no way for me to say "OK, I will train you for six months or two months or one year and after this you will be a shaman!" It depends on you. What is always true though is that the person who has chosen this path must believe in the cycles of times not in calendars and the illusions of linear time.'

He continued: 'The student must also be clear about what apprenticeship means. A lot of people want "initiation" into Andean medicine but this is an ill-defined word. For Westerners it usually means an ending or an accomplishment: to *be* "an initiate". In my tradition the term initiation simply does not exist but even its true meaning in the West is "a *beginning*" and this beginning never really ends because every day you are alive you learn a little more.

Apprenticeship is not just about the accumulation of knowledge but the achievement of wisdom. Knowledge may come easily to you so you may learn how to perform a particular ceremony in just a few days for example but wisdom – understanding what the rituals mean, the forces they invoke and when to use these processes – might take you a lifetime.'

'It is important for people to know as well that becoming a shaman does not make you a god or a guru, only a healer, so the apprenticeship must be entered into with the right spirit and not from a place of ego... The intention of the healer then is to do his best for people while acknowledging the light and the darkness - the humanity - within all of us, including himself, and denying nothing, for to repress it is to give it power.'

Once you have learned the practical skills and have knowledge of energy medicine and the plants, to *be* a shaman, then, means only having the confidence to say 'I *am* a shaman'. To *know* San Pedro means only to be able to say 'I understand this plant. I will always be learning more but *for now* I know enough'.

I was almost at this stage with San Pedro. I will always drink it and trust it to teach me more, as it had been doing for the last 14 years and intensively in the last three in all aspects of my life, but the real learning from the plant is not what *it* does but what *we* do – how we behave and the intent that we have – by putting its lessons into practice. San Pedro cannot compel us to be better people, only we can do that. It can show us our problems, our patterns and our issues but only we can change.

My life had been a process of change, transformation and evolution for the last few years of love, marriage and separation. Had I learned *all* that there was to learn from this? Have I righted *all* of my wrongs or become an expert on love and relationships? Not in the slightest, but at least I know what the issues are now so each day I can work on them more. But that is a lifelong process – an initiation which will continue every day I'm alive.

There was one other thing I wanted to do however before I would call myself ready. I wanted to diet Lime. I remembered a day in Peru, walking through a market with Jane, when I had been drawn to a stall selling Limes and somehow 'knew' that this was one of San Pedro's 'secret' ingredients. Nobody told me this – shamans do not teach that way – but I had a sense of it. Later, I asked La Bruja about it and she said 'Yes, of course. San Pedro loves Lime!' – which is curious since on most shamanic diets with any plant, Lemons and Limes are taboo, the shamans believing that citrus fruits have the ability to cut through magic and can damage or kill a delicate plant spirit. 'Bah!' said La Bruja. 'San Pedro is stronger than that!'

Now I did some research and discovered that Lime, chemically at least, is the *perfect* addition to San Pedro as it breaks down the alkaloids in the cactus and makes the brew more potent. 'Adding lemon or lime converts the alkaloids to the soluble citrate salts' the scientist and poet Dale Pendell writes in his book, *PharmakoGnosis*. He goes on: 'But this is not done in Peru, where lemons [and Limes] would be considered 'wet' while 'dry' is considered to be more powerful.' The latter may be true in his experience – for the reason I mentioned above – but it is not true in mine.

I began dieting Lime in February, the juice of three fruits freshly squeezed into a glass and drunk first thing in the morning for three days, the rest of the diet proceeding in the standard way for 14 days.

The first thing I noticed was the clarity it produced. It felt fresh and cleansing, like standing beneath a cold waterfall (that was the first image that came to my mind when I closed my eyes and drank the juice – a waterfall that cascaded down my spine, washing away the moment as well as residues of the past). The next effects were those it produced on my dreams. My dream world became intensely vivid and real – great colourful landscapes painted in bright contrasting tones, like the artwork that is produced in the Andes and is itself influenced by San Pedro.[46]

More than that, though, these dreams were lucid. I was fully present in them and could control the direction they took. I might find myself in a particular scenario for example and hear one part of my mind (the rational part) asking 'I wonder what that symbol means' or 'What would happen if I approached that person and said something to them', and another part of my mind (the dreaming part) would answer 'Well, let's go find out'; then I would be in exactly the situation I had willed. In this way I could navigate the dreamscape to gather information and knowledge. I subsequently recommended Lime on healing diets for two clients, without telling them what to expect from it, and they experienced the same influences on their dreaming. It feels like San Pedro itself but the experience is delivered while sleeping instead of awake.

Scientists who have studied San Pedro (and there are very few of them) have tended to concentrate on the mescaline content of the cactus, which they take to be its 'active' ingredient and most important component but perhaps shamans, our ancient chemists, had a knowledge in this regard which is more advanced than our own, for it is the *mixture* of plants used in a brew, not just a single compound found in one, which produces its effects.

Two of the 'secret' ingredients of San Pedro are *Nicotiana rustica* (Mapacho) and Lime, for example. The former has a concentration of nicotine up to nine times more than North American varieties and comparatively high levels of MAOI beta-carbolines including alkaloids which give it visionary effects, while Lime enlivens and enriches the dream state. These two plants are, in their own way, just as essential to the full San Pedro experience as any single ingredient such as mescaline.

The shamans knew that 3,500 years ago - which is the date of our current archaeological evidence for the first use of the cactus - although they would not have been talking then (or even now) in scientific jargon about MAOIs and beta-carbolines, of course - and they used San Pedro as a carrier for the effects of Lime just as much as they used Lime to enable the effects of the cactus by breaking down its alkaloids.

Lime: the great dreaming plant.

Lily and I continued to discuss the idea of Spain and our move there. By now we had familiar names for each other. I called her Bodge and she called me... Bodge (the name of one of the great – and invisible – pioneers of psychedelic research whose identity and contribution to the work must always remain hidden). It made for some quizzical looks in public – 'Would you like a coffee, Bodge?' 'Yes please Bodge'. We had codes and secrets of our own; things that only we knew. We decided to give Spain a try, combining living there for a while with a project I had been developing for a year or so.

THE CACTUS OF VISION

A snake and a ring-tailed lemur are coming to my theatre...
A clown with the saddest eyes is coming to my theatre
The Circus Master

2012. August

The Circus Master is a character who arrived in my dreams on the night of a San Pedro ceremony in August 2012. He was dressed in a bright red jacket, white trousers, white gloves and a black top hat and boots: the archetypal image of a Victorian circus impresario. He was handing out flyers advertising forthcoming attractions, which included a snake and a ring-tailed lemur and a clown with the saddest eyes. I thought he was fascinating as a dream image and a character in his own right. His message was about the nature of life – that it appears, like a circus, to be a random collection of people and events, freaks and curiosities who have come together in a strange and magical artificial world to entertain each other and an audience which sits in darkness and cannot be seen. And yet it is not truly random. The performers are there for a reason and have been assembled deliberately by the Circus Master. Together they form an organism which we call 'circus' but which we might also call life or 'reality' during the time we are in it. In this sense the Circus Master (or perhaps our audience of shadows) is 'God'.

Jane and I had two plant dreams. Given the 'randomness' of life, when they came true she was not there for either of them but Lily was present for both. The first was for a 10-day workshop in Europe where people could experience Ayahuasca, Salvia and San Pedro without having to travel to Peru or Mexico to do so; the second was for a ceremonial week led by La Bruja who would make her first visit to Spain so that people could work with her medicine. The first of these events was called *Plant Spirit Wisdom* and went ahead in September 2011. Some of the findings from that workshop are included in my book on Salvia and the event has become an annual one.

In August 2012 our second dream came true. Lily arrived before the workshop and we spent time together, sight-seeing in Cordova with its mosques and Moorish architecture, visiting la Cueva de los Murciélagos where the body of an ancient Poppy shaman was found, and the local towns to eat tapas and relax. There was an Ayahuasca ceremony for her birthday and we stayed in a beautiful valley – 30 acres of springs, streams and mountains: the place I had seen in my Salvia vision during our diet at New Year. After England, the open landscapes of Spain were a breath of fresh air – literally.[47]

La Bruja arrived on August 1. 'You look so much better than the last time I saw you' she said. It was a strange remark because the last time we were together was at my wedding, so I asked what she meant. 'Ross, she hypnotised you with sex' she replied bluntly.

It wasn't the first time I'd heard comments like this. There was Trudy's warning in the jungle about Jane using me to get to Cusco ('she doesn't want you as a boyfriend. She says you remind her more of her father') and a volunteer at our Centre who said more or less the same thing, having heard her say that she would 'do whatever it took' to get to the Andes with me. Then, back in England Doris had run into her at a festival a few months after her return and Jane had told her how much she had loved me. 'I wasn't just using him' she said. That 'just' says a lot.

It wasn't any surprise to me. One of my first impressions of JJ was that she had arrived at a sort of business relationship with life: to use and be used in equal measure, and I imagine that I *was* used, or at least it started off like that. Her 'mistake' was to fall in love along the way and believe for a moment that a new dream might be possible – before the old one dragged her home again.

From this perspective I suppose that I used her too, although it was never my intention. I got a good time girl to travel with, a fun companion and the 'special someone' I had always wanted to explore the plants with. It would have been a perfect arrangement if that had been our agreement to start with and we had stuck to it but when we fell in love our relationship and commitments to each other – as temporary and contingent as they turned out to be – changed, and that caused problems of its own. As Jodorowsky remarks: 'The objects that surround and accompany us form part of the language of the unconscious. In this way, putting a ring on a person can imprison him [or her], while taking away the ring can relieve him'.[48] Such entrapments may lead to illness – or to the surfacing of an illness we have dormant within us – as the dynamic between us changes.

Whatever had happened between Jane and I, it really didn't matter anymore. The woman I loved was dead and JJ had taken her place again. It was the lessons which were important now. If she used me I hope – genuinely - that she got full value from it and I wish her well. I also hope – genuinely - that she dodges some of the karma she has created. What I was more impressed with at the time was how little I cared and how much healing had therefore been done by San Pedro.

'From a certain point of view, illnesses are dreams that reveal unresolved problems...For the extraordinary to occur it is necessary for the sick to firmly believe in the possibility of a cure and to accept the existence of miracles'[49] – and this is what San Pedro does: it inspires us to new beliefs and healing.

There were three ceremonies that week and more than a dozen people drank. As ever, there were remarkable cures. A medical doctor from Greece who no longer believed in his profession and was fearful and unable to form healthy and loving relationships was transformed over the course of them into a man capable of love, able to laugh at his own anxieties, and no longer so trapped in his past. A Swedish woman who felt locked in herself and lacking in confidence climbed a mountain and, from its peak, began singing a song she had just made up, sending her voice out across the whole valley. A young man from England, so out of touch with nature and so conditioned to ask permission of others that he was literally unable to feel the strong Spanish sun on his skin until he was told by somebody else how hot it was, became a more confident and resourceful person, no longer so concerned with the thoughts of others and excited to be expressing himself through art. One of the pieces he left for us is painted with two mottos, his new ideals for living: 'Choose again' and 'I need do nothing'.

As dramatic as these healings were and as profound as they were for those who experienced them, they are not the deepest or most 'miraculous' I have seen with San Pedro. In *The Hummingbird's Journey to God*, for example, I tell the story of Deborah, a woman from South Africa who did not believe in the power of the cactus and who refused ever to drink it, until the events of her life made it totally necessary.

Deborah's husband had recently died – the result of a disease which meant it took him a year to waste away while she nursed him through it. Then, just three months later, her son was murdered at the age of only 26. She was shattered and when La Bruja met her she was 'lifeless, like the walking dead.' Soon afterwards she had a stroke which paralysed her left arm and from the shock (*manchare, susto*) of all she had been through she developed diabetes as well.

Doctors could not help her (how can a physician put a soul back together?) and with few other choices available she eventually asked to try San Pedro. La Bruja continues the story: 'I gave her the tiniest amount possible, but it was just perfect for her, as San Pedro always is, and then she lay in my arms and cried her heart out for five hours.' That is a good expression for what happened actually, because I had drunk San Pedro too and through its eyes I saw strands of energy coming from her heart and circling her chest and arm like a tourniquet. I began pulling them from her and throwing them away.

'The next morning there was a miracle. Her arm, which had been totally paralysed, had regained its movement. When she returned to South Africa she saw a specialist who tested her diabetes and that had gone too. I asked her about her San Pedro experience later and she said that as she went through it she felt a lot of pain in her heart, which is where I had seen the energy of grief that was binding her. As well as curing her physical problems, then, San Pedro showed her *why* she had them: because of the emotional distress she had been unable to let go of'.

What we learn from this is that illness is not a 'thing' that is 'in' us; it is not 'diabetes' or 'a stroke' or 'grief'. It is a *belief* we carry: that we must mourn for those we have lost, for example – or for ourselves – through a pain or disability that makes our suffering obvious. Illness is a thoughtform; a negative pattern we hold onto and reproduce. San Pedro not only heals us but shows us this thoughtform too. Then the next time it arises we know it and can make a conscious decision to think and act differently.

David is another case in point. When he moved to Peru following his divorce he discovered that he had cancer. He was recommended for chemotherapy but told he should expect only limited success. 'I had no money for treatment and, given the prognosis, there didn't seem much point anyway' he says. 'A friend of mine knew some shamans however, and arranged a healing for me at his house. I wasn't there but they drank San Pedro and sent me prayers for good health. I found out later that the energy was so strong at that ceremony that every electrical socket blew in the house. The shaman said it was a sign that the energy causing my cancer had unblocked and my tumours were gone.'

'The next day I visited the hospital to see how much chemo I was going to need. The consultant made more tests and said the results were strange: there was a "signature" of cancer in my platelets but no lumps in my body anymore and no need for treatment.'

'A few weeks later I agreed to take part in a ceremony myself. Not long into it I experienced tremendous pain, like my heart was breaking. I stood up and started to vomit. What I threw up I can only describe as unearthly. It looked like wafers of glass which were rock hard and had bubbles of air inside them. They were completely solid and transparent. I could pick them up and look through them. I asked the shaman what they were. "They are energy which was stuck inside you" he said. "They have been blocking your heart for years so you could not love and were inclined towards death. Now they are out and you are free of cancer"'.

'I tried to stay sceptical but he was right. I have been well now for the last nine years and was tested a year ago and told I was totally clear.[50] What went through my mind when I threw up that glass was rage over my divorce. I don't know if emotions like that cause cancer but I am open-minded now and from that day I have never had a problem. I am happier, more relaxed and no longer angry. I have a new direction in life'.

In their book *PHIKAL*, about the therapeutic work they have done with MDMA, Alexander (Sasha) and Ann Shulgin write about a similar healing they were involved in with a woman in her late forties who they call Miriam O and who reminds me in some ways of my own client, the one I mentioned earlier who suffered from cervical cancer.[51] According to Sasha, it was 'a day I will never forget'.

Deep into her experience and somewhat panicky Miriam had a sense that she was being poisoned. 'I'm not fooling around' she said. 'I'm really being poisoned and I want out'.

'Then get yourself out. You're in charge' Sasha answered.

'There was no comment for a minute. Then she said it: Can you give yourself cancer?'

'You certainly can. Almost everyone who has cancer has

gotten it for some reason that seems quite adequate. Where is yours?'

'In my stomach.'

'She gently touched her stomach to indicate the site of the enemy. She then unfolded one of the most complex stories I had ever heard, all of which boiled down to the fact that she'd had stomach cancer for some time and always carried round in her purse some thirty Dilaudid tablets so that if the pain got too much she could end the whole thing. I asked the only question that occurred to me: Why do you need cancer?

'That broke the dam. She dissolved in tears and blurted out her secret. Many years before, her mother had suffered from cancer of the stomach and was in such intractable pain that, finally, Miriam and her stepfather had smothered her with a pillow, releasing her from her agony. She was a teenager and she had helped kill her mother. She told me that she'd had total amnesia for all events in her life from that time until her early 20s. I wept with her...

'What she emerged with was an understanding of how repressed grief and guilt had planted itself in her own body, giving symptoms which were signals to her of something dark which needed to be exposed and opened up to consciousness before she did, indeed, succeed in giving herself her mother's cancer. When we talked again several days later she told me – almost casually – that she had thrown away the Dilaudid'.

Sasha points out that in her case, unlike David or my cervical cancer client, Miriam did not actually have cancer; she had the *symptoms* of cancer and *behaved as if* she had the disease itself. Her pain however was real and her 'imaginary' illness was just as debilitating. Our imaginations are powerful things and believing something to be true will usually make it so. As the Ketamine explorer and scientist John Lilly put it: 'Whatever one believes to be true *is* true or *becomes* true in one's own mind'. The intervention of MDMA therefore had life-changing and perhaps life-saving consequences for Miriam.

Cara is another example of how the mind and its suppressed pain can end up controlling us. Cara was a journalist – 'a *hardened* reporter', as she expressed it, who I met in Peru. It was there that she told me her story.

'My first time with San Pedro was to heal a relationship problem with my dad' she said. 'Things had been difficult between us for years and it was affecting my relationships with other men, my relationship to love and intimacy in general, and especially my relationships with children. Because of what I had experienced [in my own childhood] I was actually afraid of them and although I might one day have wanted children of my own I wouldn't allow any child near me. I felt dirty, as if they might get polluted by just being close to me. I didn't know it then but I was desperate, nearly dying, when San Pedro found me '

'As soon as I drank it, I dissolved. I became the sky, the clouds, the flowers, and I saw the beauty in all things, including myself and my relationship with my father. I realised, at some deeper level than we are ever usually aware of, that *everything* is exactly as it is meant to be.'

It is what it is...

'I saw the connection between my father and myself more clearly and it now seemed obvious to me that we had made a contract between us before I was even born so that everything that had happened was predestined and ultimately an act of love, sacrifice and connection – on his part too. I had a dream [vision] of a white flower opening and embracing me. It pulled my face towards it and kissed me and then we rested, head to head, as it were, and I knew that this was a blessing from my dad's soul to mine.'

'It gave me a new understanding of what my relationship with my dad was really about and it also changed something in me. Within two weeks of drinking San Pedro I met the man who would become my husband and, within a few weeks of that, I was pregnant. There's no bigger way to say that it healed my relationship problems because none of that would have been possible without it. Before this I was afraid to be near children. San Pedro gave me my daughter.'

For the healer, sometimes it is a case of simply getting out of the way and allowing San Pedro (or MDMA in the case of the Shulgins) to do its work. Or else it is about simplicity – what I now call 'yoghurt healing', following La Bruja's example: listening quietly to someone without judgement and with respect, being a witness to their journey, making an occasional loving gesture with a sympathetic word, a touch or a 'sweep' of the body to remove more shadowy energies. Shamanism does not always have to be dramatic battles with 'negative spirits' or journeying to lower worlds to find 'power animals'; more often, and usually more effectively, it is about just being present in *this* world with someone that you share a moment of closeness with in an attitude of love and acceptance – and an act of faith that your love is stronger than whatever unhelpful forces have taken ownership of the person you are with.

I am your gravity, I hold you
From the icaro for Chanca Piedra

Another example given by Sasha is that of Janice, with whom he took MDMA. About 40 minutes into the experience Janice began to feel increasing discomfort.

'My throat is dry'.

'I'll get you a glass of water' (It did no good).

'I'm having trouble breathing'.

'So breathe the best you can'. ('I noticed by the reflection in the window where we were, at the back of the house, that she had no difficulty breathing when I wasn't watching her...')

'Do you think I smoke too much?'

'Do *you* think you smoke too much?'

'I don't think so'.

'Then the answer is probably no'.

Then came what Sasha called 'the unexpected question, the "off the wall" question', although all of Janice's other comments had been building up to it: 'Is it all right to be alive?'

'You bet your sweet ass it's alright to be alive! It's a grace to be alive!'

Sasha continues: 'That was it. She plunged into the MDMA state and started running down the hill, calling out that it was alright to be alive. All the greens became living greens and all the sticks and stones became vital sticks and stones. I caught up with her and her face was radiant. She told me some of her personal history... with which she had never come to peace'

'She had come into the world by an unexpected Caesarean section and her mother had died during the delivery. And for fifty years she had lived with the guilt of having had her life given at the cost of her mother's life. She had been in therapy with her family physician for about three years largely addressing this problem, and apparently what she needed was the acknowledgement that it was alright to be alive. I didn't hear from her for a couple of months. When she did call she volunteered that she still felt very much at peace and had discontinued her therapy'.

Confirmation, validation, gentleness, subtlety: these are the keys to San Pedro healing – on the surface, at least. But there is another force at play too, which I have called faith. It is a real energy - a power of the mind, combined with intention – an act of the will – which is directed (through a song, an icaro, the use of incense, the breath, by prayer or some other means) to create a positive change in someone who needs our help. Ann Shulgin describes how she first discovered it while working with Peyote, a relative of San Pedro:

'As I looked at [Sam's] back, a few feet ahead, it occurred to me that I could reach out with my mind and actually touch him, and when I wondered about how best to go about doing it, an image came of peeling layers of Sam away – like an onion – until I got to the core of him and I would be able to touch that directly. I simply knew I could do it...'

'I began mentally peeling Sam's layers, one by one, gently, as I followed him. After a while I sensed a shining thing that had no shape in the middle of his body and I reached out with the will and poked it at the shining. Sam jumped in mid-step and turned, both hands spread against his back. He looked at me standing there grinning and said, "What the hell...?"'

'I apologised, not meaning it, and told him what I'd discovered I could do. I was very pleased with myself. It was like being a kid with a very powerful brand new toy, I thought, and the message came that I should be careful and responsible, even though it was an awful lot of fun to play with.'

La Bruja left at the end of the week, our workshop participants soon afterwards, and Lily and I were alone. 'So what do you reckon, Bodge; do you think you could live here?' I asked as we looked out over our peaceful valley, stretching into the distance of trees and streams and hills to the mountains beyond.

'I love it here, Bodge' she said, the sunlight bright on her face.

So that was it, another circle completing itself: from Peru to Spain to England and now back to Spain; from a single life to a relationship, marriage, divorce and now back to living with someone; from community to separation and now a new community forming. When one circle completes, something new is always created and another circle begins, one that I would travel with Lily now, while applying the lessons that San Pedro had given me through Jane.

That night I watched a star die. The moon was full, a halo of light around it, and the sky was filled with stars. Lily and I were looking up at them, marvelling at how many there were, when one of them just went out. One second it was there, the next there was nothing. *Now there's a hole in the sky.* I don't know what that means but I know it means something.

To love, to be loved
To never forget your own insignificance...
To seek joy in the saddest places, to pursue beauty to its lair
To never simplify what is complicated or complicate what is simple...
Above all, to watch, to never look away –
And never, never to forget
Arundhati Roy, *The End of Imagination*

THE END – AND A BEGINNING

Master, to whom shall we go? You have the words of eternal life
Saint Peter (John 6:68)

Angel – formerly The Man With No Name – made his way from town to town, spreading the message of San Pedro. Most people could not hear it though – or rather, they heard it but could not understand. For, in truth, it was a strange gospel that he was delivering. Simply this:

I know nothing
And nor do you.
Even more so now

San Pedro is also the medicine of the Fool.

The greatest enemy of knowledge is not ignorance.
It is the *illusion* of knowledge
Stephen Hawking, scientist

You are only what you are without asking what you are...
Do you understand?
Ejo Takata, Zen Master

For the explorer there are no true beliefs
John Lilly, scientist

THE PLANTS

The biodiversity of the tropical rainforest is so immense that less than 1% of its million species have been studied by scientists... [yet] we are losing more than 137 species of plants and animals every single day because of rainforest deforestation
Leslie Taylor, *The Healing Power of Rainforest Herbs*

JERGON SACHA

The Snake-Plant

Appearance

A single divided leaf which grows from an underground tuber on a long thin mottled stem, rising to around two metres in height.

The Ally

Jergon is a 'signature plant', its spiritual essence (or ally) advertising its presence and healing intentions through its appearance. The look and colouration of its stem resembles a poisonous snake indigenous to the area in which it grows and a medicine made from the root of the plant is the only known antidote to a bite from this snake. The plant is therefore a lifesaver when a root poultice is applied to the bite and an infusion of the rhizome in water is drunk.

Pharmaceutical companies produce the commercial antivenom from this plant based on the rainforest knowledge of shamans. According to these shamans however, the success rate of the chemical in saving lives is no better than the plant. It is, however, exorbitantly pricey (around $240 a vial) given that the plant grows freely and does the job just as well, and highly impractical since you cannot refrigerate vials of the antidote in the jungle where there is no electricity. Thus, the area (and the people that shamanic plant experts represent) which gave the world this treatment benefits hardly at all from its production.

Spirit of the Plant

The male (*macho*) is rather effeminate; the female (*embra*) rather masculine. Both plants find a use for viruses and virotes which is positive, extracting negative energy from human beings and employing it in a way which is useful and life-affirming in the spirit world, thus ensuring that this energy stays in flow.

Evidence of Healing

Jergon Sacha is also used by native people as an antidote for stingray wounds, spider bites and poison (curare) arrow wounds. Shamanically, it is used to extract spiritual poisons (virotes) sent as infections by rivals into the energy body (or soul) of a victim. The spiritual intention of Jergon Sacha is therefore to remove poisons (viruses or entities which prey upon us) in all their forms and to cleanse the physical and spiritual body, which is why it is also effective in the treatment of HIV and AIDS.

AYAHUASCA

The Vine of Souls

Appearance

Ayahuasca is a mixture of two jungle plants: the Ayahuasca vine (*Banisteriopsis caapi* - also known as the rope of the dead) and Chacruna (*Psychotria viridis*) which are brewed together for several hours to produce a bitter tea with visionary properties. It has been drunk for millennia by rainforest shamans to heal the body, mind and soul, to find purpose and to understand the desires of the spirit. They believe that it brings us closer to God and reveals what is truly important.

The Ally

Shamans say she is a beautiful lady dressed in white who embraces you like a mother, caresses you like a lover and shows you the truth of things, although she can also be confusing and contrary: '70% of what she shows you is true, 30% is illusion' – Percy Garcia, Amazonian shaman.

Spirit of the Plant

The vine itself is said to be "born of a boa", the great snake of the jungle, the spirit of the Earth, and this is how she may also appear in visions: as a colossal serpent who wraps you in her coils and drags you deeper into yourself. Visions of snakes are common in fact and some (such as Jeremy Narby in his book *The Cosmic Serpent*) draw parallels to the winding structure of DNA, suggesting that Ayahuasca enables us to see ourselves at a deeper-than-cellular level, the place where our angels and demons, our Heaven and Hell co-exist, and so gives us the possibility of creating positive change by shedding new light on the darker things we may find there.

Evidence of Healing

Little research has been carried out into the healing properties of Ayahuasca. Current scientific thinking proposes that there are none, the plant having only a visionary (hallucinogenic) effect. Stories from the jungle however (from shamans and patients alike) suggest its promise as a cure for cancer, ME (myalgic encephalopathy), CFS (chronic fatigue syndrome), Parkinson's disease, post-traumatic stress syndrome, grief and emotional issues and various forms of addiction. I have witnessed recoveries from these in a number of cases and conducted healings of my own for some clients which have relieved them of these diseases. One topical piece of research comes from the Takiwasi Center for Drug Addiction Treatment and Traditional Medicines in Taropoto, Peru, from where Dr Jaques Mabit has published several papers which show that Ayahuasca is up to 70% effective in curing alcoholism and drug addictions, compared to a Western success rate of 30% at best. Quite possibly – and a fact overlooked by scientists who dismiss Ayahuasca as simply hallucinogenic - it is the visionary qualities of the vine themselves which account for these results by showing us the root of our problems and the strengths we have within us for dealing with them.

SAN PEDRO: HUACHUMA

The Cactus of Vision or Cactus of Mystery

Appearance

San Pedro is a tall cactus which grows in Peru as well as parts of America and can also be cultivated in countries like Spain with a Mediterranean climate. In Peru it especially enjoys the high regions such as the Yunga and Quechua areas (2,300 metres and 3,500 metres above sea level respectively).

The Ally

Shamans say he is male, "as straight as an arrow – one who will never deceive you" (Hampejs; Calderon); others, "a beautiful man" (La Gringa/Myburgh). Some (including me) see him as a matador dressed in a bullfighter's *traje de luces* ('suit of lights') although he also has a warrior aspect and in this form is more alien and insect-like (Heaven; Lily).

Spirit of the Plant

Another name for the cactus is *pene de Dios* – the 'penis of God' – and there is a suggestion that its juice may have been drunk during sex magic rituals in the early Chavin and other cultures. Alexander Shulgin, who produced MDMA ('Ecstasy' or 'E') following his own research with mescaline cactus, reports in his book *PIHKAL: A Chemical Love Story* that the synthetic version is also an aphrodisiac and creates waves of closeness and empathetic understanding, sometimes leading to sex, but cautions that while MDMA can be a huge turn-on for women the sympathomimetics it contains can create problems for men in developing and sustaining erection. The spirit of the plant is in any case archetypally male, with qualities of power, endurance and resilience. Some shamans say that in the old days workers would drink a small cupful each morning to give them strength for a hard day's labour.

Evidence of Healing

I have met and worked with people who, just through drinking San Pedro, have recovered from cancer, diabetes, alcoholism, paralysis, grief and emotional issues (there are several case studies in my books *The Hummingbird's Journey to God* and *Cactus of Mystery*). Homeopathic provings and work with plant essences confirm its effectiveness for calming strong emotions and drives (compulsions, addictions and aggressive states), releasing stress and helping with issues of sensitivity, sensuality, and one's relationship to the self.

TOBACCO: NICOTIANA RUSTICA

The Mother Plant

Appearance

Nicotiana rustica, known in South America as *Mapacho,* is a plant of the solanaceae family and a potent form of Tobacco. Its seeds are minute, ranging from 0.4mm to 1.3mm in diameter but the plant itself can grow up to two metres in height, with huge green leaves and sweet-smelling flowers ranging in colour from white to purple, pink, red or yellow.

The concentration of nicotine in its leaves is up to nine times more than North American varieties such as *N. tabacum* and it also has comparatively high levels of MAOI beta-carbolines including the harmala alkaloids harman and norharman which give it visionary effects.

Recreational smoking of Tobacco is rare among Amazonian Indians except in areas where tribal customs are breaking down due to acculturation and the availability of commercial cigarettes. In ceremonies where Ayahuasca is taken however, the use of Tobacco smoke is a staple healing practice and cigars as long as 36 inches (also called Mapachos) may be smoked. The Jivaros (Shuar) of Ecuador also smoke these cigars as part of a festival to celebrate the initiation of a youth into manhood.

The Witotos mix powdered Coca with Tobacco and take it as a snuff through tubes made of hollow bird bones or long reeds. Chewing the leaves is a common practice among numerous tribes. Some, such as the Waika, keep a quid of Tobacco leaves in the lower lip all day. For visionary healing the Jivaros mix it with Ayahuasca or maikoa (*Brugmansia:* Tohay). Because of its potency, among some tribes only the shaman may take Tobacco juice through the nostrils while the rest of the (male) population drink it (women never drink). Tobacco (Mapacho) is used alone by *tabaqueros* (experts in Tobacco and the magic of smoke) or in combination with other plants as a source of visions and healing.

The Ally

She is seen by some shamans as a beautiful woman dressed in white, by others as a black smoke-like shape and by others as the plant itself but in gigantic multi-leaved form and in brilliant colours. Her attitude is motherly, healing and loving but she does demand absolute adherence to the diet and the consequences of breaking it can be severe. It is therefore not a plant to be trifled with.

Spirit of the Plant

Tobacco is both a healer and a destroyer. It may be used by the shaman to cure pulmonary illnesses, breathing problems and cancers but will also aid spirit extraction by suffocating and weakening negative entities. The greater ('mother') spirit of the plant also contains other allies with specific functions such as warriorship and healing. Many years could be spent exploring her 'chambers' and locating new helpful spirits.

Evidence of Healing

Tobacco is an adaptable and highly useful plant which is employed by various rainforest tribes as a cure for many different ailments. It may be taken as a leaf decoction to soothe sprains and bruises, used as a poultice to heal skin problems and wounds, drunk as a therapeutic juice for chills and snake bites and in snuff form to treat pulmonary complaints. For other tribal uses see R Schultes and R Raffauf, *The Healing Forest: Medicinal and Toxic Plants of the Northwest Amazonia*. In the Western world it has recently been identified as a potential treatment for cancer.

ORTEGA

The Virote Killer

Appearance

Growing to around two metres in height, Ortega (Nettle) produces pointed stinging leaves and yellow-white flowers. The genus name *Urtica* comes from the Latin verb *wrere*: 'to burn'. The species name *dioica* means 'two houses' because the plant contains either male (*macho*) or female (*embra*) flowers.

The Ally

When seen shamanically the plant resembles a short thick snake made of bright green leaves which enters the body of a patient (usually through the stomach or solar plexus) and begins the process of stinging or burning out any intrusive energy it finds.

Spirit of the Plant

Like Jergon Sacha, Ortega is used to extract spiritual poisons, often sent as infections by rivals into the body of a victim. Its intention is to thoroughly cleanse the physical and spiritual body.

Evidence of Healing

Nettle 'reduces allergies, cleanses blood, reduces inflammation, relieves pain, lowers blood pressure, heals wounds...'

'In folk medicine Nettle plants have been used as a diuretic, to build the blood, for arthritis and for rheumatism...ulcers, asthma, diabetes, intestinal inflammation, nosebleeds...'

'Several of Nettle's lectin chemicals have demonstrated marked antiviral actions (against HIV and several common upper respiratory viruses). Other chemicals... have been documented with interesting immune stimulant actions... In one study, a Nettle root extract was shown to inhibit the growth of prostate cells by 30% in five days. Another reported it inhibited BPH [benign prostatic hyperplasia] in mice by 51.4% (which suggested it could be used as a preventative as well as a treatment)' – Leslie Taylor, *The Healing Power of Rainforest Herbs*.

SALVIA DIVINORUM

The Dimension-Shifter

Appearance

A perennial herb in the mint family. Native to Oaxaca, Mexico, it grows in the humid forests of the Sierra Mazateca at altitudes of between 750 and 1500 metres. It can grow to over a metre in height and has large green leaves, hollow square stems and white flowers with purple calyces.

The Ally

Most of the names given to Salvia by Mazatec shamans associate her with the Virgin Mary (such as *hojas de la Maria*). It may not be that simple however since Salvia is a plant of paradox. She is however very direct and no-nonsense.

Spirit of the Plant

Aside from its healing properties Salvia is known for its divinatory powers when prepared and drunk as an infusion of leaves. The plant will then foretell the future and provide answers to detailed questions.

Evidence of Healing

Salvia is used as a medicine as well as for visions. Mazatec shamans prescribe a tea made from five pairs of leaves to cure anaemia, relieve headaches and rheumatism and regulate alimentary function (for example to stop diarrhoea or aid defecation in the case of stomach blockages). The anthropologist Diaz reported that there is also a magical disease which is cured by Salvia, known as *panzón de borrego* ("lamb belly") which takes the form of a swollen stomach as a result of a curse made by a *brujo* (sorcerer) who has placed a stone inside the sufferer. Salvia removes it and the stomach returns to normal. Healers also take Salvia to learn how to identify and use medicinal plants. Mazatecs believe that there is a tree in Heaven on which all healing plants grow and under the influence of Salvia they are able to talk to God and the saints and learn the uses of these plants.

Researchers from the University of California and California Pacific Medical Center Research Institute conducted a survey of 500 Salvia users which demonstrated healing effects which might last for days or more after taking Salvia. These included: increased insight (47% of respondents), improved mood (44.8%), feelings of calmness (42.2%), increased connection with the universe and nature (39.8%), increased self-confidence (21.6%) and improved concentration (19.4%).

Salvia may also have longer-term therapeutic potential Professor Bryan Roth believes that drugs derived from it could be useful in combating diseases such as Alzheimer's, depression, schizophrenia, chronic pain and AIDS. Thomas Prisinzano, assistant professor of medicinal and natural products chemistry at the University of Iowa suggests that Salvia may also help to treat cocaine addiction: 'You can give a rat free access to cocaine [then] give them free access to salvinorin A and they stop taking cocaine'. Clinical pharmacologist John Mendelsohn notes that 'There may be some derivatives that... would actually be active against cancer and HIV... there are a lot of therapeutic targets that have many people excited.'

Some of these targets include treatments for eating disorders, convulsions, ischemic brain damage, hypertension, depression, arrhythmia and for heroin, cocaine, alcohol and amphetamine dependency. Other possible applications include rheumatoid arthritis, systemic lupus erythematosis, Sjogren's Syndrome, multiple sclerosis, chronic lymphocytic leukemia, Type 1 diabetes, Epstein-Barr virus, coronavirus and cytomegalovirus.

MUCURA

The Sorcerer's Plant

Appearance

A herbaceous perennial, up to a metre in height, with green leaves and white-flowered spikes growing up through them. It has the odour of garlic and is sometimes referred to as 'garlic weed'.

The Ally

In appearance the ally is somewhat like the plant but in human form: tall and spindly with many arms.

Spirit of the Plant

Its essence is the removal of 'witchcraft' and negative energies. More fundamentally it is about protection.

Evidence of Healing

Mucura has been shown to kill cancerous cells and prevent tumours. It will also kill viruses and strengthen the immune response. Mucura was one of just 34 plants identified with active properties against cancer in a University of Illinois study of more than 1400 plant extracts. In another study whole herb water extracts were shown to be toxic to leukemia and lymphoma cancer cells. Others have shown it to be toxic against liver and brain cancer cells.

It may also be effective as a treatment for diabetes (a traditional use for the plant in the rainforest): 'Researchers in 1990 demonstrated the *in vivo* hypoglycemic effect of [Mucura], showing that [it] decreased blood sugar levels by more than 60% one hour after administration to mice' – Leslie Taylor, *The Healing Power of Rainforest Herbs*.

WHITE ROSE: ROSA BLANCA

The Emotional Releaser

Appearance

Serrated leaves and woody stems with thorns producing seed pods (hips) and white flowers.

The Ally

A woman dressed in white, with long dark hair, who appears in a landscape of snow and ice and tends the souls of the heartbroken and lost who are frozen in fear and grief.

Spirit of the Plant

An ally to soul retrieval and reconnection with positive emotions.

Evidence of Healing

Rose petal tea has been used in the treatment of stress, depression, colds, digestive ailments, nausea, insomnia, PMS, menopausal symptoms, reduced libido and eating disorders. Rose oil is used externally to regenerate skin, to promote feelings of well-being and to purify the body. Its scent is a gentle sedative which is soothing for the nervous system and can help stop panic attacks and overcome grief, resentment and anger. Rose hips may be used as a kidney tonic, with one cup equal in vitamin C to more than 140 oranges.

POPPY

The Ancestral Healer

Appearance
Green stems covered in fine hairs, producing delicate red flowers with black seeds at their centre.

The Ally
Unknown (or unremembered from what Jane said of her) but according to her and to Lynne, perceived as female, with 'hermaphrodite qualities'.

Spirit of the Plant
Appearance and identity unknown but an 'opener' and 'softener' and an aid to healing ancestral wounds.

Evidence of Healing
Red Poppy is not the same as opium Poppy and does not have its narcotic strength although the *Physician's Desk Reference for Herbal Medicines* [PDR] lists it as a mild pain reliever due to its slight opium content. The US Library of Medicine lists potential benefits in the treatment of asthma and other respiratory disorders, including bronchitis and whooping cough. The PDR adds that a cough syrup made from Poppy petals can soothe irritated throats although clinical studies confirming these results are lacking. Poppy may also be beneficial in easing anxiety or agitation, reports the PDR, its alkaloids acting as a mild mental relaxant and sedative.

SEAWEED

The Plant of Riches

Appearance
Botanically, seaweeds are classified as Green, Brown or Red. Their appearance varies, from lettuce-like structures to a thinner and finer hair-like appearance.

The Ally
Described by Lily as 'a slim, energetic emerald green lady with a velvet voice'.

Spirit of the Plant
According to Lily, 'a welcoming hostess spirit with a very nurturing, protective side... good for "women's problems", a loss of *joie de vivre*, retrieving lost or repressed memories and regaining power.'

Evidence of Healing
No land plant approaches Seaweed as a source of minerals. They are 20-50% dry weight mineral, rich in potassium, sodium, calcium, magnesium, zinc, copper, chloride, sulfur, phosphorous, vanadium, cobalt, manganese, selenium, bromine, iodine, iron and fluorine.

To explore just a few of these, potassium is essential for nerve and muscle functioning and as a transporter ion for neurotransmitters and hormones. Adding high-potassium foods, especially Seaweed, to the diets of ADD sufferers (instead of Ritalin) significantly improves behaviour and mental functioning. Fibromyalgia patients and those with anxiety disorders and depression are also improved. By eating Seaweed women are able to reduce PMS symptoms. Men also benefit since they usually have a much higher selenium demand than women because, like zinc, it is secreted in sperm and must be replaced to maintain ejaculate production and fertility.

Asthma is the leading cause of school absenteeism today and is also increasingly a problem for adults. Red algae containing carrageenan can help with this and have been used for millennia as treatments for respiratory ailments, especially sinus infections and pneumonia. *In vitro* tests show that some red algae are also strongly antiviral and one carrageenan derivative demonstrated strong anti-HIV activity when used as a contraceptive vaginal foam.

CACAO

The Food of the Gods

Appearance

The botanist Linnaeus named Cacao *Theobroma*: 'food of the gods'. The tree grows to around 16 feet high, with lanceolate leaves and small reddish flowers. The fruit is a smooth yellowy-red capsule containing about 25 seeds. The gathering season is June and December, when these capsules are cut open and the beans surrounded by their pulp are allowed to ferment so they separate more easily from the shell. The beans are then dried in the sun.

The Ally

According to Lily, a male spirit with 'many faces', including those of 'the lover, the warrior, half beast/half man, a cuddly lovely being and a psychedelic Mayan God.'

Spirit of the Plant

According to Lily, 'on a very fundamental level he is about Love'. He brings qualities of optimism, psychic abilities and alertness. 'Cacao gives a strong sense of melting away sorrow... His warrior side gives a sense of power, physical prowess and fearlessness. His spirit has a strong connection with the heart so he could be useful for people with heart conditions.'

Evidence of Healing

Cacao seeds contain 2% theobromine and the shells about 1%. Theobromine is an alkaloid resembling caffeine in its action although its effect on the nervous system is milder.

It is used principally for its diuretic effect and is especially useful where there is an accumulation of fluid in the body resulting from cardiac failure, when it is often given with digitalis to relieve dilatation. It is also used in cases of hypertension as it dilates the blood vessels.

Oil of Theobroma (or Cacao butter) is used as an ingredient in cosmetic ointments, has excellent emollient properties and will soften and protect chapped hands and lips. In pharmacies it is used for coating pills and preparing suppositories.

LIME

The Lucid Dreamer

Appearance
Common Lime – a round, green citrus fruit 3-6cm in diameter, containing sour, acidic pulp.

The Ally
Appears as a female with blonde hair, wearing a long, pale green (Lime-coloured) dress decorated with flowers and leaves.

Spirit of the Plant
Lime cuts. It will cut through magic, negativity and the chatter of the rational mind so that the soul can be more clearly heard and will talk to us in lucid dreams.

Evidence of Healing
Lime is an excellent source of citric acid, natural sugar, vitamin C, calcium and phosphorus. Vitamin C increases the body's resistance to disease, aids the healing of wounds and prevents damage to the eyes. It is also helpful in maintaining the health of teeth and bones and as a preventative against scurvy (Board of Trade regulations make it compulsory for ships to carry a supply of Lime juice when fresh vegetables are not available).

Lime is also beneficial in the treatment of digestive disorders and will help stop vomiting, indigestion and burning in the chest due to stomach acidity. It has been used in the treatment of peptic ulcers since citric acid produces an alkaline reaction which helps the digestion by assisting the absorption of fats and alcohol and neutralising excessive bile from the liver.

Lime has also proven effective in the treatment of tonsillitis, eye disorders (a few drops of warm Lime juice diluted with water can be used in the eyes in case of conjunctivitis, and regular use with Rose water in the ratio of 1:4 is helpful in preventing cataracts) and cystitis (a teaspoonful of Lime juice is added to 180gm of boiling water which is then allowed to cool and 60gm of this water is then given every two hours to relieve the burning and stop bleeding).

It is also good for weight reduction (tests show that a glass of Lime juice mixed with water and drunk each morning will help reduce weight in two to three months).

It has a sedative effect on the nerves.

AFTERWORD:
A NOTE FROM THE AUTHOR

The truth is rarely pure and never simple
Oscar Wilde, *The Importance of Being Earnest*

As far as anything can be said to be true, as far as we even know what 'truth' is, every word of this book is true. It happened just as I wrote it, although I have changed the names of the people in it to protect the innocent and not so innocent.

A number of synchronicities happened while I was writing it, usually at times when I had doubts and was wondering whether I should put down on paper the things that were on my mind. One was when I wrote the story of Angel who, lost in the desert, was the first person to discover and drink San Pedro. No-one – not even the shamans – know who first discovered San Pedro or under what circumstances so this part is a complete invention; a fabrication or a modern fable, although it must have happened something like that. Still, I was unsure whether to include it until I opened my emails that day and discovered that the first was from a man called lo_ost who was enquiring about my ceremonies with the cactus. I took that as a sign from San Pedro that the story of Angel (lost in the desert and lost in spirit) should be included and that perhaps there is some truth in it.

Another was when I was writing the chapter on love and addiction. As I had it open on my screen, the post arrived: a single item that day, a magazine called Spearhead. Spearhead is the journal of the 'men's movement', something I was involved with years ago before moving to Spain. As such it usually contains short articles on 'warriorship', 'leadership' and similar subjects, most of them pretty dry. I hardly ever read it anymore but because I was in a reflective mood that day I flicked through it and found that the main article was on love and addiction. Let me tell you how unusual that is. Firstly, Spearhead articles tend to be just a page or so in length; this was four pages. More importantly, the magazine never addresses subjects like this and the 'condition' itself is rare enough. Not only did I leave the chapter just as I'd written it, I included a quote from the article. I have learned now never to ignore these whispers from spirit.

Of the people who appear in this book, Trudy is in the process of building a new healing Centre in Peru after the slow political death of the last, where she aims to concentrate once again on addictions cures.

Selva long ago lost his job with her due to over-indulgences of his own, or to internal politics (maybe both, maybe neither), depending on who you listen to. He is married now to Nora and may be moving back to Europe to join the resurgence of his native tradition.

JJ will no doubt be sitting on a plane, escaping to another nowhere dressed up as somewhere. I hope for her sake that one day she stops running just for a moment and takes another compassionate and forgiving look at herself, as she did once in our jungle and on our mountains. If she did she might go further than a plane could ever take her and maybe even find the *real* freedom and happiness she has spent half her life chasing. But that's her choice. All I know is that she deserves love, and the chance to allow herself to fully experience it, and that remains my prayer for her.

It is curious how we all came together – Trudy, Selva, Jane and I – in a jungle thousands of miles from any of our homes, linked by a common theme which we were all more or less unaware of and in some cases still are. Trudy is not without her own issues but chose at least to kick her addictions and is, in many ways, the cleanest of us all although, thanks to San Pedro, I see my patterns now too and try not to go there.

The teachings of San Pedro were tough this time but the last few years were also the richest and most amazing of my life. I got exactly what I asked for and I cannot regret a moment of them. I am grateful for every second.

I would say this though: that if you are tempted to take this journey yourself to learn about love and healing, be clear on your intentions and careful what you ask for. It will be rewarding and you will be a better man or woman for it, but it may hurt just a little. Sometimes.

But *it is what it is...bueno suerte.*

DEDICATION

For Bodge, the unsung hero of psychedelia, for my children and Indie Nevaeh.

Thank you to those who shared my journey (especially Les, Bobby, Emily, Teertha, Tania, Suzanne, Jeannie, Carlye, Daryl, Jodie and Mili), those who faded away (Jungle, Tracie) and those who are ancient history.

This ends the saRAH cycle. You're absolutely forgiven and loved. You're also completely alone now; perhaps you always were.

ABOUT THE AUTHOR

Ross Heaven is a shaman, psychologist and director of The Four Gates Foundation (www.thefourgates.org) which runs training programmes, workshops and plant medicine ceremonies in the UK, Europe and Peru. He is the author of more than a dozen books on shamanism and healing. He lives in Spain and is very decidedly not married.

Endnotes

1. 'When the donkey saw the angel of the Lord standing in the road with a drawn sword in his hand, it turned off the road into a field. Balaam beat it to get it back on the road'. Numbers 22: 23

2. Teacher plants are those regarded by shamans as having special powers not just as healers but as allies and educators who are able to open "the doors of perception" for us so that we learn and grow from them. In Peru they include Ayahuasca, San Pedro and Tohay (datura). In Mexico they are *Teonanácatl* ('magic mushrooms'), Peyote, Salvia and Morning Glory. Every culture will have its own.

3. A female healer or 'shaman'. La Bruja, in Spanish, means 'The Sorceress': a woman capable of magic.

4. One company did try it and took out a patent on the Amazonian vine Ayahuasca but their claim was thrown out on appeal.

5. Jerome Burne, Turn Over a New Leaf, London Independent newspaper, May 10, 2005.

6. Jerome Burne, op cit.

7. Red Poppy differs from opium Poppy and is non-addictive. See later in this book.

8. In Ross Heaven, *Plant Spirit Shamanism*. Inner Traditions, 2006.

9. In Douglas Sharon, *Wizard of the Four Winds: A Shaman's Story*. Free Press, 1978

10. *Cactus of Mystery* and *The Hummingbird's Journey to God*.

11. Alexander and Ann Shulgin, *Pihkal: A Chemical Love Story*. Transform Press, 1990

12. Aeclectic Tarot. http://www.aeclectic.net/tarot/learn/meanings/ fool.shtml. Alejandro Jodorowsky and Marianne Costa offer a similar interpretation of The Fool in their book, *The Way of Tarot: The Spiritual Teacher in the Cards* (Kindle Edition, 2009): 'Key words: Freedom, energy, travel, seeking, origin, wandering, essence, liberating force' and, on the other hand, 'the irrational, chaos, flight, madness... The Fool depicts the eternal traveller wandering

through the world with no ties or nationality. He could also be a pilgrim making his way to a sacred site. Or, in the reductive sense that many tarot analysts have given him he could even be a madman wandering aimlessly towards his destruction'.

13. For more on the nature of the diet see my books, *Shamanic Quest for the Spirit of Salvia* and *Plant Spirit Shamanism*. Inner Traditions, 2013 and 2006 respectively.

14. For more on the nature of the diet see my books, *Shamanic Quest for the Spirit of Salvia* and *Plant Spirit Shamanism*. Inner Traditions, 2013 and 2006 respectively.

15. Daniel Pinchbeck (author of *Breaking Open the Head*) made a related and relevant comment on his Facebook page (September 24). While we should, in fairness, bear in mind that Pinchbeck and Chimbre (the retreat Centre he mentions in Peru where a young man had recently died in mysterious circumstances related to his drinking Ayahuasca there) have 'history' together, his overall point is, in my view and my experience, entirely valid:

'The tragedy at Chimbre serves as a tragic reminder of how naive we still are about what we call "shamanism"... in the Amazon, mastery of ayahuasca was an ambiguous skill, as the power gained from its use could be used to heal or kill. In many tribes, "shamans" or sorcerers would drink ayahuasca to shoot magical darts at their enemies. Power - *gained in any realm* - always has this potential for dangerous ambiguity.'

'Our language and concepts are not sophisticated enough yet to fully articulate the layers of ambiguity and complexity in practices that may ultimately be more magical than spiritual. In fact, the concept of "spiritual" is a major problem for us. "Spirituality" becomes an avoidance mechanism for many people. Personally, I don't think someone is "spiritual" if they meditate, do yoga, talk about Buddhism or drink ayahuasca - even if they do "energy work" or "Tantric healings" or whatever. All of that can be done to bring pleasure to the ego or enhance narcissism – in any case, these days it is not hip to not be "spiritual" in some way.'

'I also feel that "spiritual" as a concept presupposes a dichotomy or dualistic split between spirit and matter that is an error in our understanding. The "true person" of the Tao would be one who had integrated spirit *and* matter - the split only exists in our minds in any case. If we are forced to use the term "spiritual," I would reserve it for those who have dedicated themselves to service in the world, and whose daily lives reflect their inner intention. I would measure their "spirituality" by tangible results, by their impact on other people and on the physical world, not by *avowed* ideals. Clearly we need to become less naïve about shamanism – as well as spirituality in general. Shamans are not all good-hearted healers…'

16. Alborado is a band of Andean musicians who sing in their native Quechua language. Their words here roughly translate as 'What pain, what pain causes what you are telling me', the first question asked by all shamans and healers (if only to themselves) about the patient who life has brought to them.

17. The ritual temple where ceremonies are held.

18. See http://www.theglobeandmail.com/life/health/new-health/health-news/can-tobacco-be-used-to-cure-cancer/article2321906/.

19. The Creator of All Reality

20. In *El Oro de Pachacamac* by Luis Enrique Tord.

21. Although there is some confusion about this and I, personally, do not believe it – see my book *Shamanic Quest for the Spirit of Salvia* for details.

22. See my book *Plant Spirit Shamanism* for a discussion of these.

23. See my book *The Hummingbird's Journey to God* to read this story.

24. By tea or quid.

25. This seemingly stupid observation would turn out later to be much more prophetic and important than I thought.

26. Plants, whatever else they may show us, reveal areas of ourselves which require attention or where healing may be needed. Another way of interpreting a vision like this therefore – from a psychological or metaphorical perspective rather than a metaphysical one – might be to say that each of these different landscapes repre-

sented one aspect of the participant's personality - one of her 'selves' that she could further explore to understand its particular view of her life or the healing needs of that part of her personality, its drives and 'issues' and so on. From this analytical point of view it is probably also significant (and disturbing) that reality was ending in each of these landscapes (and for each of the separate personalities that these scenes represented) and that the predominant character (the blue entity) was in control of the annihilation process. Freud, Nietzsche and others have written about *thanatos*, the unconscious 'will to death' or desire for final endings, which may, in the context of this participant's vision, be a drive that is part of her 'master programme' or controlling personality. This is something that she might therefore give urgent attention to since the image could be read as a warning of her own death, telling her why and how it will happen unless she chooses to change her programming.

27. More than two years after this diet and the 'crazy' suggestion by Salvia that we are not human but part of a computer game being played by someone or something else, I came across the following article: *Physicists Say There May Be a Way To Prove That We Live in a Computer Simulation.* 'Back in 2003, Oxford professor Nick Bostrom suggested that we may be living in a computer simulation. In his paper, Bostrom offered very little science to support his hypothesis - though he did calculate the computational requirements needed to pull off such a feat. And indeed, a philosophical claim is one thing, actually proving it is quite another. But now, a team of physicists say proof might be possible...' You can read the rest of this article at http://decryptedmatrix.com/live/physicists-say-there-may-be-a-way-to-prove-that-we-live-in-a-computer-simulation/?utm_source=feedburner.

28. In *Psychomagic: The Transformative Power of Shamanic Psychotherapy.* Alejandro Jodorowsky. Inner Traditions, 2004.

29. And in fact Trudy left too just a few years later and under its new management the facility has become a tourist lodge more than a

healing Centre.

30. During my diets the plants had suggested a three-stage process to healing or progress of any kind: the *thesis*, where an idea or a new situation arises; the *antithesis*, where this idea is challenged and its opposite may manifest; and finally *synthesis*, where the two states are brought together and a 'third way', a resolution or a movement towards unity emerges. The thesis is the first idea, the antithesis is its challenge and the synthesis becomes a new hypothesis for the future.

31. The Spanish do not have a word for 'housewife'; rather, married women are referred to by the more poetic and beautiful expression, *alma del casa*: the soul of the house.

32. In Douglas Sharon, *Wizard of the Four Winds: A Shaman's Story*. Free Press, 1979.

33. For more information on the mesa and how to work with it see my book, *Cactus of Mystery*. Inner Traditions, 2012.

34. Spearhead magazine, summer 2012.

35. The title is based on Philip Larkin's poem, *This be the Verse*.

36. Does beauty even exist when you have no-one to share it with? That is another question. San Pedro's answer was: 'Yes, when it is absorbed by you so it becomes part of the human world and that beauty is reflected in beautiful acts of your own'.

37. This story is told in detail by Alexia herself in my book *Cactus of Mystery*.

38. 'Star' is his term for the ribs since San Pedro slices, when viewed from the top, do resemble stars.

39. A line from the film, *Magnolia*.

40. 'Set refers to the personality, past experiences, mood, motivations, intelligence, imagination, attitudes, current life activities and the expectations of the person [taking a substance]... Setting refers to the conditions of use, including the physical, social and emotional environment and the other people present' – Karl Jansen MD, *Ketamine: Dreams and Realities*

41. 'To enter into a person's difficulties is to enter into his family... We

are all marked, not to say contaminated, by the psychological universe of our people. A number of people have associated with them a personality that is not theirs, one that is borrowed from one or more members of their emotional environment. To be born into a family is to be, if I may say it this way, possessed. This possession is transmitted from generation to generation: the enchanted becomes the enchanter in projecting onto his children what was projected onto him – unless an awakening comes to break the cycle'. Alejandro Jodorowsky, *Psychomagic*. Op cit.

42. In *Ketamine: Dreams and Realities*, op cit.

43. *The Spiritual Journey of Alejandro Jodorowsky: The Creator of El Topo*. Park Street Press, 2008.

44. The following interpretations are from Jodorowsky's work with the original Marseilles tarot and the first meanings of the cards (see Alejandro Jodorowsky and Marianne Costa. *The Way of Tarot: The Spiritual Teacher in the Cards*).

The lover. 'Key words: Eros, heart, choice, emotional domain, conflict, ambiguity, trio, social life, community, siblings, doing what you love'. In the *Tarot de Marseille*, the card is called the Lovers not the Lover. It depicts *six* lovers (the Sun, the Earth, the angel/cupid, the man in the middle, the woman on the right and the woman/hermaphrodite on the left). Who the querent chooses as *the* lover (singular) from this set may be significant in itself. 'This is a card of union and disunion, of social and emotional choices... In a reading this ambiguous card prompts us to question our own emotional state: how is our emotional life going? Are we enjoying peace or experiencing conflict? Are we doing what we love?... Does the situation that is our chief concern have roots in our past and if so what are they?'

The Hierophant (Pope). 'Key words: Wisdom, ideal, communication, teaching, verticality, plan, mediator, faith, guide, example, to marry, spiritual power, saintliness'.

The World. 'Key words: Realisation, soul, world, fullness, success, heroism, genius, holiness, dance, ecstasy, universal fulfilment, totality'.

45. My interview with Dr Orellana and with other Peruvian shamans can be read in full in my book, *Cactus of Mystery*. Inner Traditions, 2012.

46. See my book *Cactus of Mystery* for a discussion of the influence of San Pedro on music and art.

47. Andalusia is the second largest of the autonomous regions of Spain, with a surface area of 87,597 square kilometres (33,821 square miles) and represents more than 17% of the entire territory of Spain, making it comparable to many smaller European countries. Home to just 8,424,102 people however, its population is roughly equivalent to that of Greater London (8,174,000 people) – which means there is space, freedom and unpolluted fresh air, as well as sunshine, blue skies, and none of the tensions of cities like London.

48. Alejandro Jodorowsky, Psychomagic. Op cit.

49. Alejandro Jodorowsky, Psychomagic. Op cit.

50. I first heard this story from David in 2008 and he is still well today, so at the time of writing his remission has now lasted 13 years. His attitudes towards San Pedro have also changed and he now helps out on my *Cactus of Vision* trips to Peru so that others can receive healing from the plant as he did.

51. MDMA – street name, Ecstasy – is a synthetic form of mescaline which was developed and popularised by Alexander Shulgin following his work with the Peyote and San Pedro.

Moon Books invites you to begin or deepen your encounter with Paganism, in all its rich, creative, flourishing forms.